teach
yourself

biblical hebrew
sarah nicholson

Launched in 1938, the **teach yourself** series
grew rapidly in response to the world's wartime
needs. Loved and trusted by over 50 million
readers, the series has continued to respond to
society's changing interests and passions and
now, 70 years on, includes over 500 titles,
from Arabic and Beekeeping to Yoga and Zulu.
What would you like to learn?

be where you want to be with **teach yourself**

The author wishes to extend special thanks to Ginny Catmur and to Calum Smith for their help in preparing this book.

For UK order enquiries: please contact Bookpoint Ltd, 130 Milton Park, Abingdon, Oxon, OX14 4SB. Telephone: +44 (0) 1235 827720. Fax: +44 (0) 1235 400454. Lines are open 09.00–17.00, Monday to Saturday, with a 24-hour message answering service. Details about our titles and how to order are available at www.teachyourself.co.uk

For USA order enquiries: please contact McGraw-Hill Customer Services, PO Box 545, Blacklick, OH 43004-0545, USA. Telephone: 1-800-722-4726. Fax: 1-614-755-5645.

For Canada order enquiries: please contact McGraw-Hill Ryerson Ltd, 300 Water St, Whitby, Ontario, L1N 9B6, Canada. Telephone: 905 430 5000. Fax: 905 430 5020.

Long renowned as the authoritative source for self-guided learning – with more than 50 million copies sold worldwide – the **teach yourself** series includes over 500 titles in the fields of languages, crafts, hobbies, business, computing and education.

British Library Cataloguing in Publication Data: a catalogue record for this title is available from the British Library.

Library of Congress Catalog Card Number: on file.

First published in UK 2006 by Hodder Education, part of Hachette Livre UK, 338 Euston Road, London, NW1 3BH.

First published in US 2006 by The McGraw-Hill Companies, Inc.

This edition published 2006.

The **teach yourself** name is a registered trade mark of Hodder Headline.

Typeset by WorldAccent.
Printed in Great Britain for Hodder Education, an Hachette Livre UK Company, 338 Euston Road, London NW1 3BH, by CPI Cox and Wyman, Reading, Berkshire RG1 8EX.

The publisher has used its best endeavours to ensure that the URLs for external websites referred to in this book are correct and active at the time of going to press. However, the publisher and the author have no responsibility for the websites and can make no guarantee that a site will remain live or that the content will remain relevant, decent or appropriate.

Hachette Livre UK's policy is to use papers that are natural, renewable and recyclable products and made from wood grown in sustainable forests. The logging and manufacturing processes are expected to conform to the environmental regulations of the country of origin.

Impression number   10 9 8 7 6 5 4 3
Year   2010 2009 2008

contents

Biblical Hebrew is not a difficult language to learn. Native English speakers might initially feel daunted at the prospect of learning a new alphabet, or learning to read from right to left, and yet these two aspects of biblical Hebrew can usually be mastered very quickly indeed.

English is an Indo-European language, whereas Hebrew is a Semitic language. This means that, unlike other Indo-European such as French or German, Hebrew words may sound very 'foreign' to us. Learning other Indo-European languages might feel easier because of their similarities to English. Those who have learned German, for example, may have taken comfort from the familiarity of the sounds of basic words: the word for *she* is pronounced 'zee', the word for *me* is pronounced 'meekh' and the word for *fish* is pronounced 'fish'. In contrast, the Hebrew for *she* is pronounced 'he'; the word for *he* is pronounced 'who' and the word for *who* is pronounced 'me'. The word for *fish* is pronounced 'dog'.

However, despite the unfamiliar sound of Hebrew words, the vocabulary is actually quite small. Estimates vary as to the number of words in the Hebrew Bible (it depends how you count them), but a figure often mentioned is 4,000 words. Compare that with estimates of over 800,000 words in the English language! Readers of this book should not expect to learn all the words in the Hebrew Bible, but the small vocabulary does make the language easier to learn.

Moreover, the grammar of biblical Hebrew is (arguably) simpler than that of many Indo-European languages. For example, in biblical Hebrew there are no complex tense constructions like 'I would have had to leave'. The pronunciation is utterly regular, and there are none of the tricky combinations of letters that abound in the English language, such as the *ough* that sounds different in *cough*, *rough* and *though*.

Most importantly, though, learning biblical Hebrew can be very exciting. To engage with the biblical texts in their original languages can provide a sense of insight and a level of understanding that even the best translations cannot quite match. It can also be very interesting to discover how different translations have handled difficulties in the Hebrew text. But ultimately, learning the language can give us a fresh perspective on texts that have been the subject of debate, inspiration and comfort for centuries.

Aims

The aim of this book is to present the basics of biblical Hebrew clearly enough that in due course a reader will be able to read passages of the Bible in Hebrew. It can take time to achieve fluency in biblical Hebrew, and readers should not expect to be fluent by the end of this book. However, the book should give readers a fundamental knowledge of the language, and the skills to develop their Hebrew beyond the limits of an introductory book. By the time they reach the end of this book, readers should have acquired a knowledge of some fundamental vocabulary and grammar and should have acquired the skills to read and translate simple passages from the biblical text.

Methods

The method used in this book is as inductive as possible. In addition to setting exercises for the purpose of memorizing points of grammar, readers are encouraged to see how Hebrew is actually used in the Bible. Therefore, some of the work involves reading and translating real biblical passages. It is hoped that engaging with the Bible as soon as possible might be more motivating than simply presenting a series of grammatically correct but sterile exercises.

To get the best results you should spend up to ten hours of learning time on each unit. This is not just the time taken to read the unit and do the exercises and translations, but also to re-read and to practise using the new material in the unit. Many people find that doing a little each day is more effective than attempting to work through a whole unit at once. Learning a language can be quite tiring and less is often more.

Learning styles

Different readers may have different learning styles. Some readers enjoy learning lists of vocabulary and grammatical forms; others find it easier to learn how words work within a text. Most people learn best if they employ a variety of learning styles, and so this book encourages different ways of learning. If you find some of the suggestions unhelpful or irrelevant you can simply ignore them, but you are advised at least to try them for a few weeks to see if they work for you.

How to use this book

This book contains 20 units. Each unit explains some points of Hebrew grammar and then discusses a passage from the Bible. It is probably best to work through it in order, since later units build on material presented in earlier units.

In the early units, the Hebrew words are accompanied by approximate pronunciation. The suggestions in this book represent one way of pronouncing Hebrew, but this is by no means the only way. The suggestions in this book are also very approximate and may be open to debate. The approximate pronunciation is intended to be of use to people who are trying to learn Hebrew by themselves and who need support in pronouncing the words. If anyone is reading this book to supplement a Hebrew class, they should be guided by their teacher's pronunciation. And of course any reader who finds the approximate pronunciation unhelpful should simply ignore it.

Much of the textual focus of this book is on translation. Learning an ancient language is not a conversational enterprise in the same way as learning a modern language, and so understanding the texts often involves translating them. Naturally, there are differing ideas about what a translation should be and how we should go about it. The method used in this book involves translating into idiomatic English, since understanding a text in one's own language is a crucial step towards learning how the language works. There is a place for more literal translation, but it is generally most useful to people who are already very familiar with the vocabulary and syntax of the original language. Therefore this book emphasizes idiomatic translation.

Other reading

This book is a basic introduction to biblical Hebrew. It is not an Introduction to the Old Testament/Tanakh; neither is it a traditional grammar of biblical Hebrew. There are many very interesting things to learn about the Bible that are outside the scope of this book, and so it may be useful to read other books as well if you are curious about questions such as the history, authorship, contents or theology of the Bible. A few general possibilities are listed below.

Introductions

Readers might be interested in reading an Introduction to the Old Testament alongside or after this book. An Introduction will often be entitled just that: *Introduction to the Old Testament*. There are many of them available and they encompass a range of academic and theological perspectives. It is not the intention to recommend a particular Introduction; readers are advised to visit a library and browse. Of course, the internet can also be a useful source.

Websites

There are, naturally, many websites that focus on biblical Hebrew and on issues of biblical interpretation. Many of them are very good; many others are mediocre. If you are interested in exploring the material available online, you are reminded that almost anyone can put up a web page, so information found online may not be accurate or may represent a very minority position.

Grammars

Although this book introduces the basics of the grammar of biblical Hebrew, it is not exhaustive. A traditional grammar will set out these points in more detail, often without the textual work that appears in this book. There are many grammars available and they might be useful to a reader who has worked through this book and wishes to continue learning Hebrew.

Commentaries

Commentaries are books that seek to explain in some detail each verse of a particular book of the Bible. Some commentaries discuss the whole Bible. Some commentaries have a devotional leaning; others focus on academic matters. Some, though not all, discuss the Hebrew. Readers of this book might be interested in reading a commentary on Genesis, particularly one that comments on the use of Hebrew.

Dictionaries and lexicons

Any reader who wishes to continue with Hebrew after this book should try to invest in a dictionary or a lexicon. Dictionaries and lexicons for biblical Hebrew (as opposed to modern Hebrew) are usually Hebrew to English only and list the grammatical roots of words. It can be difficult to get the hang of using a dictionary until you have a good grasp of Hebrew grammar. It can take time to learn how to used a Hebrew dictionary or lexicon. There is a basic lexicon at the back of this book, but it does not cover the vocabulary of the entire biblical text.

1.1 Introduction

This book is about biblical Hebrew, which is an ancient language. There are other forms of Hebrew, such as Mishnaic Hebrew and modern Hebrew, which are somewhat different and, though interesting, beyond the scope of this book. Hebrew is a Semitic language and has features in common with other Semitic languages (such as Arabic). By contrast, English is Indo-European, and more closely related to languages like French and German. There are some notable differences between the two language families, and hence between Hebrew and English.

In English, we write from left to right; but in Hebrew, it's the other way around: right to left. This means that books written in Hebrew usually open at what looks (to English speakers) like the back cover. In English, we write the vowels next to the consonants; in Hebrew, we usually write them underneath or above the consonants. In Hebrew, most words are derived from a three-letter verbal root. For example, there is a verb, *shamar* (*to guard*), and from the three-letter root שׁמר we get words like the following:

shomer	שֹׁמֵר	a *guard*
shamrah	שָׁמְרָה	a *watch*; i.e. a period where one guards
shemurah	שְׁמֻרָה	an *eyelid*, because it guards the eye
shimur	שִׁמֻּר	a *vigil*
mishmar	מִשְׁמָר	a *prison*
mishmeret	מִשְׁמֶרֶת	an *injunction* (like a law; something you have to keep)

Notice how the shape שׁמר occurs in the words above. When you have learned the alphabet, you will be able to pronounce these words for yourself. Note: the words in the list above are not the only words from the root שׁמר. Many other words come from the same root, such as words meaning *they have guarded*, and *we will be guarded* and *I am guarding*. The words above are simply examples.

1.2 The alphabet

You will find a summary of how to form the Hebrew characters in Appendix 1.

Grammar: consonants and vowels

In English, the vowels are *a*, *e*, *i*, *o* and *u*. All the other letters are consonants. In English, the vowels appear in the alphabet mixed in with the consonants; but in Hebrew, the vowels are learned separately from the consonants.

'The Hebrew alphabet' really means the Hebrew consonants, and there are 22 of them. In Hebrew, the vowels are considered to be quite separate from the consonants (there are 14 vowels, if you count all the possibilities). In fact, sometimes the vowels are simply left out. It is easy enough to understand a sentence written without vowels in a language you already know, but it is hard to learn to pronounce words with no vowels. So in this book, we are going to use the vowels. However, we will focus on the consonants first.

There are different ways of pronouncing biblical Hebrew. The version presented in this book is common in universities, but in synagogues several other pronunciations are used. Modern Hebrew is slightly different again. Pronunciation isn't as crucial as it might be if you were learning to speak a modern language. You will not need to order food or book a room in biblical Hebrew; making yourself understood in real life is not the issue. However, you will find it much easier to read the text if you learn to pronounce the words properly. Mixing up letters, for example, could lead to misunderstanding the text. Do take as much time as you need to learn how the letters sound. You can find a summary pronunciation chart in Appendix 2.

Consonants

The very first letter is called *alef*: א. It is a silent letter, and thus easy to pronounce. When you see it in a word, you pronounce the vowel underneath it.

Try writing it a few times: _____

The second letter is called *bet* (say *bait*): ב. Sometimes there is a dot, called a *dagesh*, inside it: בּ. Without the *dagesh* it's *v* (as in *van*); with the *dagesh* it's *b* (as in *book*). *Dagesh* will be explained in more detail in Unit 3.

Practise writing it a few times: _____

The third letter is called *gimel* (say *gimel* with a hard *g*; not *jimel*): ג. It is always pronounced with a hard *g* (as in *gold*); never with a soft *g* (as in *gin*).

Try writing it a few times: _____

The fourth letter is *dalet*: ד. It is pronounced *d* (as in *door*).

Practise writing it a few times: _____

The fifth letter is *he* (say it *hay*). It looks like this: ה and is pronounced *h* (as in *help*), although it is silent at the end of a word.

Try writing it a few times: _____

The best way to practise these is with a vowel, so we'll look at two to begin with. The first is a short *a* vowel called *patach*, pronounced *a* as in *pat*. It is a short line written underneath a consonant; e.g. אַ. The second is a short *e* vowel called *segol*, pronounced *e* as in *set*. It is made up of three little dots written underneath a consonant; e.g. בֶ.

Try pronouncing these, reading from right to left (the first few have a key to guide you):

הַ	דַ	גַ	בַ	אַ
ha	*da*	*ga*	*va*	*a*

הֶ	דֶ	גֶ	בֶּ	אֶ
heh	deh	geh	beh	e

Don't forget: *a* as in *pat* and *e* as in *set*. Here are some more:

הַ	דַ	גַ	בַ	אַ
הֶ	דֶ	גֶ	בֶ	אֶ
גַ	בֶ	בַּ	הֶ	דַ
גֶ	בַ	דֶ	הַ	אֶ

The next consonant is *vav*: ו. It is pronounced *v* as in *van*, just the same as ב without *dagesh*.

Write it a few times: _____

Then we have *zayin*: ז. It is pronounced *z* as in *zone*. Be sure not to confuse it with *vav* (ו).

Write it a few times: _____

After that comes *chet*: ח. Be sure to distinguish it from ה. *Chet* is pronounced *ch* as in the Scottish word *loch*. It is never *ch* as in *cheese*. This can be a challenging sound for some, particularly for people from England or North America (to whom it's not unlike the sound of gargling), but with a bit of practice it can be achieved.

Write it a few times: _____

The ninth consonant is *tet*: ט, which is pronounced *t* as in *time*.

Write it a few times: _____

And then the tenth letter is *yod* י, which is pronounced *y* as in *young*. It is a very small letter and is written above the line. Notice how small it is compared with other consonants: חָיָה (this word is *chayah*, meaning *to live*).

Write it a few times: _____

Now practise saying these consonants with some vowels (read from right to left):

וַ	זַ	חַ	טַ	יַ
va	za	cha	ta	ya
וֶ	זֶ	חֶ	טֶ	יֶ
ve	ze	che	te	ye
חַ	יֶ	זַ	טֶ	וֶ
זֶ	וַ	זַ	יַ	חֶ

The Hebrew consonants also have a numerical value; if you look in a Hebrew Bible, you may see the verses are numbered with these consonants, so these letters have the values 1 to 10. I am sorry to say that the letters don't actually translate the numbers; while you can use ד as the equivalent of 4, if you want to say *four* in Hebrew you have to say *arbah*. It's not too confusing when we remember that when Italian speakers see 4 they say *quattro*, while Scots Gaelic speakers say *ceithir*. So when we see א at the beginning of a verse, we know it's verse 1.

The next consonant is *kaf*: כ. Like *bet*, it's pronounced differently when written with *dagesh* (כּ), in which case it is pronounced *k* as in *king*. Without *dagesh* (כ) it is pronounced ch as in *loch* (just the same as ח). Be sure not to confuse it with *beth* (ב).

Write it a few times: _____

Then comes *lamed*: ל. It is pronounced *l* as in *land*.

Write it a few times: _____

It is followed by *mem* (say *maim*): מ, which is pronounced *m* as in *milk*.

Write it a few times: _____

The next letter is *nun* (say it *noon*): נ, which is pronounced *n* as in *not*. Be sure not to confuse it with *gimel* (ג).

Write it a few times: _____

Then comes *samech* ס, which is pronounced *s* as in *sock*. Be sure not to confuse it with *tet* (ט).

Write it a few times: _____

And next there is *ayin* ע (say it *eye-in*), which is silent, like *alef*.

Write it a few times: _____

Here are some syllables to help you practise pronouncing these consonants. Remember: *a* as in *pat* and *e* as in *set*.

כַ	לַ	מַ	נַ	סַ	עַ
cha	la	ma	na	sa	a
כֶּ	לֶ	מֶ	נֶ	סֶ	עֶ
ke	le	me	ne	se	e
מַ	סַ	כַּ	נַ	צַ	לַ
סַ	עַ	לַ	כַ	נַ	מַ

There are only a few more consonants to learn. The next one is *pe* (say *pay*) פ, which is another letter that changes pronunciation with *dagesh*. Without *dagesh* it's pronounced *f*, as in *fin*, and with dagesh (פּ) it's pronounced *p* as in *pin*.

Write it a few times: _____

Then there is *tsade* צ (say it *tsad-ay*), which is pronounced *ts*, as in *tsar*. Be sure not to confuse it with *ayin* (ע).

Write it a few times: _____

Next comes *qof* ק (say it *kofe*), pronounced *k* as in *king*.

Write it a few times: _____

After *qof* is *resh* ר, pronounced *r* as in *run*. Be sure not to confuse it with *dalet* (ד).

Write it a few times: _____

The next letter is really two letters, distinguished by the placing of the dot.

This one שׂ is called *sin*, and is pronounced *s* as in *sock*.

This one שׁ is called *shin* and is pronounced *sh* as in *shock*.

Write *sin* (שׂ) a few times: _____

Write *shin* (שׁ) a few times: _____

And the last letter of the alphabet is *tav*: ת, which, just like ט, is pronounced *t* as in *time*.

Write it a few times: _____

Try pronouncing these (remember to read right to left):

תַ	שַׁ	שַׂ	קַ	צַ	פַ
ta	sha	sa	ka	tsa	fa

תֶ	שֶׁ	שֶׂ	קֶ	צֶ	פֶ
teh	sheh	seh	keh	tseh	peh

שַׁ	צַ	תָ	פַ	קֶ	שָׁ
פֶ	שַׂ	שֶׂ	קַ	צֶ	תַ

1.3 Reading practice

It is very important to be able to remember and pronounce the letters. The consonants are set out below, at random and with vowels, to give you the opportunity to practise. Most people find they learn best if they read out loud, rather than silently.

וֶ	פָּ	רַ	כָ	דַ	שֶׁ	צַ	סַ	זִ	אַ	קֶ	שָׁ
קַ	לְ	חַ	עֲ	מֶ	טַ	נֶ	הֶ	יִ	בֶּ	גַ	תַ
שָׁ	מָ	בַ	כַ	זִ	חַ	הַ	פַּ	סֶ	עַ	תֶ	שַׁ
עַ	נֶ	וַ	צַ	לְ	כָ	טֶ	גָ	דֶ	אָ	יְ	רֶ

And some practice at distinguishing letters of similar appearance:

ב כ ע צ ו ז ס ט ה ה ח ת

ד ר שׁ שׂ

Finally, here are some real Hebrew words to pronounce. Suggested pronunciation and meanings are below the words (*light* here is *light* as in *not heavy* rather than *light* as in *not dark*). Remember that ה is silent at the end of a word.

אֶל קַל חַד פַּח עַז שֶׂה רַב פַּר עַד מַה

ma	ad	par	rav	se	az	pach	chad	kal	el
what	until	ox	many	lamb	strong	snare	sharp	light	to

1.4 Suggestions

- Write out all the consonants in order at least three times. When you come to use a dictionary, it will be helpful to have learned the order.

- Do the reading practice above every day for a few days until you are certain you have learned to pronounce all the letters.

- Learn the meanings of the Hebrew words in section 1.3 above.

1.5 Summary

In this unit, we have learned that

- Hebrew is read from right to left

- the vowels are written below (or sometimes above) the consonants

- we have learned all the consonants in order, and two of the vowels.

Once these have been mastered, you will be ready to learn more vowels in Unit 2.

2.1 Short and long vowels

The distinction between short and long vowels is convenient rather than strictly accurate. In fact, we do not really know exactly how vowels were pronounced by the people who wrote down the biblical texts. However, it is useful for learning biblical Hebrew.

We have learned two of the vowels so far. Now it is time to learn the rest.

Short vowels

patach	_	a as in pat
segol	ֶ	e as in set
chireq	.	i as in hit
qamets chatuf	ֳ	o as in hot
qibbuts	ֻ	u as in put

It is easier to see how the vowels work when we put them together with a consonant. Remember to pronounce the vowels as described above. For example, don't pronounce _so_ below as the word _so_, and don't pronounce _si_ below like the Spanish word for _yes_.

| שֻ | שֹ | שִ | שֶ | שַ |
| su | so | si | se | sa |

Try reading these out loud, from right to left (don't forget: ח and כ are _ch_ as in _loch_):

כְ   יְ   שָׂ   ח   ז   ו   ה   דָ   גּ   בּ   א

תָּ   שׁ   רְ   קֶ   צָ   פּ   עֲ   ס   נָ   מְ   ל

Long vowels

Consonants appear in three of the long vowels. This might appear confusing at first but in practice it causes few difficulties. You might like to think of the ו as holding the dot in place in long *o* and long *u*, whereas the י simply lengthens the short-*i* vowel.

qamets	ָ	*a* as in *pa*
tsere	ֵ	*e* as in *blasé*
hireq yod	ִי	*i* as in *routine*
cholem	וֹ	*o* as in *cone*
shureq	וּ	*u* as in *Peru*

Again, it's easier to pronounce them with a consonant. The approximate pronunciation below is based on the table in Appendix 2.

תוּ	תוֹ	תִי	תֵ	תָ
too	*tō*	*tee*	*tay*	*tā*

Here are the long vowels with random consonants. The first line includes approximate pronunciation.

חָ	וָ	גוֹ	הִי	דֵ	אָ	זוּ	טוֹ	יֵ	בִי	כָ
chā	*vā*	*gō*	*hee*	*day*	*ā*	*zoo*	*tō*	*yay*	*vee*	*kā*

תֵ	צִי	קוֹ	סוּ	שָׁ	פֵּ	מִי	נוֹ	רוּ	עֲ	לֶ

Note: the vowel ָ is sometimes pronounced *ah* (when used as a long vowel) and sometimes pronounced *o* as in *hot* (when used as a short vowel). In practice, it is almost always *ah*, but later we will learn the contexts in which it is pronounced *o*.

However, for some people (such as those who speak with certain North American accents) the two sounds are indistinguishable. In the approximate pronunciation found in this book, *ah* represents long *a*, as in *tah* (תָ) above. If you pronounce the *a* in *raw* the same way as the *o* in *hot*, then you might be unable to distinguish between short *o* and long *a*.

Learning the names of all the vowels isn't absolutely necessary; however, you do need to be able to recognize them. It can be easier to think of them as, e.g., 'short *e*' (ֶ) and 'long *e*' (ֵ).

So far we have been practising chiefly with meaningless syllables, but now we can try some more real Hebrew words. Many people find the easiest way to learn vocabulary is to write new words in a vocabulary book. Remember also to add the words from Unit 1.

good	טוֹב	tōv
evil, bad	רַע	ra
with	עִם	im
on	עַל	al
white	חָר	chur
therefore	כֵּן	kayn
he	הוּא	hoo
she	הִיא	hee
man	אִישׁ	eesh
mountain	הַר	har

Note: sometimes the long-*o* vowel is written without the ו to hold it up. If טוֹב were written that way, it would look like this: טֹב. It would be pronounced just the same, though: *tōv*.

2.2 Exercise 1

Writing practice: write the words in the list above in Hebrew.

Write the following words in Hebrew (from Unit 1) and write their meanings next to them:

_____ _____ מַה

_____ _____ עַד

_____ _____ פַּר

_____ _____ רַב

_____ _____ שֶׁה

_____ _____ עַז

_____ _____ פַּח

_____ _____ חַד

_____ _____ קַל

_____ _____ אֶל

2.3 *Sheva* and composite vowels

Sheva

There is also a vowel called *sheva* (pronounced *sha-VA*) that corresponds to the way we usually pronounce the first *o* in *tomato*. It looks like ֽ and is sometimes silent, but is sometimes vocalized. When vocalized, it is simplest to represent its pronunciation with a symbol: [a]. For example, if we were to write the way tomato is pronounced, we could write *t[a]-MA-to*.

Here are a couple of examples:

silent *sheva*	מִדְבָּר	*mid-BAR* (a *desert*)
vocalized *sheva*	מְשֹׁל	*m[a]-SHŌL* (*to rule*)

Composite vowels

The last three vowels are composite vowels made up of the *sheva* and one of the short *a*, *e* or *o* vowels. They look like this:

chatef patach   ֲ   (don't forget: *ch* is pronounced as in the Scottish word *loch*) *chatef segol* ֱ

chatef qamets chatuf ֳ

These are pronounced just like their short-vowel equivalents and occur with the letters ה ע א and ח. These letters can take other vowels, but they cannot usually take a simple *sheva*.

Practise saying these out loud (approximate pronunciation is suggested):

חָ	חֶ	חַ	הָ	הֶ	הַ	עָ	עֶ	עַ	אָ	אֶ	אַ
cho	che	cha	ho	he	ha	o	e	a	o	e	a

2.4 Exercise 2

Complete the table of vowels.

	SHORT VOWELS	LONG VOWELS	COMPOSITE VOWELS
a			ֲ
e		ֵ	
i		ִי	
o	ֹ		
u		וּ	

2.5 Final forms

Five of the consonants change shape if they are the last letter of a word. They are:

	kaf	mem	nun	pe	tsadhe
beginning or middle	כ	מ	נ	פ	צ
end of word	ך	ם	ן	ף	ץ

Notice how four of them (excepting *mem*) seem to grow a tail that comes straight down below the line. Be sure to distinguish final *kaf* ך from *dalet* ד; final *mem* ם from *samek* ס; and final *nun* ן from *vav* ו.

Try writing them a few times:

Final *kaf* ך _____

Final *mem* ם _____

Final *nun* ן _____

Final *pe* ף _____

Final *tsadhe* ץ _____

Here are some examples of how they are used in words:

a people	עַם	am
from	מִן	min
palm (of hand)	כַּף	kaf
tree	עֵץ	ayts
but	אַך	ach

A note about consonants and vowels: in English we can string several consonants together, such as the combination 'tchphr' in *catchphrase*, but in Hebrew this kind of consonant string would be unpronounceable. In Hebrew, every consonant in a word takes a vowel, except the very last consonant. There are occasional exceptions, such as final *kaf*, which usually takes a *sheva* (ךְ) but can sometimes be ך.

2.6 Reading practice

Here are some more Hebrew words. Read them out loud, from right to left. Approximate pronunciation and meanings are given below the words.

אָח	בַּת	בֵּן	אֵם	אָב
ach	bat	bayn	aym	āv
brother	daughter	son	mother	father

יוֹם	סוּס	יָד	חוֹל	יָם
yōm	soos	yād	chōl	yām
day	horse	hand	sand	sea

Here are random combinations of vowels and consonants to practise reading out loud:

סִי	דַ	גֻ	טוּ	לַ	צוֹ	וְ	נָ	זֶ	כֵ	בְּ	מְ
כַ	בָּ	שָׁ	קֶ	עֲ	שִׁי	אֱ	רָ	הַ	תָ	פִ	חֶ
אֵף	לָךְ	טֶם	גִין	דוֹב	אֵד	נַף	צַת	מוּל	בֵּץ	כָּשׁ	זָק
הֵל	תוֹם	יַץ	שׁוֹה	רֵךְ	עֵף	תֻגג	הֶם	שָׁן	קִיד	חָס	פֵּק
בִּיל	קֵל	חוּס	לֵב	מַר	יָח	בּוֹעַ	בֵּר	דַן	אָה	בֵל	עַז
חוֹשׁ	נוּךְ	פִּית	גֵל	שָׁץ	אָה	עוּל	מַן	פֵּד	נָא	מֶה	טִישׁ

2.7 Suggestions

- Do the reading practice above every day for a few days until you are sure you have mastered all the vowels and consonants.

- Learn the new vocabulary.

2.8 Summary

In this unit we have looked at

- the short and long vowels
- the *sheva* and composite *sheva*
- the five final forms
- 25 new words found in biblical Hebrew.

3.1 *Dagesh*

In Unit 1, we noted the occasional presence of a dot inside a letter: a dot called *dagesh*. *Dagesh* is sometimes described as a kind of doubling of the letter without writing it twice. However, there are various reasons for using *dagesh*, as we will discover.

The three letters we previously noted in connection with *dagesh* (ב כ and פ) were pronounced differently when they took a *dagesh*. A reminder:

v as in *van*	ב	*b* as in *book*	בּ
ch as in *loch*	כ	*k* as in *king*	כּ
f as in *fin*	פ	*p* as in *pin*	פּ

Other letters can take *dagesh*, but none of the others changes the way it is pronounced when it takes *dagesh*. A consonant can take *dagesh* for various reasons, and we will encounter these reasons in due course.

One example is that certain letters take *dagesh* when they come at the beginning of a word. The letters in question are פ כ ד ג ב and ת. So in the word בַּת (meaning *daughter*), the ב has a *dagesh* because it comes at the beginning of a word. And because it has a *dagesh*, the word is pronounced *bat* rather than *vat*. Similarly, in the word גָּן (meaning *garden*) the ג has a *dagesh* because it comes at the beginning of the word, but doesn't change its pronunciation with *dagesh*. (In fact, the letters ג ד and ת used to change pronunciation, but the change is no longer widely observed in the pronunciation system we are following.)

Five letters never take *dagesh*: א ה ע ח and ר. Four of these consonants, א ה ע and ח, are commonly known as *gutturals*. There may be some debate about the accuracy of the term, but the four letters do have particular properties, and it is worth pointing them out. We will discuss their peculiarities as we encounter them. The letter ר is not really a guttural, but sometimes behaves like one.

3.2 Exercise 1

Write out the alphabet in order, from memory, with a *dagesh* in each letter that can take *dagesh*.

Then check your work against Unit 1. Did you get the order right? Did you remember which letters do not take *dagesh*?

3.3 The conjunction ו

> **Grammar: Conjunctions**
>
> Consider these sentences:
>
> *The daughter is good and the son is good.*
>
> *The daughter is good but the son is evil.*
>
> The words *and* and *but* in these two sentences are conjunctions. Conjunctions join words or phrases together. Other examples in English are words like *if*, *because* and *that*.

In English *and* is a word in its own right, but in Hebrew it is the letter ו added to the beginning of a word. The vowel underneath it is usually a *sheva*. Here are some examples:

bad and good	רַע וְטוֹב	ra vᵃ-tōv
sand and sea	חוֹל וְיָם	chōl vᵃ-yām

When the conjunction ו comes before the letters ב מ and פ, it changes to a *u* vowel to make the word easier to pronounce:

daughter and son	בַּת וּבֵן	bat oo-VAYN
man and ox	אִישׁ וּפָר	eesh oo-FAR

Note: we would normally expect the word בֵּן to be written with *dagesh* in the ב. However, with the conjunction placed at the beginning of the word, the word no longer begins with ב and so does not require *dagesh*; the same is true of פַּר. Note also that when ו changes to a *u* vowel, it is no longer written with *sheva*. Since it has become a vowel, it no longer takes a vowel.

The change from וְ to וּ also happens when the conjunction is placed in front of a word whose first vowel is a *sheva*. For example, the first vowel in the name דְּבוֹרָה (pronounced *de-vō-RĀ*; the name usually rendered *Deborah* in English) is a *sheva*. So *and Deborah* would be וּדְבוֹרָה.

The conjunction ו can also mean *but* in sentences where a contrast is implied. We will discuss this later, when we are ready for whole sentences.

3.4 Exercise 2

sister	אָחוֹת	ach-ŌT
garden	גַּן	gan
woman	אִשָּׁה	ish-ĀH (note the *dagesh* in the שׁ; this is simply how the word is spelled)
land	אֶרֶץ	ER-ets
voice	קוֹל	kōl
heart	לֵבָב	lay-VĀV

Read the following out loud. Write them in Hebrew and then translate them into English:

_____	_____	אָב וְאֵם
_____	_____	גַּן וָעֵץ
_____	_____	סוּס וְשֶׂה
_____	_____	יָם וְהַר
_____	_____	אָחוֹת וְאָח
_____	_____	יָד וְכַף
_____	_____	חַד וְקַל

אִשָּׁה וְאִישׁ   _____   _____

אֶרֶץ וְעַם   _____   _____

לֵבָב וְקוֹל   _____   _____

3.5 The name of God

In biblical Hebrew there are two words for the deity. One is
אֱלֹהִים, pronounced *el-ō-HEEM*, which simply means *God*.
The other is God's name, יְהוָה. The latter is often represented
in English translations as *the LORD*. Although it is vocalized
(given vowels) in the biblical text, the convention is not to
pronounce it as written, but instead to say אֲדֹנָי, pronounced
a-dō-NĪ, which means *my Lord*. The word אֱלֹהִים is usually
translated *God*, except on occasions where it refers to several
gods. The word יְהוָה may be translated *the LORD* or *Yhwh*.
The *w* in Yhwh dates from a time when *vav* was called *waw*
and pronounced *w*.

3.6 Text: Psalm 25:8

It is always challenging to find simple and appropriate texts in
biblical Hebrew with which to demonstrate points of grammar.
Sometimes it is easier to invent non-biblical sentences, or to
adapt biblical texts to simplify their grammar. However, looking
at the real biblical text can be tremendously exciting, even if it
may be a little more ambitious. Learning grammatical points
can be supported with exercises, but in order to get a sense of
how the grammar is used in the Bible it is necessary to look at
the real thing.

Reading real biblical texts will involve encountering some
grammatical ideas before we have properly dealt with them. For
example, we have not yet looked at verbs, and so if we would
like to look at a real biblical passage at this point we will have to
accept that we will not understand the verbs. This can be a little
frustrating, but this frustration may be tempered with patience,
and the thrill of reading the Bible itself may compensate for the
delay in understanding every word perfectly. You will return to
these texts later, with greater knowledge.

Points to look out for in this text:

- Words we have already encountered.
- The divine name.
- *Dagesh*.
- Use of the conjunction וֹ.

If you are making your own vocabulary book, copy these words into it:

a way, path	דֶּרֶךְ	DER-ek
a sinner	חַטָּא	cha-TĀ
good	טוֹב	tōv (you should have this word in your vocabulary already)
to show, teach, instruct	יָרָה	yā-RĀ
just, upright	יָשָׁר	yā-SHĀR
name of God	יְהוָה	a-dō-NĪ
therefore	עַל־כֵּן	al kayn

Text

Read the verse aloud two or three times to be sure you know how the words sound. These words are longer than the words we've seen already, but there are only a few of them.

טוֹב־וְיָשָׁר יְהוָה
עַל־כֵּן יוֹרֶה חַטָּאִים בַּדָּרֶךְ׃

Approximate pronunciation:

TŌV vᵃ-yā-SHĀR a-dō-NĪ al kayn yō-RE cha-tā-EEM ba-DĀR-ek.

Now match each word of the text with the vocabulary above, as far as you can. Some of the words above are not precisely the same as the words in the list of vocabulary. The words in the vocabulary are the dictionary forms. In English, if we want to know the meaning of the word *brought* we need to look up *bring* in the dictionary. Similarly, if we want to know the meaning of יוֹרֶה, we have to look up יָרָה in the dictionary. Once you have matched the words in the text with the vocabulary, you should begin to have a sense of the meaning of the verse.

Notes

It should have been possible to match the first few words of the text to the vocabulary without too much difficulty. The last three words of the text are a little more complicated. There are also a few other points to deal with, so we will look at each word in the text.

טוֹב־

The line joining this word to the next word is called *maqqef*. It joins words in a manner rather like a hyphen in English, as in the phrase *happy-go-lucky*.

וְיָשָׁר

Notice the conjunction at the beginning of the word.

עַל־כֵּן

This word is made up of two words: עַל and כֵּן, joined by *maqqef*. Together they mean *therefore*. There is a *dagesh* in כ because it is at the beginning of the word.

יוֹרֶה

This word means *he teaches* or *he instructs*.

חַטָּאִים

This is a plural word meaning *sinners*. The ending יﬦ indicates a plural, as we will see later. There is a *dagesh* in the ט simply because that is how the word is spelled. (There is a more complex orthographical explanation, but it requires an advanced understanding of Hebrew nouns.)

בַּדֶּרֶךְ

This means *in the way*. The first letter, ב, is a preposition meaning *in*. We will learn about prepositions later. But it is worth noting that it is a single letter attached to the front of the word, just like ו. Notice also that the ב is written with *dagesh* because it is at the beginning of the word. The symbol : after בְּדָרֶךְ indicates that this is the end of the verse. It is not the same as a full stop (or period) in English; it occurs only at the end of a verse, even if the verse is made up of several sentences. Notice also that there is an *a* vowel instead of an *e* vowel in the middle syllable of the word. This has happened because it is the last word in the verse. It is said to be 'in pause', because a reader pauses at the last word in the verse and, in Hebrew, this can mean a vowel is lengthened (in this case from short *e* to long *a*.)

By this point your word-matching should have produced something like: *good and just Yhwh therefore he teaches sinners in the way*.

It is now necessary to turn this into a sentence in idiomatic English, which is (arguably) the most difficult task of translation. Hebrew word order is not the same as English word order. You will need to juggle the words until they make sense in English, while still retaining the meaning of the Hebrew.

Possible translation

Yhwh is good and just; therefore he teaches sinners in the way.

There are two points to note here. First, there is no word meaning *is* in the Hebrew text. It is common for this word to be absent in Hebrew, and we need to add the word *is* if the sentence is to make sense in English. This way of constructing sentences will be explained in more detail later. Second, the word order has been changed in the possible translation. This is because in today's English, we usually say *the house is white* rather than *white is the house*. But of course, this is a psalm; it is poetry and we can be a little more flexible with word order than we can in prose. It would be perfectly appropriate to translate the phrase: *Good and just is Yhwh*. And, of course, we can substitute *the LORD* for *Yhwh*.

3.7 Suggestions

- Memorize the letters that take *dagesh* at the beginning of a word.
- Learn what ו does before מ, ב and פ.
- Learn all new vocabulary.

- Practise reading the text of Psalm 25:8 aloud. Go very slowly at first.

- Practise reading out loud all the vocabulary you have learned so far.

3.8 Summary

In this unit we have looked at

- *dagesh*
- the conjunction ו, which means *and* or *but*
- the name of God
- the text of Psalm 25:8
- *maqqef.*

4.1 The definite article

> **Grammar: the definite article**
>
> In English, we have definite and indefinite articles. The word *the* is the definite article, as in *the house*, meaning a particular house. The word *a* is the indefinite article, as in *a house*, meaning an unspecified house.

The definite article in Hebrew is not a separate word (as it is in English), but instead is attached to the word that follows it, just like the conjunction ו. The definite article comprises the letter ה, usually with a short-*a* vowel, and a *dagesh* in the following letter. Here are some examples:

the day	הַיּוֹם
the horse	הַסּוּס

Note the *dagesh* in י and ס.

As we noted above, some letters take *dagesh* at the beginning of a word, and these continue to take a *dagesh* (only one *dagesh*: we do not add a second *dagesh* to indicate the definite article). Here are some examples:

the son	הַבֵּן
the garden	הַגָּן

And some letters do not take *dagesh* at all, so they cannot take *dagesh* with the definite article. However, in these cases the vowel under the ה sometimes changes to a long-*a* vowel. Here are some examples:

| the man | הָאִישׁ |
| the father | הָאָב |

However, this vowel change is not inevitable. For example, *the sand* is הַחוֹל with a short-*a* vowel.

Occasionally the vowel under the ה will change to a short-*e* vowel:

| a feast | חַג |
| the feast | הֶחָג |

There is a common word that changes with the definite article, and it is worth learning the change:

| land | אֶרֶץ |
| the land | הָאָרֶץ |

There is no indefinite article in Hebrew. The word סוּס can mean either *horse* or *a horse*. Context will usually determine whether we translate it with an indefinite article in English.

4.2 Exercise 1

a) Put the definite article in front of the following words and write the meaning of the word next to it (the first is done for you). Don't forget to add the *dagesh* in letters that take *dagesh*.

Example:

Meaning: _____*the day*_____ הַיּוֹם

Meaning: _____ בַּת

Meaning: _____ גַּן

Meaning: _____ חוֹל

Meaning: _____ יָד

Meaning: _____ לֵבָב

Meaning: _____ דֶּרֶךְ

Meaning: _____ קוֹל

Meaning: _____ אֶרֶץ

Meaning: _____ אִישׁ

b) Translate:

הָאִישׁ וְהָאִשָּׁה _____

הָאָב וְהָאֵם _____

הַחוֹל וְהַיָּם _____

הַסּוּס וְהַפָּר _____

הָאָח וְהָאָחוֹת _____

4.3 Gender and number

Grammar: number and gender

In English, words can be singular (s) (e.g. the *apple*) or plural (p) (e.g. the *oranges*). We call this *number*. If you ask me to describe the grammatical number of the word *bananas* I would tell you it was plural. I don't know how many bananas there are; I know only there is more than one. This applies to many words: *she* is singular; *they* is plural.

In Hebrew, as well as being singular or plural, words can be masculine (m) or feminine (f). The word for *land* is feminine and the word for *garden* is masculine. In English, gardens are neither masculine nor feminine, since English does not have gender. We may assume that *a prince* is masculine and *a princess* is feminine, but they are not grammatically so.

In Unit 6 we will also encounter common (c) gender.

A number of the words we have learned already are feminine. Many people find it helpful to make a note of the gender of words in their vocabulary books, so if you are keeping a book you might like to note that the following words are feminine:

כַּף   יָד   הִיא   בַּת   אִשָּׁה   אֶרֶץ   אֵם   אַחַת

It is unsurprising that words for female people are grammatically feminine, though this is not inevitable. There is no particular logic to the gender of other words. One might guess at reasons why a *tree* should be masculine and a *spring* feminine, but often there is no way to predict a word's gender, and it must be learned. However, words that end with הָ are usually feminine, e.g.:

woman	אִשָּׁה	*i-SHĀ*
cow	פָּרָה	*pa-RĀ*
princess	שָׂרָה	*sa-RĀ*

A noteable exception is the word for *night*, לַיְלָה (*LĪ-lā*), which is masculine. For pronunciation see Appendix 2.

Grammar: nouns and verbs

It can be useful to distinguish different categories of words. This can be complicated, because some words are categorized according to context. Consider the word *respect*. In the sentence *I respect you* the word *respect* is a verb. But in the sentence *Please treat everybody with respect* the word *respect* is a noun.

A verb is often described as a 'doing word'. It describes activities like *walk*, *run*, *swim*; and also other things we do, like *think*, *owe*, *respect*. If you can put *to* in front of it, it's probably a verb. *To think* makes sense; *to window* doesn't. But many words, like *respect*, can be either nouns or verbs.

A noun is often described as an 'object' or a 'thing'. It can be a real object, like *window*, *fish*, *shoe*; or it can be abstract, like *integrity*, *love*, *respect*. If you can put *the* in front of it, it's probably a noun. *The window* makes sense; *the think* doesn't. Names are sometimes known as *proper nouns*. Most of the words we have learned so far are nouns.

Plurals are formed by adding *suffixes* (extra letters at the end of a word). In English, we usually add *s* (e.g. *cow*; *cows*), though some words in English have no distinct plural (e.g. *sheep*; *sheep*) and some have irregular plurals, which are left over from an earlier stage in the development of the English language (e.g. *ox*; *oxen*). Hebrew also adds suffixes to make plurals.

In Hebrew, masculine plurals add the suffix יִם. We have already seen a masculine plural in Pslam 25: the word חַטָּא has the plural חַטָּאִים. Here are some more examples:

horse	סוס		*horses*	סוּסִים	*soos-EEM*
ox	פַּר		*oxen*	פָּרִים	*par-EEM*
prince	שַׂר	*sar*	*princes*	שָׂרִים	*sar-EEM*

Feminine plurals change the ה to וֹת:

mare	סוּסָה	*soo-SĀ*	*mares*	סוּסוֹת	*soo-SŌT*
cow	פָּרָה	*pa-RĀ*	*cows*	פָּרוֹת	*pa-RŌT*
princess	שָׂרָה	*sa-RĀ*	*princesses*	שָׂרוֹת	*sa-RŌT*

Dual form

In Hebrew, there is a special ending for things that come in pairs, such as *hands* and *feet*. These words are typically feminine. This form is called the *dual* form and looks very much like the masculine ending, but with an extra *a* vowel:

hand	יָד	*yād*	*hands*	יָדַיִם	*yā-DĪ-im*
foot	רֶגֶל	*RE-gel*	*feet*	רַגְלַיִם	*rag-LĪ-im*
knee	בֶּרֶךְ	*BE-rek*	*knees*	בִּרְכַּיִם	*bir-KĪ-im*
lip	שָׂפָה	*sā-FĀ*	*lips*	שְׂפָתַיִם	*s^a-fā-TĪ-im*
ear	אֹזֶן	*Ō-zen*	*ears*	אָזְנַיִם	*oz-NĪ-yim*
eye	עַיִן	*A-yin*	*eyes*	עֵינַיִם	*ay-NĪ-yim*

Notice that the vowels have changed in most of the plural forms: e.g. the vowels in רֶגֶל have changed to and in רַגְלַיִם. There are reasons for this, and we will discuss these later. For now it is important merely to notice that there are differences.

4.4 Exercise 2

a) Write the plurals of the following nouns and give the meaning:

Example:

Meaning: _____*mares*_____ Plural: _____סוּסוֹת_____ Singular: סוּסָה

Meaning: _____*the oxen*_____ Plural: _____הַפָּרִים_____ Singular: הַפָּר

Meaning: _____ Plural: _____ Singular: סוּס

Meaning: _____ Plural: _____ Singular: עַיִן

Meaning: _____ Plural: _____ Singular: הַשֹּׁר

Meaning: _____ Plural: _____ Singular: הַשָּׂרָה

Meaning: _____ Plural: _____ Singular: קוֹל

Meaning: _____ Plural: _____ Singular: פָּרָה

Meaning: _____ Plural: _____ Singular: הַיָּד

Meaning: _____ Plural: _____ Singular: רֶגֶל

b) Translate

יָדַיִם וְרַגְלַיִם _____

סוּסִים וְסוּסוֹת _____

הֶהָרִים וְהַיַּמִּים _____

הַגַּנִּים וְהַדְּרָכִים _____

Hint: If the last of these seems difficult, perhaps it is because both nouns end in letters that have final forms. Check your vocabulary book for words that begin with the right letter and see if you can find them.

4.5 Irregular plurals

Not all feminine nouns end in ה ; e.g., בַּת is feminine but doesn't end in ה . Sometimes these feminine nouns form plurals differently, and indeed some of the common masculine nouns have irregular plurals. Moreover, we have already encountered a word that appears to have the form of a feminine plural, since it ends with וֹת, but in fact it is singular. The word is אָחוֹת (*sister*). Here are a few examples of irregular plurals, which you must learn:

man	אִישׁ	*men*	אֲנָשִׁים	*a-nā-SHEEM*
woman	אִשָּׁה	*women*	נָשִׁים	*nā-SHEEM*
son	בֵּן	*sons*	בָּנִים	*bā-NEEM*
daughter	בַּת	*daughters*	בָּנוֹת	*bā-NŌT*
brother	אָח	*brothers*	אַחִים	*a-CHEEM*
sister	אָחוֹת	*sisters*	אֲחָיוֹת	*ach-AĪ-ōt*
father	אָב	*fathers*	אָבוֹת	*ā-VŌT*
mother	אֵם	*mothers*	אִמּוֹת	*im-MŌT*

A feminine word with an apparently masculine ending:

city	עִיר	*cities*	עָרִים	*ā-REEM*

A masculine word with an apparently feminine ending:

night	לַיְלָה	*nights*	לֵילוֹת	*LAY-lōt*

Plurals that are easily confused:

day	יוֹם	*days*	יָמִים	*yā-MEEM*
sea	יָם	*seas*	יַמִּים	*ya-MEEM*

4.6 Exercise 3

Write the following in Hebrew:

a man _____   *the men* _____

a daughter _____   *the daughters* _____

the mother _____   *mothers* _____

night _____   *nights* _____

the days and the nights _____

cities and princes _____

4.7 Text: Genesis 1:1

There is no ideal verse in the Bible with which to demonstrate the definite article and the use of plurals at this stage. Verses with straightforward plurals often have complicated verbs or other difficult grammatical features. The advantage of Genesis 1:1 is that it is familiar to many people and it does show definite articles and plurals in action, though perhaps not as effectively as exercises designed for the purpose. However, I hope it is a little more interesting than a mere exercise.

Points to look out for in this text:

- Words we have already encountered.

- Use of the definite article.

- Plural forms.

object marker (no English word translates it)	אֵת	*ayt*
verb: *to create, to form, to make*	בָּרָא	*bā-RĀ*
noun (f): *a beginning, a former time*	רֵאשִׁית	*ray-SHEET*
noun: *heaven*	שָׁמַיִם	*sha-MĪ-yim*

Text

As in Unit 3, read the verse aloud a few times to be sure of the pronunciation.

בְּרֵאשִׁית בָּרָא אֱלֹהִים אֵת הַשָּׁמַיִם וְאֵת הָאָרֶץ:

Approximate pronunciation:

Bᵃ-ray-SHEET bā-RĀ elō-HEEM ayt ha-shā-MĪ-yim vᵃ-ayt hā-ĀR-ets

As you did in Unit 3, try to match each word of the text with the vocabulary above, as far as you can. Remember, some of the words above are not precisely the same as the words in the list of vocabulary. The words in the vocabulary are the dictionary forms. Once you have matched the words in the text with the vocabulary, you should begin to have a sense of the meaning of the verse. Of course, many readers will find this verse very familiar: the meaning is obvious. Or is it?

Notes

בְּרֵאשִׁית

The letter בּ at the beginning of this word means *in*. We will look at this in more detail later. The whole word is usually translated *in the beginning*, though translations vary. Notice that there is no vowel under the *alef*. This is fairly common in Hebrew; it is often treated as a silent letter (a little like the *h* in *honest*) and left unvocalized.

בָּרָא

This word means *he created*. Notice that the meaning given in the vocabulary above for בָּרָא is *to create* but we are translating exactly the same word here as *he created*. Also, the word for *he* (הוּא) is not used here. We will explore the reasons for this later.

אֱלֹהִים

The word for *God* (see Unit 2). This word is plural in form but is not usually translated as a plural, unless it refers to the gods of other nations.

אֵת

This word is known as the 'object marker', and will be discussed later. There is no English word for אֵת, so we leave it untranslated.

הַשָּׁמַיִם

The definite article and the word for *heaven*. The word has a dual ending, but usually in idiomatic English we talk about *heaven* rather than *the heavens*, except perhaps in contexts where biblical idiom is common (e.g. in some religious institutions). However, many translations translate this word *the heavens*, and it would not be wrong to follow their lead.

וְאֵת

The conjunction וֹ (clearly meaning *and* rather than *but* in this context) and the object marker again. We simply translate this word *and*.

הָאָרֶץ

The definite article and the word for earth.

Possible translations

In the beginning God created the heavens and the earth.

In the beginning God created heaven and earth.

4.8 Suggestions

- Learn all the new vocabulary (and continue to do this after each unit).

- Learn the plural forms in this unit. Be sure you understand the distinction between plural and dual forms.

- Learn the irregular plural forms; these are common words, so you may encounter them frequently in the Bible.

4.9 Summary

In this unit we have looked at

- the definite article
- plural and dual forms
- the text of Genesis 1:1.

unit 05

5.1 Subject pronouns

> A pronoun is a word that takes the place of a noun. Examples are
> words like *she* and *they*.

Personal pronouns in Hebrew have to be learned by heart – there's
no easy way to remember them. There are many pronouns in
Hebrew (just like in English). In this unit we're going to focus
on pronouns meaning *he, she, you, I, they* and *we*.

SINGULAR			PLURAL		
he	הוּא	*hoo*	*they* (m)	הֵמָּה or הֵם	*HAY-mā* or *haym*
she	הִיא	*hee*	*they* (f)	הֵנָּה	*HAY-nā*
you (m)	אַתָּה	*at-TĀ*	*you* (m)	אַתֶּם	*a-TEM*
you (f)	אַתְּ	*at*	*you* (f)	אַתֶּן	*a-TEN*
I	אָנֹכִי or אֲנִי	*ā-no-CHEE* or *a-NEE*	*we*	אֲנַחְנוּ	*a-NACH-noo*

In biblical Hebrew, there are four ways of saying *you*; it depends
on whether we are addressing one person or more, and whether
those people are male or female. If we are addressing a group
of men and women, the masculine plural is used. The feminine
plural is used only for addressing two or more women. Since
there aren't many groups of women in the Hebrew Bible, we
don't see the feminine plural much, though there are quite a few
in the book of Ruth.

The pronouns above are used only when they are the subject of a
verb. That's why they're called *subject pronouns*. In the sentence
She gave the book to him, she is the subject; *him* is the object.

So הוּא is the pronoun used as the subject: it means *he* but not *him*. Later, in Unit 10, we'll look at object pronouns (words for *me*, *him*, *her* etc.)

5.2 Exercise 1

Fill in the blanks.

SINGULAR		PLURAL	
he	_____	*they* (m)	_____
_____	הִיא	_____	הֵנָּה
you (m)	_____	_____	אַתֶּם
_____ (f)	אַתְּ	*you* (f)	_____
I	_____	_____	אֲנַחְנוּ

5.3 Sentences without verbs

If we want to use English grammar correctly, we need to put verbs in our sentences (e.g. I *am* the king). However, in Hebrew we can make simple sentences using just pronouns and nouns.

In Hebrew, the present tense of the verb *to be* is understood without needing to be written. If you know the Hebrew for *I* (אֲנִי) and for the *king* (מֶלֶךְ MEL-ech), you can say, *I am the king*:

אֲנִי הַמֶּלֶךְ

Here are some more examples of verbless sentences:

You are the father.	אַתָּה הָאָב
She is the princess.	הִיא הַשָּׂרָה

The words הוּא and הִיא can also mean *it*:

It is the garden.	הוּא הַגַּן
It is the city.	הִיא הָעִיר

We use הוּא with הַגַּן because גַּן is masculine, and הִיא with הָעִיר because עִיר is feminine.

5.4 Exercise 2

Complete the sentences.

He is the prince.	_____	הוּא
She is the woman.	_____	הִיא
You are the brother.	הָאָח _____	
You are the princess.	_____	אַתְּ
I am the king.	הַמֶּלֶךְ _____	
It is the mountain.	הָהָר _____	
It is the cow.	_____	הִיא
They are the sons.	הַבָּנִים _____	
They are the women.	הַנָּשִׁים _____	
You are the fathers.	_____	אַתֶּם
You are the daughters.	_____	אַתֵּן
We are the princes.	הַשָּׂרִים _____	
They are the horses.	הַסּוּסִים _____	
They are the cows.	_____	הֵנָּה

5.5 Text: 2 Samuel 12:7a

verb: *to say*	אָמַר	ā-MAR
name: *David*	דָּוִד	dā-VID
name: *Nathan*	נָתָן	nā-TĀN

Text

Read the verse aloud a few times to be sure of the pronunciation.

וַיֹּאמֶר נָתָן אֶל־דָּוִד אַתָּה הָאִישׁ

Approximate pronunciation:

va-YO-mer nā-TĀN el dā-VID at-TĀ hā-EESH

Notes

וַיֹּאמֶר

This word means *and he said*. We haven't learned about verbs yet; we will learn this form later. Notice, though, the ו at the beginning of the word, meaning *and*.

נָתָן

The name Nathan.

אֶל־דָּוִד

We have seen the word אֶל before: it means *to*. Here it is joined with *maqqef* to the name *David*.

אַתָּה

This pronoun means *you*. It is masculine and singular.

הָאִישׁ

You have encountered this word several times already: it means *the man*.

By now you should have something like: *And he said Nathan to David you are the man*. Notice that the word order in Hebrew differs from English. The verb comes first in the sentence (*and he said*), followed by the subject (*Nathan*) and then the object (*David*). Also, Hebrew has no quotation marks for indicating direct speech. But when we translate into English, it is appropriate to use quotation marks if a person in the text speaks directly to another.

Possible translation

And Nathan said to David, 'You are the man.'

5.6 Suggestion

Write out the pronouns on a sheet of paper and put it in your purse or wallet. Then read the pronouns aloud every day for a week.

5.7 Summary

In this unit we have looked at:

- personal pronouns for the subject of the verb
- the construction of Hebrew sentences without the verb *to be*
- the text of 2 Samuel 12:7a.

5.8 Self-assessment

The self-assessment is intended to test your knowledge and understanding of the points of grammar covered in Units 1 to 5.

Answer all questions as fully as possible. Try to answer the questions without looking up the answers.

1) Write out the alphabet in order (it's easy to forget the order after the first couple of weeks). Include final forms where they exist.

3 marks

2) Write out the following:

  a) short vowels
  b) long vowels
  c) *sheva*
  d) composite *sheva* vowels

4 marks

3) a) Which letters always take dagesh at the beginning of a word?

  b) Which letters never take *dagesh*?

2 marks

4) Write in Hebrew:

   a) *the king*

   b) *the hand*

   c) *the man*

   d) *the mother*

                                  4 marks

5) Write in Hebrew:

   a) *man and woman*

   b) *princess and prince*

   c) *night and day*

   d) *city and mountain*

   e) *horse and mare*

   f) *land and sea*

                                    6 marks

6) Write in English:

   a) הוּא הָאִישׁ

   b) הֵמָּה הַשָּׂרִים

   c) אֲנַחְנוּ הַבָּנוֹת

   d) הִיא הָעִיר

   e) אַתֶּן הַנָּשִׁים

   f) אֲנִי הָאָחוֹת

                                    6 marks

The answers to the self-assessment are in the Key to the exercises at the back of the book.

Scoring: Each correct answer gets one mark. (For question 1, divide the alphabet into 3 sections: א to ז and ח to ס and ע to ת.) You lose a mark if you make a mistake. A mistake means a missing letter or a missing vowel, or other missing or incorrect information. The final score will be a number out of 25. Multiply by 4 to find your percentage.

If you make any mistakes (and almost everyone will make a few), make sure you understand where you went wrong before you continue with Unit 6.

Note: learning a language often involves making silly little errors. People learning Hebrew tend to find their commonest mistakes are missing or incorrect vowels. It can seem unfair to lose a whole mark for a missing vowel. However, if you were learning English, you would want to include all the vowels! Nevertheless, you are marking this yourself, so you can be as tough or as lenient as you choose. The important thing is that you learn from your mistakes.

At this point you have already learned a significant amount. You are familiar with a new alphabet and you are becoming more comfortable using it. Reading and writing from right to left is probably something you barely notice now. You have learned quite a bit of useful vocabulary: you know about 80 words, and you could probably recognize at least one word on every page of a Hebrew Bible. Furthermore, you have started to read the Bible in Hebrew. The next five units will draw on the skills and knowledge you have already gained.

6.1 Nouns with pronominal suffixes

Grammar: person

The idea of *person* is used to indicate the relationship between the speaker or writer and the listener or reader. It is probably easiest to grasp by means of an example:

I told you that he was happy.

If we describe the pronouns in this sentence, we would say that *I* is first person, *you* is second person and *he* is third person.

Here are the English pronouns categorized by person:

I, me, my, mine, we, our, ours	first person
You, your, yours	second person
He, him, his, she, her, hers, it, its, they, their, theirs	third person

These pronouns can be singular: *I, you, he, she, it*; or plural: *we, you* (as in *all of you*), *they*.

In Hebrew, the pronouns can also be masculine (m) אָנֹכִי; feminine (f) הִיא אַתְּ הֵנָּה אַתֵּן; or common (c) הוּא אַתָּה הֵמָּה אַתֶּם אֲנַחְנוּ. Common gender is not exactly like the concept of neuter gender in other languages, but it is similar. In Hebrew, first-person pronouns are always common gender. However, Hebrew nouns are rarely common gender.

The idea of person does not apply only to pronouns; it can also apply to verbs, as we will discover in due course.

We can use shorthand to indicate person, gender and number. For example, הוּא is 3ms (third person masculine singular).

In English, if I want to indicate that a house belongs to me, I can describe it as *my house*. In Hebrew the idea is conveyed by adding a suffix to the word for *house*. These suffixes are called *pronominal* suffixes because they are related to the personal pronouns we have already learned.

Here is the word סוּס with pronominal suffixes:

his horse (3ms)	סוּסוֹ	soo-SŌ
her horse (3fs)	סוּסָהּ	soo-SĀCH
your horse (2ms)	סוּסְךָ	soo-sᵃ-CHĀ
your horse (2ms)	סוּסֶךָ	soo-SAYCH
my horse (1cs)	סוּסִי	soo-SEE
their horse (3mp)	סוּסָם	soo-SĀM
their horse (3fp)	סוּסָן	soo-SĀN
your horse (2mp)	סוּסְכֶם	soo-sᵃ-CHEM
your horse (2fp)	סוּסְכֶן	soo-sᵃ-CHEN
our horse (1cp)	סוּסָנוּ	soo-SAY-noo

Four words can be translated *your horse*. The word used depends on whether the *you* referred to is one man (2ms), one woman (2fs), a group of men or a mixed group (2mp), or a group of women (2fp).

Note the dot in the final ה of סוּסָהּ, *her horse*. This looks exactly the same as a *dagesh* but is called *mappiq*. *Mappiq* occurs only in a final ה. Of course, ה cannot take *dagesh*, so if you see a dot in a ה it must be *mappiq*. When you see הּ you pronounce it *ch* as in *loch*. Thus סוּסָהּ is *soos-ACH*.

The same suffixes are used if a noun is feminine, although if the noun ends in הָ , the ה changes to ת. Here is the word סוּסָה with pronominal suffixes:

his mare (3ms)	סוּסָתוֹ	soo-sā-TŌ
her mare (3fs)	סוּסָתָהּ	soo-sā-TĀCH
your mare (2ms)	סוּסָתְךָ	soo-sā-tᵃ-CHĀ
your mare (2fs)	סוּסָתֵךְ	soo-sā-TAYCH
my mare (1cs)	סוּסָתִי	soo-sā-TEE
their mare (3mp)	סוּסָתָם	soo-sā-TĀM
their mare (3fp)	סוּסָתָן	soo-sā-TĀN
your mare (2mp)	סוּסַתְכֶם	soo-sat-CHEM
your mare (2fp)	סוּסַתְכֶן	soo-sat-CHEN
our mare (1cp)	סוּסָתֵנוּ	soo-sā-TAY-noo

If more than one horse is being described, slightly different suffixes are added to a modified form of the plural noun. Here is the word סוּסִים with pronominal suffixes:

his horses	סוּסָיו	soo-SAV
her horses	סוּסֶיהָ	soo-SAY-hā
your horses	סוּסֶיךָ	soo-SAY-chā
your horses	סוּסַיִךְ	soo-SĪ-yich
my horses	סוּסַי	soo-SĪ
their horses	סוּסֵיהֶם	soo-say-HEM
their horses	סוּסֵיהֶן	soo-say-HEN
your horses	סוּסֵיכֶם	soo-say-CHEM
your horses	סוּסֵיכֶן	soo-say-CHEN
our horses	סוּסֵינוּ	soo-SAY-noo

The pronominal suffixes for feminine plural nouns are the same, even to the extent of preserving the ' of the masculine plural. Here is the word סוּסוֹת with pronominal suffixes:

his mares	סוּסוֹתָיו	soo-sō-TĀV
her mares	סוּסוֹתֶיהָ	soo-sō-TAY-hā
your mares	סוּסוֹתֶיךָ	soo-sō-TAY-chā
your mares	סוּסוֹתַיִךְ	soo-sō-TĪ-yich
my mares	סוּסוֹתַי	soo-sō-TĪ

their mares	סוּסוֹתֵיהֶם	soo-sō-tay-HEM
their mares	סוּסוֹתֵיהֶן	soo-sō-tay-HEN
your mares	סוּסוֹתֵיכֶם	soo-sō-tay-CHEM
your mares	סוּסוֹתֵיכֶן	soo-sō-tay-CHEN
our mares	סוּסוֹתֵינוּ	soo-sō-TAY-noo

6.2 Exercise 1

Write the following in the correct places in the table and give meanings:

קוֹלוֹ קוֹלִי קוֹלְכֶם קוֹלֵךְ קוֹלָן קוֹלְכֶן קוֹלֵנוּ קוֹלָהּ קוֹלָם קוֹלֶךָ

3ms _____ meaning _____

3fs _____ meaning _____

2ms _____ meaning _____

2fs _____ meaning _____

1cs _____ meaning _____

3mp _____ meaning _____

3fp _____ meaning _____

2mp _____ meaning _____

2fp _____ meaning _____

1cp _____ meaning _____

Write out פָּרָה with pronominal suffixes:

3ms _____ meaning _____

3fs _____ meaning _____

2ms _____ meaning _____

2fs _____ meaning _____

1cs _____ meaning _____

3mp _____ meaning _____

3fp _____ meaning _____

2mp _____ meaning _____

2fp _____ meaning _____

1cp _____ meaning _____

Give meanings for the following:

אָבִי _____

יָדֶיךָ _____

אֱלֹהֵינוּ _____

מַלְכֵיהֶם _____

אִמּוֹ _____

Hint: the absolute forms of the words above (i.e. the forms you would find in a dictionary) are:

אָב יָד אֱלֹהִים מֶלֶךְ אֵם

6.3 Adjectives in verbless sentences

> **Grammar: adjectives**
>
> An adjective is a word that describes a noun. In the sentence *The door is red* the word *door* is a noun and the word *red* is an adjective. Other examples of adjectives are *good*, *bad*, *sharp*, *just* (as in upright), *strong*, *white*, *many*, *light* (as in not heavy). We have already encountered the Hebrew words for these adjectives:
>
> טוֹב רַע חַד יָשָׁר עַז חָר רַב קַל

In Unit 5, we looked at sentences without verbs; e.g. אֲנִי הַמֶּלֶךְ *I am the king*. The present tense of the verb *to be* is understood without being written.

Similarly, if we want to say *the man is good* or *the horse is strong* in Hebrew, we leave out the verb *to be*. We also have to put the adjective before the noun. Read these examples (and all examples) out loud:

the man is good   טוֹב הָאִישׁ

my horse is strong   עַז סוּסִי

We have already seen an example of this construction in Psalm 25:8 (see Unit 3).

In English, adjectives generally do not change. We can say *the door is red* or *the doors are red*; *red* remains the same. One exception, perhaps, is *blond*: we might say *the man is blond*, but *the woman is blonde*. This kind of change is called *agreement*. The word *blond* is masculine, so it agrees with the word *man*. The letter *e* is added to the word (hence *blonde*) in order to agree with the word *woman*.

In Hebrew, all adjectives have to agree with the noun they are describing. If the adjective describes a feminine noun, it takes a feminine form:

the woman is good	טוֹבָה הָאִשָּׁה	tō-VĀ hah-i-SHĀ
his mare is strong	עַזָּה סוּסָתוֹ	a-ZĀ soo-sā-TŌ

If the adjective describes a plural noun, it takes a plural form:

the men are good	טוֹבִים הָאֲנָשִׁים	tō-VEEM hā-a-nā-SHEEM
our sons are bad	רָעִים בָּנֵינוּ	rā-EEM bā-NAY-noo

A noun that is both feminine and plural requires an adjective that is both feminine and plural:

the mothers are good	טוֹבוֹת הָאִמּוֹת	tō-VŌT ha-i-MŌT
the princesses are bad	רָעוֹת הַשָּׂרוֹת	rā-ŌT ha-sā-RŌT

You may remember that some nouns have irregular forms. For example, לַיְלָה looks like a feminine noun but is in fact masculine. And the word for *women* looks like a masculine plural but is in fact feminine. In cases like this, the form of the adjective should be the usual form. The same applies to nouns with dual endings. For example:

the nights are good	טוֹבִים הַלֵּילוֹת	tō-VEEM ha-lay-LŌT
the fathers are good	טוֹבִים הָאָבוֹת	tō-VEEM hah-a-VŌT
the women are good	טוֹבוֹת הַנָּשִׁים	tō-VŌT ha-nā-SHEEM
the hands are good	טוֹבוֹת הַיָּדַיִם	tō-VŌT ha-yā-DĪ-yim

Many nouns and adjectives are vocalized differently (i.e. they have different vowels) when they appear in feminine or plural forms. Others aquire a *dagesh*. For example, compare the adjectives in the following:

the horse is strong   עַז הַסּוּס

the mare is strong   עַזָּה הַסּוּסָה

Note the *dagesh* in עַזָּה. There are reasons for such changes, and a Hebrew grammar will explain them. The changes do not usually interfere with recognition; if you know a word in its absolute (basic) form, you should be able to recognize it in plural or feminine forms. And even if you don't know the word, the changes are not usually significant enough to cause difficulty in finding the word in a dictionary.

Negatives

In Hebrew, negatives are introduced with the negative particle לֹא. This is how it works:

the king is good   טוֹב הַמֶּלֶךְ

the king is not good   לֹא טוֹב הַמֶּלֶךְ

the horse is strong but the   עַז הַסּוּס וְלֹא עַזָּה הַסּוּסָה
mare is not strong

(You might remember that the conjunction וְ can mean *but* when a contrast is implied.)

6.4 Exercise 2

Adjectives

great, large	גָּדוֹל	gā-DŌL
new	חָדָשׁ	chā-DĀSH
wise	חָכָם	chā-CHĀM
beautiful	יָפֶה	yā-FE (f יָפָה yā-FĀ)
holy	קָדוֹשׁ	kā-DŌSH
small	קָטֹן	kā-TŌN (f קְטַנָּה k^a-ta-NĀ)

| empty | רֵיק | rayk |

Nouns

love (f)	אַהֲבָה	a-ha-VĀ
food (f)	אָכְלָה	och-LĀ
house (m)	בַּיִת	BA-yit (p בָּתִּים bāt-TEEM)
blessing (f)	בְּרָכָה	bᵃ-rā-CHĀ (p בְּרָכוֹת bᵃ-rā-CHŌT)
word, thing (m)	דָּבָר	dā-VĀR (p דְּבָרִים dᵃ-vā-REEM)
knowledge (f)	דַּעַת	DA-at
sword (f)	חֶרֶב	CHE-rev (p חֲרָבוֹת cha-rā-VŌT)
priest (m)	כֹּהֵן	cō-HAYN (p כֹּהֲנִים cō-ha-NEEM)
place (m)	מָקוֹם	mā-KŌM (p מְקוֹמוֹת mᵃ-kō-MŌT)

Note that מָקוֹם is a masculine noun with an irregular plural ending that looks feminine. It takes masculine adjectives.

Choose the correct adjective from the options given, and give the meanings of the sentences:

קְטַנָּם	קָטָן	קְטַנָּה	הַכֹּהֵן _____
חַדּוֹת	חַדָּה	חַד	חֲרָבוֹת _____
קָדוֹשׁ	קְדוֹשִׁים	קְדוֹשׁוֹת	הַמְּקוֹמוֹת _____
רַע	רָעָה	רָעוֹת	הַשָּׂר _____
טוֹבוֹת	טוֹבָה	טוֹב	הָאָכְלָה _____
רֵיקוֹת	רֵיקָה	רֵיק	הַבַּיִת _____
יָפוֹת	יָפָה	יָפֶה	אַהֲבָתוֹ _____
חֲכָמִים	חֲכָמוֹת	חָכָם	דְּבָרֵינוּ _____
גְּדוֹלָה	גָּדוֹל	גְּדוֹלוֹת	דַּעְתִּי _____
חֲדָשׁוֹת	חֲדָשָׁה	חֲדָשִׁים	בִּרְכוֹתֵיכֶם _____

6.5 Adjectives (attributive)

There are other ways to use adjectives in English. Compare the following:

a) *The man is good.*

b) *the good man*

Both of these describe the man in the same way and have much the same meaning. However, example a) is a complete sentence, whereas example b) is just part of a sentence. Example b) needs more information (generally a verb) to make it a sentence; e.g. *The good man rested*, or *Abraham is a good man*. This kind of use of adjectives is called *attributive*.

In English, an attributive adjective comes before the noun, but in Hebrew (like French and many other languages) it comes after the noun. Notice also that both words have the definite article:

the good man	הָאִישׁ הַטּוֹב
the holy word	הַדָּבָר הַקָּדוֹשׁ

If we wanted to say *a good man* or *a holy word*, we would omit the definite articles on both noun and adjective:

a good man	אִישׁ טוֹב
a holy word	דָּבָר קָדוֹשׁ

The adjective must always agree with the noun, as we saw in section 6.3 above:

ms	*the great priest*	הַכֹּהֵן הַגָּדוֹל
mp	*the great priests*	הַכֹּהֲנִים הַגְּדוֹלִים
fs	*the small cow*	הַפָּרָה הַקְּטַנָּה
fp	*the small cows*	הַפָּרוֹת הַקְּטַנּוֹת

To use this kind of adjectival construction in a sentence, a verb is needed. Verbs generally come at the beginning of a sentence in Hebrew. The verb in this example is *to rest*:

The good man rested.	שָׁבַת הָאִישׁ הַטּוֹב	shā-VAT hā-EESH ha-TŌV

Literally this means *He rested the man the good* but in English we would say *The good man rested*.

If the verb is the present tense of the verb *to be*, it is not necessary to write it in Hebrew because the sense is understood implicitly, as we have seen previously. For example:

Abraham is a good man.   אִישׁ טוֹב אַבְרָהָם

Literally, this means *A man a good (is) Abraham* but in English we would say *Abraham is a good man.*

6.6 Exercise 3

Write in English:

הַחֶרֶב הַחַד

הָעִיר הַגְּדוֹלָה

הַשָּׂרוֹת הַחֲכָמוֹת

הַדְּבָרִים הַקְּדוֹשִׁים

הַנָּשִׁים הַיָּפוֹת

6.7 Text: Psalm 76:2 (76:1 in English)

Points to look out for in this text:

- Words we have already encountered.
- Use of pronominal suffixes.
- Use of adjectives.

verb: *to know*	יָדַע	*yā-DĀ*
place name: *Judah*	יְהוּדָה	*yᵃ-hoo-DĀ*
place name: *Israel*	יִשְׂרָאֵל	*yis-rā-AYL*
noun (m): *name*	שֵׁם	*shaym*

Text

Read the verse aloud a few times to be sure of the pronunciation.

נוֹדָע בִּיהוּדָה אֱלֹהִים

בְּיִשְׂרָאֵל גָּדוֹל שְׁמוֹ:

Approximate pronunciation:

nō-DĀ bee-hoo-DĀ e-lo-HEEM bª-yis-rā-AYL gā-DŌL shª-MŌ

Write the words you know beneath the words in the text, and match the others to the words in the vocabulary.

Notes

a) נוֹדָע This word is a verb and we will look at verbs later. For now, it means *it is known*. The verb is the basis for the word דַּעַת, which we encountered earlier in the unit.

b) בִּיהוּדָה This is *Judah* with the prefix בְּ. It is the same prefix we saw in Unit 4 in the word בְּרֵאשִׁית and we will learn more about it later. The whole word, therefore, means *in Judah*.

c) אֱלֹהִים No doubt the word for God is quite familiar by now.

d) בְּיִשְׂרָאֵל Like בִּיהוּדָה, this is a place name with the prefix בְּ. The whole word, therefore, means *in Israel*.

e) גָּדוֹל This word should be familiar from the vocabulary in section 6.4.

f) שְׁמוֹ This word is שֵׁם with the third person singular pronominal suffix. So it means *his name*.

Possible translation

God is known in Judah;

In Israel his name is great.

We could, of course, translate the second phrase as *His name is great in Israel*, which would also be correct English. The choice involves deciding which translation best captures the meaning and style of the Hebrew. This verse is a psalm and therefore poetry; if it were prose we might expect to see

גָּדוֹל שְׁמוֹ בְּיִשְׂרָאֵל

6.8 Suggestions

- Learn the pronominal suffixes.

- The distinction between הָאִישׁ טוֹב and הָאִישׁ הַטּוֹב is often difficult to grasp. Write out the following and memorize it:

The man is good.   טוֹב הָאִישׁ

The good man (rested).   (שָׁבַת) הָאִישׁ הַטּוֹב

6.9 Summary

In this unit we have looked at

- pronominal suffixes

- adjectives in verbless sentences

- attributive adjectives

- the text of Psalm 76:2.

7.1 Demonstratives

Grammar: demonstratives

Demonstratives indicate which particular thing (or things) is (or are) being referred to. Demonstratives can be used as adjectives or as pronouns. In English, demonstratives are words like *this, these, that, those.*

When they are used as adjectives, they describe a noun; e.g.:

This house is new.

When they are used as pronouns they stand in place of a noun; e.g.:

This is new (i.e. *this house is new*).

This is the new house (i.e. *this house is the new house*).

These sentences are similar in meaning:

This house is new.

This is the new house.

In fact, the distinction between them can usually be understood without determining whether the demonstrative is being used as an adjective or as a pronoun.

The demonstratives in Hebrew are:

this (m)	זֶה	ze
this (f)	זֹאת	zōt
these (m and f)	אֵלֶּה	AY-le
that (m)	הוּא	hoo
that (f)	הִיא	hee
those (m)	הֵם	haym
those (f)	הֵנָּה	HAY-nā

Note: the words for *that* and *those* are the same as the subject pronouns meaning *he, she, they* (m) and *they* (f).

When they are used to qualify a noun, they come after the noun (like other adjectives) and they take the definite article:

this man	הָאִישׁ הַזֶּה
that woman	הָאִשָּׁה הַזֹּאת
these men	הָאֲנָשִׁים הָאֵלֶּה
these women	הַנָּשִׁים הָאֵלֶּה
that son	הַבֵּן הַהוּא
that daughter	הַבַּת הַהִיא
those sons	הַבָּנִים הָהֵם
those daughters	הַבָּנוֹת הָהֵנָּה

When demonstratives are used as pronouns they follow the usual word order for pronouns. Remember:

You are the father.	אַתָּה הָאָב

Similarly:

This is the father.	זֶה הָאָב
This is the mother.	זֹאת הָאֵם
These are the brothers.	אֵלֶּה הָאַחִים
These are the sisters.	אֵלֶּה הָאֲחָיוֹת

That is the father.	הוּא הָאָב
That is the mother.	הִיא הָאֵם
Those are the brothers.	הֵם הָאַחִים
Those are the sisters.	הֵנָּה הָאֲחָיוֹת

Of course, since the word הוּא also means *he*, we could translate the above Hebrew sentences *He is the father*, *She is the mother* etc. The context will determine whether to translate with a personal pronoun or a demonstrative pronoun. If it is not clear from the context of the Hebrew text, then the sense will always be ambiguous.

A noun with a pronominal suffix does not need a definite article, since the suffix makes it definite:

This is my mother.	זֶה אִמִּי
That is my father.	הוּא אָבִי

Again, the second example could also be translated *He is my father*.

A noun can be qualified by several words at the same time, by adjectives and demonstrative pronouns, as in the examples in the grammar box above:

This house is new.	חָדָשׁ הַבַּיִת הַזֶּה

This means literally *New (is) this house*. Compare the word order with טוֹב הָאִישׁ.

This is the new house.	זֶה הַבַּיִת הֶחָדָשׁ

This means literally *This (is) the house the new one*. Compare the word order with הָאִישׁ הַטּוֹב.

This is the good and just man.	זֶה הָאִישׁ הַטּוֹב וְהַיָּשָׁר

This means literally *This (is) the man the good and the just*.

This man is good and just.	טוֹב וְיָשָׁר הָאִישׁ הַזֶּה

This means literally *Good and just (is) the man the this*.

This is my small cow. זֹאת פָּרָתִי הַקְּטַנָּה

This means literally *This is my cow the small.*

7.2 Exercise 1

Give meanings for the following:

Example: *This horse* הַסּוּס הַזֶּה

הַשֵּׁם הַזֶּה

הָאֲכָלָה הַזֹּאת

הַדְּבָרִים הָאֵלֶּה

הַבְּרָכוֹת הָאֵלֶּה

הַבַּיִת הַהוּא

הָאַהֲבָה הַהִיא

הַמְּקוֹמוֹת הָהֵם

הֶחָרָבוֹת הָהֵנָּה

Choose the appropriate demonstrative and give meanings:

זֶה	הֵנָּה	אֵלֶּה	הַכֹּהֵן _____
זֹאת	הִיא	הוּא	הַלֵּבָב _____
אֵלֶּה	זֹאת	הוּא	הָאָרֶץ _____
הֵנָּה	זֶה	אֵלֶּה	הַלֵּילוֹת _____
הֵנָּה	הֵם	זֹאת	הַשָּׁמַיִם _____
זֹאת	הוּא	אֵלֶּה	סוּסוֹתֵכֶם _____
הִיא	הוּא	אֵלֶּה	פָּרָתוֹ _____
זֹאת	הֵם	הֵנָּה	הַנָּשִׁים _____

7.3 The construct

There is no word for *of* in Hebrew. To indicate possession, Hebrew places one noun before another:

the voice of the king   קוֹל הַמֶּלֶךְ

In idiomatic English, we would be more likely to say *the king's voice*.

In this sentence, the word קוֹל is said to be in a *construct relationship* to the word הַמֶּלֶךְ.

The word קוֹל does not change when it is in a construct relationship to another noun. Many words do not change in the construct state.

However, many words do change a little. If we were talking about the king's word or his law (תּוֹרָה *toh-RAH*) rather than his voice, for example, we would say:

the king's word (ms)	דְּבַר הַמֶּלֶךְ	*dᵃ-VAR ha-ME-lech*
the king's words (mp)	דִּבְרֵי הַמֶּלֶךְ	*div-RAY ha-ME-lech*
the king's law (fs)	תּוֹרַת הַמֶּלֶךְ	*tō-RAT ha-ME-lech*
the king's laws (fp)	תּוֹרוֹת הַמֶּלֶךְ	*tō-RŌT ha-ME-lech*

These forms are the most straightforward and are very common. The main points to note are as follows:

Masculine singular: shortened vowels. The two long a vowels in דָּבָר have reduced to ְ and ַ .

Masculine plural: shortened vowels and the י of the plural form without the ם.

Feminine singular: the וֹת ending changes to ַת (as it does before pronominal suffixes).

Feminine plural: frequently unchanged, though there are sometimes vowel changes.

It is usually possible to recognize a construct even if you do not recognize the form. See if you can guess what these phrases mean (see the end of this section for the answers):

a) כֹּהֲנֵי יהוה

b) מַלְכֵי הָאָרֶץ

c) אַהֲבַת הָאִשָּׁה

d) חָרְבוֹת דָּוִד

e) אֱלֹהֵי אָבִי

A number of construct forms are irregular or unusual. These are the construct forms of some common words:

	SINGULAR	CONSTRUCT SINGULAR	PLURAL	CONSTRUCT PLURAL
father	אָב	אֲבִי	אָבוֹת	אֲבוֹת
brother	אָח	אֲחִי	אַחִים	אֲחֵי
man	אִישׁ	אִישׁ	אֲנָשִׁים	אַנְשֵׁי
woman	אִשָּׁה	אֵשֶׁת	נָשִׁים	נְשֵׁי
land	אֶרֶץ	אֶרֶץ	אֲרָצוֹת	אַרְצוֹת
house	בַּיִת	בֵּית	בָּתִּים	בָּתֵּי
son	בֵּן	בֶּן	בָּנִים	בְּנֵי
daughter	בַּת	בַּת	בָּנוֹת	בְּנוֹת
day	יוֹם	יוֹם	יָמִים	יְמֵי
eye	עַיִן	עֵין	עֵינַיִם	עֵינֵי
city	עִיר	עִיר	עָרִים	עָרֵי

In Hebrew, we sometimes encounter several construct forms in a chain, e.g.:

the words of the daughters of the men of Israel   דִּבְרֵי בְּנוֹת אַנְשֵׁי יִשְׂרָאֵל

We could translate this *Israel's men's daughters' words*. However, with a construct chain it is often clumsy to translate in this way. It is easier to use the word *of* several times instead of a chain of English possessive nouns.

However, there can be exceptions. In Hebrew, the words אִישׁ and אִשָּׁה (and their construct forms) can be used to indicate *husband* and *wife*. The phrase בְּנוֹת אֵשֶׁת הָאִישׁ is probably better translated the *man's wife's daughters* rather than *the daughters of the wife of the man*.

So far we have looked at examples of the construct that are definite: *the* voice of *the* king. The word קוֹל does not need a definite article: it is assumed to be definite, because *the king* is definite. Similarly, a name is always definite; hence:

the voice of David (or *David's voice*)   קוֹל דָּוִד

the king of Israel (or *Israel's king*)   מֶלֶךְ יִשְׂרָאֵל

If we wanted to say *a voice of a king* we would say קוֹל מֶלֶךְ without the definite article on מֶלֶךְ. It is assumed that קוֹל is indefinite, because מֶלֶךְ is indefinite.

Clearly, it would be impossible to use the construct to say 'a *son of* the *man*' or 'the *son of* a *man*'. There are other ways of expressing these ideas in Hebrew, as we will see later.

The phrases above were:

a) *Yhwh's priests* (or *the LORD's priests*)

b) *the kings of the land*

c) *the woman's love*

d) *David's swords* (or *the swords of David*)

e) *my father's God* (or *the God of my father*)

Did you wonder why there is no *dagesh* in מ in the phrase מַלְכֵי הָאָרֶץ or in the כ in כֹּהֲנֵי יהוה? Words in construct relationship are considered to be a single unit, even though they are written as two separate words. Therefore the words מַלְכֵי and הָאָרֶץ are considered to be a single unit. Sometimes in cases like this, the *dagesh* is missing at the beginning of the word in the construct state. Sometimes the words in construct relationship are joined by *maqqef*; e.g. בֶּן־דָּוִד *the son of David*.

7.4 Exercise 2

Arrange the words into the sentences below, putting them into the plural and the construct where necessary.

אָבִי אִשָּׁה בֶּן בַּיִת דָּבָר דָּוִד הָאִישׁ יְהוּדָה יִשְׂרָאֵל הַכֹּהֵן הָעָם מֶלֶךְ
סוּסוֹ עַיִן עִיר שֵׁם

The man's wife.

The priest's word.

The kings of Israel.

David's son.

The people's eyes.

The cities of Judah.

His horse's name.

My father's house.

Translate:

זֹאת אֵשֶׁת אָבִי

אֵלֶּה דִּבְרֵי מַלְכְּךָ

הוּא קוֹל בְּנוֹ

הִנֵּה שִׂפְתֵי שָׂרוֹתֵינוּ

7.5 Text: Exodus 15:1a

The text we are going to look at in this unit can be found on the front of this book. If you look very closely at the cover, about a third of the way down, you might be able to make it out. This text comes from a passage known as the Song of Moses, which takes up most of Exodus 15. The song is unique in the Bible: it does not seem to be much like any particular psalm or liturgical text. It was probably associated with the Passover feast, though it is not necessarily restricted to Passover. It focuses on motifs important throughout the Hebrew Bible: on Yhwh's deliverance of his people and his incomparable power, and on the fulfilment of the promise of descendants and land.

Points to look out for in this text:

• Words we have already encountered.

• Demonstratives.

• Use of the construct.

adverb: *then, therefore*	אָז	*ahz*
name: *Moses*	מֹשֶׁה	*mō-SHE*
verb: *to sing*	שִׁיר	*sheer*
noun (f): *song*	שִׁירָה	*shee-RĀ*

Text

Read the verse aloud a few times to be sure of the pronunciation.

אָז יָשִׁר־מֹשֶׁה וּבְנֵי יִשְׂרָאֵל אֶת־הַשִּׁרָה הַזֹּאת לַיהוה

Approximate pronunciation:

āz yā-SHEER mō-SHE oov-NAY yis-rah-AYL et ha-shee-RĀ ha-ZŌT lā-dō-NĪ

Write the words you know beneath the words in the text, and match the others to the words in the vocabulary.

Notes

יָשִׁר

This means *he sang.*

וּבְנֵי

The word (*son*) in the construct plural, with the conjunction וְ. Remember that וְ becomes וּ before the letters בּ and מ and פּ. This word therefore means *and the sons of.*

אֶת

As in Genesis 1:1, this word has no direct English translation.

לַיהוה

You may remember that the letter בּ at the beginning of a word means *in*. Similarly, the letter ל at the beginning of a word indicates *to* (we will learn about these in Unit 8). This word means *to Yhwh* or *to the LORD*. Although the word יָשִׁר means *he sang*, it seems that the subject of the verb is *Moses and the sons of Israel.* This kind of construction is common in Hebrew. Sometimes the phrase בְּנֵי יִשְׂרָאֵל is translated *the children of Israel* rather than *the sons of Israel.* Another word for *song* is שִׁיר (which is masculine and looks exactly like the verb *to sing* above). It occurs in the title of the book Song of Songs: שִׁיר הַשִּׁירִים.

Possible translation

Then Moses and the children of Israel sang this song to Yhwh.

7.6 Suggestions

- Make a list of the demonstratives and learn them.
- Be sure you understand the construct.

7.7 Summary

In this unit we have looked at

- demonstratives (*this, these, that, those*)
- the construct
- the text of Exodus 15:1a.

Vocabulary for the unit will be given at the beginning from this point, although vocabulary for the text will be given immediately before the text, as in previous units.

noun (m): *enemy*	אֹיֵב	*Ō-yayv*
there is not, there are not	אֵין	*ayn*
noun (m): *beloved*	דּוֹד	*dōd*
name: *Daniel*	דָּנִאֵל	*dā-nee-AYL*
noun: (f) *wisdom*	חָכְמָה	*choch-MĀ*
noun (m): *dream*	חֲלוֹם	*cha-LŌM*
noun (m): *love, kindness*	חֶסֶד	*CHE-sed*
name: *Joshua*	יְהוֹשֻׁעַ	*ye-hō-SHOO-a*
name: *Joseph*	יוֹסֵף	*yō-SAYF*
there is, there are	יֵשׁ or יֵשׁ־	*yesh or yaysh*
all, entirety, the whole	כֹּל or כָּל־	*kōl or kol*
noun (f): *wing, skirt* (of a robe)	כָּנָף	*kā-NĀF*
noun (m): *death*	מָוֶת	*MĀ-vet* (construct: מוֹת *mōt*)
noun (m): *young man, servant*	נַעַר	*NA-ar*
noun (m): *servant*	עֶבֶד	*E-ved*
verb: *to stand*	עָמַד	*ā-MAD*
noun (m): *mouth*	פֶּה	*pe*
verb: *to open*	פָּתַח	*pā-TACH*

8.1 Prepositions

> **Grammar: prepositions**
>
> In English, prepositions are those little words like *to, of, at, by, under*. Prepositions indicate relationships between a noun or pronoun and other words in the sentence. For example:
>
> | *The angel* | *stood* | *under* | *the tree.* |
> |---|---|---|---|
> | noun | verb | preposition | noun |
>
> In this sentence, *under* describes the angel's location in relation to the tree. There are other ways in which prepositions may be used, but you do not necessarily need to understand the functions of prepositions in order to recognize them. Complications can arise when prepositions are used in unusual ways, but good commentaries will discuss the issues.

In Hebrew, the prepositions often work in a similar way to English prepositions. We have seen one example of a preposition in Unit 5:

and Nathan said to David   וַיֹּאמֶר נָתָן אֶל־דָּוִד

So the word אֶל means *to*. Here it is joined to דָּוִד by *maqqef*, which is common. However, prepositions are found without *maqqef* more often than with it.

Other prepositions are:

until, as far as	עַד	*ad*
on, upon, against	עַל	*al*
beneath	תַּחַת	*TĀ-chat*
between	בֵּין	*bayn* (remember to distinguish this from the word בֵּן, meaning *son*)

Here are some examples of these prepositions in Hebrew:

as far as the tree	עַד הָעֵץ
upon the tree	עַל הָעֵץ

| beneath the tree | תַּחַת הָעֵץ |
| between the trees | בֵּין הָעֵצִים |

The word בֵּין is used twice if something is between two different things:

| between the house and the tree | בֵּין הַבַּיִת וּבֵין הָעֵץ |

Literally: *between the house and between the tree*.

There are two words in Hebrew for *with*: עִם and אֶת:

| with the man | עִם הָאִישׁ |
| with the man | אֶת הָאִישׁ |

The word אֶת is spelled the same way as the object marker (which we saw in Unit 4 and will learn more about later) but the context should indicate when it is the object marker and when it means *with*, just as the context determines whether the word *bow* means the front of a ship or what a musician does at the end of concert.

There is another preposition that is very common and worth learning. The word לִפְנֵי (lif-NAY) literally means *before the face of*. It means *before*, usually in the sense of *in front of*. For example:

| *and he stood before (in front of) Joseph* | וַיַּעַמְדוּ לִפְנֵי יוֹסֵף |
(Genesis 43:15)

Finally, the preposition אַחֲרֵי (a-cha-RAY) means *after*. For example:

| *after the death of Joshua* | אַחֲרֵי מוֹת יְהוֹשֻׁעַ |
(Judges 1:1)

8.2 Exercise 1

Match the English with the Hebrew:

| *as far as the city* | בֵּין הָאֲנָשִׁים |
| *on the skirt* | תַּחַת הַשָּׁמֶשׁ |

with my servant	אֶל אִשְׁתּוֹ
between the men	עַד הָעִיר
with the young men	עִם עֲבְדִּי
beneath the sun	עִם אֵלָיו
with an enemy	אֶת הַנְּעָרִים
to his wife	עַל הַכָּנָף

8.3 Inseparable prepositions

Three prepositions in Hebrew work as suffixes: they are joined to a word rather like the definite article is joined to a word. These three prepositions are:

in, with	בּ
as, like	כּ
to, at, for	ל

When the noun is indefinite, these prepositions are usually vocalized with *sheva*. Here are some examples in Hebrew:

in a house	בְּבַיִת
like a house	כְּבַיִת
to a house	לְבַיִת

Notice that there is no need for *dagesh* in בּ the of בַיִת.

If the noun is definite, the definite article ה is omitted but the preposition is vocalized with ַ or another vowel. For example:

in the house	בַּבַּיִת
like the house	כַּבַּיִת
to the house	לַבַּיִת

Notice that the *dagesh* is now required in the בּ of בַּיִת because the *dagesh* is part of the definite article, even though the ה has dropped out.

Prefixing an inseparable preposition to אֱלֹהִים is slightly different:

to God   לֵאלֹהִים

The distinction between definite and indefinite nouns can be confusing if the first vowel in the noun is a composite *sheva*, because even indefinite nouns will take a vocalized preposition. So:

a dream (m)	חֲלוֹם	cha-LŌM
in a dream	בַּחֲלוֹם	ba-cha-LŌM

We have already seen inseparable prepositions in previous units:

in the path	בַּדֶּרֶךְ	(Psalm 25:8)
in the beginning	בְּרֵשִׁית	(Genesis 1:1)
in Judah	בִּיהוּדָה	(Psalm 76:2)
in Israel	בְּיִשְׂרָאֵל	(Psalm 76:2)
to Yhwh	לַיהוה	(Exodus 15:1a)

If you are wondering why we translate בְּרֵשִׁית *in* the *beginning* rather than *in* a *beginning* you are asking an important question. One simple answer is that it makes more sense in English. However, there has been some discussion of the word among scholars. Good commentaries on the Hebrew Bible will outline the technical issues and some of the possible answers.

The preposition בְּ can be used to mean *with* in the instrumental sense; e.g.:

She opens her mouth with wisdom.   פִּיהָ פָּתְחָה בְחָכְמָה
(Proverbs 31:26)
Literally *her mouth she opens with wisdom.*

It never means with in the sense of *together with*, as עִם and אֶת do.

The preposition לְ can indicate possession. For example:

The king has a horse.   יֵשׁ־לַמֶּלֶךְ סוּס
(literally *there is to the king a horse*)

The princes have no wives.   אֵין־לַשָּׂרִים נָשִׁים
(literally *there are not to the princes women*)

One preposition can either stand alone or be joined to the noun rather like an inseparable preposition. The word is מִן and means *from*. It usually remains separate from the noun when the noun has a definite article. For example:

from the earth   מִן הָאָרֶץ
from this house   מִן הַבַּיִת הַזֶּה

The word is often joined to the noun with *maqqef*; e.g.:

from heaven (from the heavens)   מִן־הַשָּׁמָיִם

When a word has no definite article, מִן is often attached to the word as a prefix, like an inseparable preposition. When it is prefixed in this way, it loses its final נ, but a *dagesh* in the first letter of the noun replaces the נ. For example:

from a house   מִבַּיִת
from a king   מִמֶּלֶךְ
from your city   מֵעִירְךָ
from Judah   מִיהוּדָה

Notice that in מֵעִירְךָ, the vowel under מ is an *e* vowel rather than an *i* vowel. This is because עִיר begins with a guttural and so cannot take a *dagesh*; the vowel under מ is lengthened. The same would be true of words beginning with other gutturals and ר.

Notice also that in מִיהוּדָה, the *sheva* under the י of יְהוּדָה has dropped out.

The preposition מִן is used idiomatically in Hebrew for comparing things. For example:

You are wiser than Daniel.   חָכָם אַתָּה מִדָּנִאֵל
(Exekiel 28:3)

This is literally *wise are you from Daniel*; i.e. *you are wise in comparison to Daniel*. Similarly:

Yhwh is greater than all the gods. גָּדוֹל יהוה מִכָּל־הָאֱלֹהִים
(Exodus 18:11 adapted)

This is literally *great is Yhwh from all the gods*; i.e. *Yhwh is great in comparison to all the gods*.

8.4 Exercise 2

Reading practice: By now you should feel quite comfortable reading Hebrew aloud. You probably will not be able to read Hebrew as fast as you can read English, but by this point you should have no problems distinguishing letters that look similar and you should have no problems recognizing the vowels. This is especially important if you are learning Hebrew on your own, since you must depend entirely on yourself for pronunciation. If you find you are still struggling a little at this stage, it will be difficult to make progress until you master reading aloud.

Read as much of the following passage as you can out loud, but stop if you become frustrated.

Psalm 100

1 מִזְמוֹר לְתוֹדָה

2 הָרִיעוּ לַיהוָה כָּל־הָאָרֶץ׃ עִבְדוּ אֶת־יְהוָה בְּשִׂמְחָה

3 בֹּאוּ לְפָנָיו בִּרְנָנָה׃ דְּעוּ כִּי־יְהוָה הוּא אֱלֹהִים

הוּא־עָשָׂנוּ וְלֹא אֲנַחנוּ עַמּוֹ וְצֹאן מַרְעִיתוֹ

4 בֹּאוּ שְׁעָרָיו בְּתוֹדָה חֲצֵרֹתָיו בִּתְהִלָּה

5 הוֹדוּ־לוֹ בָּרְכוּ שְׁמוֹ׃ כִּי־טוֹב יְהוָה לְעוֹלָם חַסְדּוֹ

וְעַד־דֹּר וָדֹר אֱמוּנָתוֹ׃

There are some familiar words and sounds in this psalm, but also some other less familiar sounds, such as the ending of the word חֲצֵרֹתָיו (pronounced ch*a*-tsay-rō-*TAV*). We are not going to translate it now because there are many forms we have not yet encountered, and there is also a textual issue we will not explore until later. The purpose for now is simply to practise pronouncing Hebrew.

If you were able to read the whole thing (even slowly) with some confidence that you were reading it correctly, then you are doing very well. Do check your pronunciation anyway, just in case you are making any mistakes you are unaware of.

If you were able to read at least half of it, you are probably doing well with familiar words and syllables but struggling a little with unfamiliar patterns. If you think this is the case, the best practice is to read as much as possible. If you have a Bible in Hebrew, read parts of it aloud: one short verse at a time until you feel more confident. Even reading words in a dictionary can help, though reading whole sentences is probaby better practice.

If you were able to read less than half of it, you may be feeling anxious about reading aloud (even to yourself), or you may find you have not yet learned the alphabet and vowels thoroughly. Either way, the best approach is also practice. Several approaches may be helpful: practice reading the texts at the end of each unit; go back to Unit 1 and look through the alphabet and short words; write out flash cards with one Hebrew word on each card and the English translation on the reverse. Another technique that can help is to look at a passage in Hebrew and practise reading the *last* syllable of each word. Sometimes the words can seem too big and we cannot take in a whole word with one glance. The end seems too far away from the beginning. Looking at the last syllable before trying to pronounce the whole word can sometimes help to dispel anxiety about what might be coming next. Checking out the last syllable before reading the whole word can also help your eye to take in the whole word.

And of course, whatever your sense of your reading level, it is important to read all the examples in this book out loud.

8.5 Prepositions with pronominal suffixes

Ideas like *to him* or *in them* are expressed in Hebrew by adding a suffix to the preposition. The suffixes are the pronominal suffixes we learned in Unit 6. The most straightforward forms are the inseparable prepositions בְּ and לְ. We will look at more complicated forms later.

These are the forms with pronominal suffixes:

in/with him (or *it*)	בּוֹ	*bō*
in/with her (or *it*)	בָּהּ	*bāch*
in/with you (ms)	בְּךָ	*ba-chā*
in/with you (fs)	בָּךְ	*bāch*
in/with me	בִּי	*bee*
in/with them (mp)	בָּהֶם	*bā-HEM*
in/with them (fp)	בָּהֶן	*bā-HEN*
in/with you (mp)	בָּכֶם	*bā-CHEM*
in/with you (fp)	בָּכֶן	*bā-CHEN*
in/with us	בָּנוּ	*bā-NOO*
to/at/for him (or *it*)	לוֹ	
to/at/for her (or *it*)	לָהּ	
to/at/for you (ms)	לְךָ	
to/at/for you (fs)	לָךְ	
to/at/for me	לִי	
to/at/for them (mp)	לָהֶם	
to/at/for them (fp)	לָהֶן	
to/at/for you (mp)	לָכֶם	
to/at/for you (fp)	לָכֶן	
to/at/for us	לָנוּ	

The approximate pronunciation for בּ should serve as a guide for לּ.

The preposition לּ with pronominal suffixes can indicate possession, just like לּ as an inseparable preposition. For example:

he has a servant (literally *there is to him a servant*)	יֶשׁ־לוֹ עֶבֶד
we have a sister	יֶשׁ־לָנוּ אָחוֹת
she has no husband (literally *there is not to her a husband*)	אֵין־לָהּ אִישׁ
I have no enemy	אֵין־לָנוּ אֹיֵב

An example from the Hebrew Bible:

My beloved is mine and I am his. דּוֹדִי לִי וַאֲנִי לוֹ
(Song of Songs 2:16)

8.6 Exercise 3

Fill in the prepositions:

1) _____ *an enemy*   כְּאוֹיֵב

2) _____ *a loud voice*   בְּקוֹל־גָּדוֹל

3) _____ *evening* _____ *morning*   מֵעֶרֶב עַד־בֹּקֶר

4) _____ *the king*   לִפְנֵי הַמֶּלֶךְ

5) _____ *this woman*   מִן־הָאִשָּׁה הַזֹּאת

Translate:

1) טוֹב חֶסֶד מִדַּעַת

2) רַע הָעָם וְלֹא בָהֶם דַּעַת

3) אַתֶּם בְּיָדִי

4) יֵשׁ לָהּ בֵּן

5) הַסּוּסִים הַגְּדוֹלִים הָאֵלֶּה לָנוּ

8.7 Text: Ruth 1:1

Points to look out for in this text:

- Words we have already encountered.
- Prepositions.
- Inseparable prepositions.

place name: *Bethlehem* (literally *house of bread*. The word for *bread* is לֶחֶם.)	בֵּית לֶחֶם	*bayt LE-chem*
verb: *to live* (temporarily)	גּוּר	*goor*
verb: *to be*	הָיָה	*hā-YĀ*
verb: *to go, walk*	הָלַךְ	*hā-LĀCH*
place name: *Moab*	מוֹאָב	*mō-ĀV*
noun (m): *famine*	רָעָב	*rā-ĀV*
noun (m): *field*	שָׂדֶה	*sā-DE*
two, both	שְׁנַיִם	*shᵃ-NĪ-im*
verb: *to judge*	שָׁפַט	*sha-FĀT*
noun (m): *judge*	שֹׁפֵט	*shō-FAYT*

Text

Read the verse aloud a few times to be sure of the pronunciation:

וַיְהִי בִּימֵי שְׁפֹט הַשֹּׁפְטִים וַיְהִי רָעָב בָּאָרֶץ וַיֵּלֶךְ אִישׁ מִבֵּית לֶחֶם
יְהוּדָה לָגוּר בִּשְׂדֵי מוֹאָב הוּא וְאִשְׁתּוֹ וּשְׁנֵי בָנָיו:

Approximate pronunciation:

*va-yᵃ-HEE bee-MAY shᵃ-FŌT ha-shō-fᵃ-TEEM va-yᵃ-HEE rā-ĀV
bā-ĀR-ets va-YAY-lech eesh mi-BAYT LE-chem yᵃ-HOO-dā lā-
GOOR bis-DAY mō-ĀV hoo vᵃ-eesh-TŌ oosh-NAY vā-NĀV.*

Write the words you know beneath the words in the text, and match the others to the words in the vocabulary.

Notes

וַיְהִי

This word is from the verb *to be*. It means *and it was*. It is a very common word in the Hebrew Bible and is often found at the beginning of a story, rather like *once upon a time* in English. It often used to be translated *and it came to pass*, though that phrase is now associated almost exclusively with biblical language. A more idiomatic translation in modern English might be *and it happened*. However, it can often be left untranslated without impairing the sense of the Hebrew.

בִּימֵי

This is the preposition בְּ prefixed to the plural of the word for *day* in construct form. So it means *in the days of*.

שְׁפֹט

This means *the judging of*. We will look at this form later.

הַשֹּׁפְטִים

This means *the judges*. By now you are probably fairly familiar with the definite article and the masculine plural form. See an Introduction to the Old Testament/Hebrew Bible (see Introduction to this book) for the role of judges in ancient Israel.

בָּאָרֶץ

The preposition בְּ is prefixed to the word אֶרֶץ. The *a* vowel under the בְּ indicates that the word is definite: *in the land of* rather than *in a land of*.

וַיֵּלֶךְ

A verb meaning *and he went* or *and he walked*.

מִבֵּית לֶחֶם

The preposition מִן prefixed to the place name בֵּית לֶחֶם. You know the word בֵּית: it is the construct of בַּיִת, so it means *house of*. The whole name means *house of bread*. It appears to be in the construct because of its relationship to the following word. So מִבֵּית לֶחֶם יְהוּדָה means *from Bethlehem of Judah*, or, more idiomatically, *from Bethlehem in Judah*.

לָגוּר

This is the preposition לְ prefixed to the verb גוּר. It means *to live* (as a foreigner).

בְּשְׂדֵי

The preposition בְּ prefixed to the construct plural form of שָׂדֶה. Hence *in the fields of*.

וְאִשְׁתּוֹ

The conjunction וְ prefixed to the word for woman with a pronominal suffix that is third person masculine singular. Thus *and his wife*.

וּשְׁנֵי

The conjunction וְ prefixed to the word for *two* or *both* in construct form. The conjunction is וּ rather than וְ because the first vowel of שְׁנַיִם is a *sheva*. Hence *and two of* or *and both of*.

בָנָיו

This is the plural of בֵּן with the third person masculine singular pronominal suffix. So it means *his sons*. If you are wondering why there is no *dagesh* in the בּ, it is because of the construct relationship with וּשְׁנֵי. The construct relationship treats the two words as if they were one, and often there is no *dagesh* in the second word where we might expect one.

You should now have something like *And it happened in the days of the judging of the judges and there was a famine in the land and a man from Bethlehem of Judah went to live in the fields of Moab, he and his wife and both of his sons.*

Possible translations

Fairly literal:

And it happened in the days when the judges judged, there was a famine in the land, and a man from Bethlehem in Judah went to live as a resident alien in the fields of Moab, he and his wife and his two sons.

Somewhat freer:

In the days when the judges ruled, there was a famine in the land. So a man from Bethlehem in Judah went to live in Moab with his wife and both his sons.

8.8 Suggestions

- Learn the prepositions.
- Learn בּ and ל with pronominal suffixes.
- Assess your reading and practise reading aloud, going back to Unit 1 if necessary.

8.9 Summary

In this unit we have looked at

- prepositions meaning *to, until/as far as, on/upon/against, beneath, between, from, before.*
- inseparable prepositions that are prefixed to nouns (בּ and כּ and ל)
- the use of pronominal suffixes with the inseparable prepositions בּ and ל
- the idiomatic use of מִן to make comparisons
- the use of ל to indicate possession
- the text of Ruth 1:1.

verb: *to love*	אָהַב	*ā-HAV*
interjection: *behold*	הִנֵּה	*hi-NEH*
adjective: *strong, powerful*	חָזָק	*chā-ZĀK*
particle: *because, that*	כִּי	*kee*
adjective: *heavy, difficult*	כָּבֵד	*kā-VAYD*
noun (m): *to turn, depart*	סוּר	*soor*
adjective: *small, young*	קָטֹן	*kā-TŌN*

9.1 The object marker

Grammar: subjects and objects

Look at this sentence:

The woman wore a hat.

In this sentence, *the woman* is the subject of the verb *wore*, and *a hat* is the object.

Another example: *The cat climbed the tree.* In this sentence *the cat* is the subject of *climbed*, and *the tree* is the object.

A verb can have several subjects and several objects; e.g.:

The boy and the girl ate a pizza, a hamburger and an apple pie.

In this sentence, the *boy* and the *girl* are the subjects; the *pizza*, the *hamburger* and the *apple pie* are the objects.

And a slightly more complicated example:

This morning my mother filled a cup with water.

Here *my mother* is the subject of the verb *filled* and the objects are *a cup* and *water*. The phrase *This morning* is neither the subject nor the object.

At a glance:

SUBJECT	VERB	OBJECT
The woman	*wore*	*a hat.*
The cat	*climbed*	*the tree.*
The boy and the girl	*ate*	*a pizza, a hamburger and an apple pie.*
My mother	*filled*	*a cup, water.*

In Hebrew, there is a word we sometimes see before the object of a verb, so it is known as the 'object marker'. The word is אֵת and we have already encountered it in Genesis 1:1. It can also be attached to the object with *maqqef*, in which case the vowel changes and it is written אֶת־. There is no word we can use to translate it into English. That does not mean it is untranslatable, however. It is translated when we translate using an object in English.

The object marker is especially helpful in Hebrew because it is not always immediately obvious from the word order what the subject or object is. In English, the word order determines which part of the sentence is the subject and which is the object. For example, in the English sentence *The father loved the son* we know that it is the father doing the loving, because of the word order. However, in Hebrew the verb usually comes first in a sentence: אָהַב הָאָב הַבֵּן. Without אֵת this could mean either *the father loved the son* or *the son loved the father*. To make the Hebrew clear we might see:

| either | אָהַב הָאָב אֶת הַבֵּן | *The father loved the son.* |
| or | אָהַב אֶת הָאָב הַבֵּן | *The son loved the father.* |

Although the word אֵת occurs frequently, it is not inevitably found before the object, so we should not expect to see it every time we encounter an object. Moreover, it has exactly the same spelling as אֵת meaning *with*, but the context should indicate whether it is an object marker or a preposition.

9.2 Further prepositions with pronominal suffixes

In Unit 8, we learned בְּ and לְ with pronominal suffixes. Other prepositions are slightly more complicated, because they introduce extra letters into the suffix. However, if you have learned the pronominal suffixes, it should be possible to identify the forms and translate them.

Often the extra letter is י, which can make the forms look like plurals. However, if you learn them carefully now, you will not be confused when you encounter them in the text; and in fact, some of the forms are so common that you will soon become familiar with them.

Reading all of these out loud several times (or even copying them out) can help you learn them. It can seem tedious, but it is usually effective. It takes time to learn these properly, but it is much easier to read Hebrew if you don't need to look up endings on prepositions, since they are such common words.

One of the commonest words is אֶל (*to*) with pronominal suffixes. It goes like this:

to *him* (or *it*)	אֵלָיו	*ay-LAV*
to *her* (or *it*)	אֵלֶיהָ	*ay-LAY-hā*
to *you* (ms)	אֵלֶיךָ	*ay-LAY-chā*
to *you* (fs)	אֵלַיִךְ	*ay-LĪ-yik*
to *me*	אֵלַי	*ay-LĪ*
to *them* (mp)	אֲלֵיהֶם	*a-lay-HEM*
to *them* (fp)	אֲלֵיהֶן	*a-lay-HEN*
to *you* (mp)	אֲלֵיכֶם	*a-lay-CHEM*
to *you* (fp)	אֲלֵיכֶן	*a-lay-CHEN*
to *us*	אֵלֵינוּ	*ay-LAY-noo*

The stress pattern in the approximate pronunciation should be familiar from סוּסוֹ. The same pattern works for all the prepositions with suffixes.

The preposition עַל (*on*) is formed in the same way:

on him (or *it*)	עָלָיו	*on them* (mp)	עֲלֵיהֶם
on her (or *it*)	עָלֶיהָ	*on them* (fp)	עֲלֵיהֶן
on you (ms)	עָלֶיךָ	*on you* (mp)	עֲלֵיכֶם
on you (fs)	עָלַיִךְ	*on you* (fp)	עֲלֵיכֶן
on me	עָלַי	*on us*	עָלֵינוּ

And similarly עַד (*as far as, until*):

as far as him (or *it*)	עָדָיו	*as far as them* (mp)	עֲדֵיהֶם
as far as her (or *it*)	עָדֶיהָ	*as far as them* (fp)	עֲדֵיהֶן
as far as you (ms)	עָדֶיךָ	*as far as you* (mp)	עֲדֵיכֶם
as far as you (fs)	עָדַיִךְ	*as far as you* (fp)	עֲדֵיכֶן
as far as me	עָדַי	*as far as us*	עָדֵינוּ

Another preposition you will see frequently with pronominal suffixes is מִן (*from*).

from him (or *it*)	מִמֶּנּוּ	*from them* (mp)	מֵהֶם
from her (or *it*)	מִמֶּנָּה	*from them* (fp)	מֵהֶן
from you (ms)	מִמְּךָ	*from you* (mp)	מִכֶּם
from you (fs)	מִמֵּךְ	*from you* (fp)	מִכֶּן
from me	מִמֶּנִּי	*from us*	מִמֶּנּוּ

Notice that the word for *from him* is the same as the word for *from us*. Context should help determine which is meant.

The pronominal suffixes on both words for *with*, אֵת and עִם, should be instantly recognizable. The main point to note about these prepositions is the *dagesh* in the ת and the מ when suffixes are added:

with him (or it)	אִתּוֹ	with them (mp)	אִתָּם
with her (or it)	אִתָּהּ	with them (fp)	אִתָּן
with you (ms)	אִתְּךָ	with you (mp)	אִתְּכֶם
with you (fs)	אִתָּךְ	with you (fp)	אִתְּכֶן
with me	אִתִּי	with us	אִתָּנוּ

with him (or it)	עִמּוֹ	with them (mp)	עִמָּם
with her (or it)	עִמָּהּ	with them (fp)	עִמָּן
with you (ms)	עִמְּךָ	with you (mp)	עִמָּכֶם
with you (fs)	עִמָּךְ	with you (fp)	עִמָּכֶן
with me	עִמִּי	with us	עִמָּנוּ

The suffixes on the word for *between* (בֵּין) are similar to בְּ and לְ until you get to the second column:

between him (or it)	בֵּינוֹ	between them (mp)	בֵּינֵיהֶם
between her (or it)	בֵּינָהּ	between them (fp)	בֵּינֵיהֶן
between you (ms)	בֵּינְךָ	between you (mp)	בֵּינֵיכֶם
between you (fs)	בֵּינֵךְ	between you (fp)	בֵּינֵיכֶן
between me	בֵּינִי	between us	בֵּינֵינוּ

When the prepositions אַחֲרֵי (*after*) and תַּחַת (*under*) take suffixes, they are formed rather like the second half of בֵּין:

after him (or it)	אַחֲרָיו	after them (mp)	אַחֲרֵיהֶם
after her (or it)	אַחֲרֶיהָ	after them (fp)	אַחֲרֵיהֶן
after you (ms)	אַחֲרֶיךָ	after you (mp)	אַחֲרֵיכֶם
after you (fs)	אַחֲרַיִךְ	after you (fp)	אַחֲרֵיכֶם
after me	אַחֲרַי	after us	אַחֲרֵינוּ

under him (or it)	תַּחְתָּיו	under them (mp)	תַּחְתֵּיהֶם
under her (or it)	תַּחְתֶּיהָ	under them (fp)	תַּחְתֵּיהֶן
under you (ms)	תַּחְתֶּיךָ	under you (mp)	תַּחְתֵּיכֶם

| *under you* (fs) | תַּחְתֵּיךְ | *under you* (fp) | תַּחְתֵּיכֶן |
| *under me* | תַּחְתַּי | *under us* | תַּחְתֵּינוּ |

The preposition לִפְנֵי follows the same form as אַחֲרֵי and תַּחַת.

The inseparable preposition כְּ is a little different:

like him (or *it*)	כָּמוֹהוּ	*like them* (mp)	כָּהֶם
like her (or *it*)	כָּמוֹהָ	*like them* (fp)	כָּהֵן
like you (ms)	כָּמוֹךָ	*like you* (mp)	כָּכֶם
like you (fs)	כָּמוֹךְ	*like you* (fp)	כָּכֵן
like me	כָּמוֹנִי	*like us*	כָּמוֹנוּ

Note the additional מ before the endings are added. These are not precisely the same as the endings on מִן, but are fairly similar.

One further point about prepositions: they can be combined. For example:

away from   מֵעִם

and it left Saul (literally: *and from with Saul it departed*)
וּמֵעִם שָׁאוּל סָר (1 Samuel 18:12)

9.3 Exercise 1

Complete the columns:

Prepositions אֶל עַל and עַד:

3ms	*until him/it*	עָדָיו	3mp	*on them*	_____
3fs	*on her/it*	_____	3fp	*to them*	_____
2ms	*as far as you*	_____	2mp	*to you*	_____
2fs	*on you*	_____	2fp	*as far as you*	_____
1s	*to me*	_____	1p	*to us*	_____

Prepositions אַחֲרֵי לִפְנֵי and תַּחַת:

| 3ms | *under him/it* | תַּחְתָּיו | 3mp | *before them* | _____ |
| 3fs | *after her/it* | _____ | 3fp | *under them* | _____ |

2ms	*under you*	_____	2mp	*before you*	_____
2fs	*after you*	_____	2fp	*after you*	_____
1s	*after me*	_____	1p	*under us*	_____

Prepositions בְּ and מִן (remember, the suffixes on בְּ are not identical to those on מִן):

3ms	*from him/it*	מִמֶּנּוּ	3mp	*like them*	_____
3fs	*like her/it*	_____	3fp	*from them*	_____
2ms	*from you*	_____	2mp	*from you*	_____
2fs	*like you*	_____	2fp	*like you*	_____
1s	*from me*	_____	1p	*from us*	_____

9.4 Comparatives and superlatives

Grammar: comparatives and superlatives

In English, we make comparatives and superlatives either by adding endings to an adjective.

holy
holier (comparative)
holiest (superlative)

or we do it by using the words *more* and *most*:

beautiful
more beautiful (comparative)
most beautiful (superlative)

Some of these forms are irregular in English; e.g.:

good
better (comparative)
best (superlative)

It is helpful to bear this in mind, and avoid translations like *To obey is more good than sacrifice.*

As we have seen, the preposition מִן is used idiomatically in Hebrew for comparing things. For example:

you are wiser that Daniel   חָכָם אַתָּה מִדָּנִאֵל
(Exekiel 28:3)
(literally *wise are you from Daniel*, i.e. *you are wise in comparison to Daniel*.)

Similarly:

Yhwh is greater than all the gods   גָּדוֹל יהוה מִכָּל־הָאֱלֹהִים
(Exodus 18:11 adapted)

The מִן construction noted above can also be used in the sense of *to... for....* For example:

they were too strong for him   חֲזָקִים הֵמָּה מִמֶּנּוּ
(Judges 18:26)

because it is too difficult for me   כִּי כָבֵד מִמֶּנִּי
(Numbers 11:14)

A number of Hebrew idioms may be translated with a superlative in English. An adjective can be used with the definite article; e.g.:

the youngest is with our father   הַקָּטֹן אֶת־אָבִינוּ
(Genesis 42:32 adapted)
(literally *the young (one) is with our father*.)

here is my eldest daughter   הִנֵּה בִתִּי הַגְּדוֹלָה
(1 Samuel 18:17)
(literally *behold my daughter, the large one*.)

Alternatively, a construct relationship can be used; e.g.:

the youngest of his sons   קְטֹן בָּנָיו
(2 Chronicles 21:17)

The word קְטֹן is the construct form of the adjective קָטֹן. Adjectives can have construct forms, just like nouns, and this one works like דָּבָר. See e.g. דְּבַר הַמֶּלֶךְ in Unit 7.

Another way of expressing a superlative is to use a noun in a construct relationship to its plural; e.g.:

the greatest song   שִׁיר הַשִּׁירִים
(literally *the song of songs*) (Song 1:1)

the holiest place   קֹדֶשׁ הַקֳּדָשִׁים
(literally *the holy of holies*) (Exodus 26:33)

the worst vanity   הֲבֵל הֲבָלִים
(literally *vanity of vanities*) (Ecclesiastes 1:2)

Superlatives can also be expressed by use of words that indicate divinity or death. For example:

a mighty prince   נְשִׂיא אֱלֹהִים
(literally *a prince of gods*) (Genesis 23:6)

for love is exceedingly strong   כִּי־עַזָּה כַמָּוֶת אַהֲבָה
(literally *for love is as strong as death*) (Song 8:6)

There are a number of other ways of expressing the superlative in Hebrew. A good Hebrew grammar should give further examples.

9.5 Exercise 2

Comprehension. Read the Hebrew and answer the questions in English:

גָּדוֹל דָּוִד מִן־יוֹסֵף וְיֵשׁ סוּסִים וּפָרוֹת וְנָשִׁים לוֹ: יֵשׁ בַּיִת
וְסוּסִים לְיוֹסֵף וְאֵין אִשָּׁה לוֹ: סוּס הַסּוּסִים לְדָוִד וְחַר קָטֹן סוּסֵי יוֹסֵף:

Who is greater than Joseph?

What does David have?

What does Joseph lack?

Who has the best horse?

Which horse is white?

9.6 Text: Deuteronomy 10:17

Points to look out for in this text:

- Words we have already encountered.
- Superlatives.

noun (m): *God/god*	אֵל	ayl
that, which, who	אֲשֶׁר	a-SHER
adjective: *strong*	גִּבֹּר	gib-BŌR
verb: *to take*	לָקַח	lā-KACH
participle: *terrible, wonderful* (we will learn about participles later)	נוֹרָא	nō-RĀ
verb: *to lift up*	נָשָׂא	nā-SĀ
noun (m): *face*	פָּנֶה	pā-NE
noun (m): *present, bribe*	שֹׁחַד	SHŌ-chad

Text

Read the verse aloud a few times to be sure of the pronunciation.

כִּי יְהוָה אֱלֹהֵיכֶם הוּא אֱלֹהֵי הָאֱלֹהִים וַאֲדֹנֵי הָאֲדֹנִים הָאֵל הַגָּדֹל
הַגִּבֹּר וְהַנּוֹרָא אֲשֶׁר לֹא־יִשָּׂא פָנִים וְלֹא יִקַּח שֹׁחַד:

Approximate pronunciation:

ki a-don-Ī e-lō-HAY-chem hoo e-lō-HAY hā-e-lō-HEEM va-a-dō-NAY hā-a-dō-NEEM, hā-AYL ha-gā-DŌL ha-gib-BŌR vᵃ-ha-nō-RĀ a-SHER lō yis-SĀ pā-NEEM vᵃ-lō yi-KACH SHŌ-chad

Write beneath the words in the text the words you know, and match the others to the words in the vocabulary.

Notes

אֱלֹהֵיכֶם

This is אֱלֹהִים with a 2mp pronominal suffix, so it means *your God*.

הוּא אֱלֹהֵי הָאֱלֹהִים

This is a verbless clause, with the verb *to be* implied: *he is the God of Gods*. Remember that the word אֱלֹהֵי is in construct relationship to הָאֱלֹהִים, so it is definite by implication (*the* God of), because הָאֱלֹהִים is definite.

וַאֲדֹנֵי הָאֲדֹנִים

Similarly, *and the lord of lords*. The word הָאֲדֹנִים is definite, and so אֲדֹנֵי is definite by virtue of being in a construct relationship to הָאֲדֹנִים.

הָאֵל הַגָּדֹל הַגִּבֹּר וְהַנּוֹרָא

This is not a verbless clause. It should not be translated *the God is great* ... because of the word order. Instead, it means *the great, strong and terrible God*. If the distinction between טוֹב הָאִישׁ (*the man is good*) and הָאִישׁ הַטּוֹב (*the good man*) is still a little confusing, look at Unit 6 again.

אֲשֶׁר

This is sometimes called the 'relative pronoun'. It means *which*, *who* or *that*. Many people translate it intuitively. In this verse, since we are speaking of a person (if God may be termed a person rather than a thing) we would translate אֲשֶׁר with *who*.

לֹא־יִשָּׂא פָנִים

The word יִשָּׂא means *he lifts up*; the נ in the verb has disappeared. It is common for the letter נ to disappear, especially if it comes at the beginning of a word. It is said to be assimilated into the next letter, which is why the שׂ has a *dagesh*. We will learn more about verbs later. This whole phrase means literally *he does not lift up faces*. A more idiomatic translation into English requires a little interpretation of the text. Some translations have something like *he does not regard persons*. Others have something like *he is not partial*. The idea of lifting up one's face can be an indication of innocence in Hebrew, so perhaps the phrase refers to an idea that God shows no favouritism. The word פָּנִים is plural, and therefore it agrees with the word אֱלֹהִים, but אֱלֹהִים was not the most recent reference to God; God has just been described as אֵל, which is singular. However, there does seem to be a lot of support for the idea that this verse refers to God's face rather than anyone else's.

יִקַּח

This verbal form means *he takes*; the ל in the verb has disappeared. This is not so common as the disappearance of the letter נ; in fact, it really only happens in לָקַח. But we will learn more about verbs later.

Possible translation

Because Yhwh your God is the God of gods and the lord of lords; the great, strong and terrible God, who is impartial and does not take bribes.

9.7 Suggestion

- Learn the prepositions with pronominal suffixes. If you learn אֶל, מִן and אַחֲרֵי thoroughly, you should be able to recognize almost any preposition with a pronominal suffix.

9.8 Summary

In this unit we have looked at

- prepositions with pronominal suffixes
- comparatives with מִן
- superlatives using adjectives, the construct and the construct of a noun with its own plural
- the text of Deuteronomy 10:17.

noun (f): *covenant*	בְּרִית	bª-REET
noun (mp): *the redeemed*	גְּאוּלִים	gª-oo-LEEM
noun (m): *redeemer*	גּוֹאֵל	gō-AYL
verb: *to live*	חָיָה	chā-YĀ
name: *Michal*	מִיכַל	mi-CHAL
place name: *Egypt*	מִצְרַיִם	mits-RĀ-yeem
noun (m): *olden time, of old*	מִקֶּדֶם	mi-KE-dem
verb: *to call*	קָרָא	kā-RĀ
name: *Solomon*	שְׁלֹמֹה	shª-LŌ-mō

10.1 Verbs: Perfect

Hebrew verbs work in a way quite different from English verbs. Some of the differences are straightforward; others take a little time to get used to. Often the best way to demonstrate the differences is by looking at an example.

The first verb form we will learn is called the Perfect. In some grammars it is known as Qatal, because the term 'Perfect' can convey ideas about Indo-European languages irrelevant to Hebrew. However, since 'Perfect' is the term found in many grammars, it seems sensible to use it here.

The Perfect usually describes a completed action in the past, though sometimes it can describe things happening in the present or future. The verb קָטַל (*to kill*) is often used as a demonstration verb when discussing Hebrew grammar; hence the name Qatal. This is what it looks like:

he killed	קָטַל	*kā-TAL*
she killed	קָטְלָה	*kā-t^a-LĀ*
you killed (ms)	קָטַלְתָּ	*kā-TAL-tā*
you killed (fs)	קָטַלְתְּ	*kā-TALT*
I killed	קָטַלְתִּי	*kā-TAL-tee*
they killed	קָטְלוּ	*kā-t^a-LOO*
you killed (mp)	קְטַלְתֶּם	*k^a-tal-TEM*
you killed (fp)	קְטַלְתֶּן	*k^a-tal-TEN*
we killed	קָטַלְנוּ	*kā-TAL-noo*

Note: in English we use the word *killed* for each person, but in Hebrew each word is slightly different.

Another point to notice is that we talk about the verb קָטַל, which means literally *he killed*, whereas in English we would talk about the verb *to kill*. The reason is that קָטַל is the simplest form of the verb. If you want to look up a verb in a Hebrew–English dictionary you need to look up the Perfect third person masculine singular. The dictionary will tell you that קָטַל means *to kill*, even though literally it means *he killed*. In fact, something similar happens in English. We talk about the verb *to kill*, but you would not look up *to kill* in the dictionary; you would look up *kill*.

The three letters that make up the third person masculine singular (in this case קטל) are known as the *root*, and endings are added to the root to form the different parts of the verb. So the first person singular ending in the Perfect is תִּי, etc.

The advantage of learning the verb קָטַל is that it is the basis of the verb tables in many grammars. However, if we want to begin using verbs, it might be more pleasant to practise with less gory verbs. Here are some examples. It's best to read them out loud.

to rule

he has ruled	מָשַׁל	*mā-SHAL*
she has ruled	מָשְׁלָה	*mā-sh^a-LĀ*
you have ruled (ms)	מָשַׁלְתָּ	*mā-SHAL-tā*

you have ruled (fs)	מָשַׁלְתְּ	mā-SHALT
I have ruled	מָשַׁלְתִּי	mā-SHAL-tee
they have ruled	מָשְׁלוּ	mā-shᵃ-LOO
you have ruled (mp)	מְשַׁלְתֶּם	mᵃ-shal-TEM
you have ruled (fp)	מְשַׁלְתֶּן	mᵃ-shal-TEN
we have ruled	מָשַׁלְנוּ	mā-SHAL-noo

to guard, to keep (e.g. a commandment)

he has guarded/kept	שָׁמַר	sha-MAR
she has guarded/kept	שָׁמְרָה	sha-mᵃ-RAH
you have guarded/kept (ms)	שָׁמַרְתָּ	sha-MAR-tah
you have guarded/kept (fs)	שָׁמַרְתְּ	sha-MART
I have guarded/kept	שָׁמַרְתִּי	sha-MAR-tee
they have guarded/kept	שָׁמְרוּ	sha-mᵃ-ROO
you have guarded/kept (mp)	שְׁמַרְתֶּם	shᵃ-mar-TEM
you have guarded/kept (fp)	שְׁמַרְתֶּן	shᵃ-mar-TEN
we have guarded/kept	שָׁמַרְנוּ	sha-MAR-noo

The approximate pronunciation for קָטַל should serve as a guide for all verbs in the Perfect.

to eat

he has eaten	אָכַל
she has eaten	אָכְלָה
you have eaten (ms)	אָכַלְתָּ
you have eaten (fs)	אָכַלְתְּ
I have eaten	אָכַלְתִּי
they have eaten	אָכְלוּ
you have eaten (mp)	אֲכַלְתֶּם
you have eaten (fp)	אֲכַלְתֶּן
we have eaten	אָכַלְנוּ

to walk

he has walked	הָלַךְ
she has walked	הָלְכָה
you have walked (ms)	הָלַכְתָּ
you have walked (fs)	הָלַכְתְּ
I have walked	הָלַכְתִּי
they have walked	הָלְכוּ
you have walked (mp)	הֲלַכְתֶּם
you have walked (fp)	הֲלַכְתֶּן
we have walked	הָלַכְנוּ

Note: in the word קְטַלְתֶּם, the first vowel is a simple *sheva*, whereas in אֲכַלְתֶּם and הֲלַכְתֶּם the first vowel is a complex *sheva*. The reason is that gutturals do not take a simple *sheva*. However, this should not cause any difficulty in understanding the word.

to take

he has taken	לָקַח
she has taken	לָקְחָה
you have taken (ms)	לָקַחְתָּ
you have taken (fs)	לָקַחְתְּ
I have taken	לָקַחְתִּי
they have taken	לָקְחוּ
you have taken (mp)	לְקַחְתֶּם
you have taken (fp)	לְקַחְתֶּן
we have taken	לָקַחְנוּ

Note: in קְטַלְתְּ there are two *shevas* next to each other. This is rare in Hebrew in general, although it is usual in the Perfect. However, gutturals do not usually take a simple *sheva*. That is why in לָקַחְתְּ the first of the *shevas* has been replaced by an *a* vowel.

Vowel changes under gutturals are common, but should not usually cause problems in understanding the Perfect.

10.2 Exercise 1

Using קָטַל as a model, write out the Perfect of the following verbs:

	to visit פָּקַד	to write כָּתַב	to remember זָכַר
3ms	_____	_____	_____
3fs	_____	_____	_____
2ms	_____	_____	_____
2fs	_____	_____	_____
1s	_____	_____	_____
3p	_____	_____	_____
2mp	_____	_____	_____
2fp	_____	_____	_____
1p	_____	_____	_____

10.3 How the Perfect is used

Hebrew word order is generally different from English. In Hebrew, the verb usually comes first in a sentence or phrase, followed by the subject, and then the object. However, a few words or phrases may come before the verb. For example:

You have not kept the covenant of God. לֹא שָׁמְרוּ בְּרִית אֱלֹהִים
(Psalm 78:10)

Therefore she called his name Dan. עַל־כֵּן קָרְאָה שְׁמוֹ דָּן
(Genesis 30:6)

(We have seen something similar in Genesis 1:1, Unit 4.)

In English, if we want to say *he walked* or *they walked* we always have to use the pronoun so that it is clear who walked. In Hebrew, the pronoun is unnecessary because it is clear from the form of the verb. The word הָלַכְנוּ means *we walked*, and there is no need to include the word אֲנַחְנוּ. If a pronoun is used, it usually indicates emphasis:

And I know that my redeemer lives.   וַאֲנִי יָדַעְתִּי גֹּאֲלִי חָי
(Job 19:25)

or *As for me, I know that my redeemer lives.*

Another technique used in Hebrew to indicate emphasis is to change the word order, placing the object before the verb:

And the darkness he called night   וְלַחֹשֶׁךְ קָרָא לָיְלָה
(Genesis 1:5)

Notice the difference in nuance between this and the phrase we might have expected: *and he called the darkness night*. The word לָיְלָה is in pause and so the first vowel has lengthened. This should not present any difficulties in understanding.

In Hebrew, a verb always has to agree with its subject. If the subject is masculine and singular, the verb has to be masculine and singular. In the phrase אָהֲבָה מִיכַל דָּוִד, it is clear from the verb that Michal loved David and it would mean the same even if the word order were changed to אָהֲבָה דָּוִד מִיכַל. If we wanted to say that David loved Michal, the verb would have to be אָהַב, so the phrase would read אָהַב דָּוִד מִיכַל.

In English, we have separate tenses to describe whether things happened in the past, the present or the future. Some of our verbal constructions can be rather complex; e.g.: *I will have been walking for ten minutes when I reach the park*. Hebrew verbs do not express time in the same way as English verbs. The Perfect can sometimes be translated with an English past tense, sometimes with a present tense, and sometimes with a future tense. Sometimes it is clear from the context, although there are some general circumstances under which it is more appropriate to choose a present tense than a past tense, for example. Some traditional grammars will explain this in detail.

It is helpful to see examples of how the Perfect can be translated by different English tenses. It may not yet be possible to understand exactly how the tense is chosen, partly because at this stage it is hard to get a sense of the wider context of the verse without knowing more Hebrew. However, at least it is possible to see that several tenses can be used to translate the Perfect:

Past tense:

In the beginning God created the heavens and the earth.

בְּרֵאשִׁית בָּרָא אֱלֹהִים אֵת הַשָּׁמַיִם וְאֵת הָאָרֶץ (Genesis 1:1)

Present tense:

I remember the days of old.

זָכַרְתִּי יָמִים מִקֶּדֶם (Psalm 143: 5)

Future tense:

And (or but) the redeemed shall walk.

וְהָלְכוּ גְאוּלִים (Isaiah 35:9)

However, for now it is probably easiest to think of the Perfect as a past tense and to translate it as demonstrated in section 10.1.

10.4 Exercise 2

Match the Hebrew sentences to the English translations:

עָמַדְתִּי בַּגָּן בֵּין הָעֵצִים

בָּרָאתָ אֶת־עֲצֵי הַשָּׂדֶה

מָשְׁלוּ דָוִד וּשְׁלֹמֹה בִּיהוּדָה

זָכְרָה שֵׁם עֶבֶד אָבִי

אָמַרְתֶּן אֵלֵינוּ אֵין מֶלֶךְ בְּיִשְׂרָאֵל

אָכְלָה הַפָּרָה הַזֹּאת אֶת־כָּל־לַחְמִי

קָרָא הַכֹּהֵן אֶל־הָעָם מִבֵּיתוֹ

שָׁמַרְתָּ אֶת־הַשָּׂרָה הַיָּפָה

לֹא שָׁבַתְנוּ בְּאֶרֶץ מִצְרַיִם

שְׁמַרְתֶּם אֶת־תּוֹרַת יְהוָה אֱלֹהֵיכֶם

The priest called to the people from his house.

She remembered the name of my father's servant.

This cow ate all my bread.

You created the trees of the field.

You guarded the beautiful princess.

I stood in the garden between the trees.

David and Solomon ruled in Judah.

You kept the law of Yhwh your God.

You said to us there is no king in Israel.

We did not rest in the land of Egypt.

10.5 Text: Job 1:21

It is very common to encounter verbs in the Perfect in the same verse as other kinds of verbs. At this point it is enough to be able to identify the verbs you are familiar with; other forms will be explained later.

Points to look out for in this text:

- Words we have already encountered.
- Forms of the Perfect.
- Word order.

noun (f): *belly, womb*	בֶּטֶן	*BE-ten*
verb: *to bless*	בֵּרֵךְ	*bā-RACH*
verb: *to go out, to be born*	יָצָא	*yā-TSĀ*
verb: *to give*	נָתַן	*nā-TAN*
adjective: *naked*	עָרֹם	*ā-RŌM*
verb: *to return*	שׁוּב	*shoov*
adverb: *there*	שָׁם	*shām*

Text

Read the verse aloud a few times to be sure of the pronunciation:

וַיֹּאמֶר עָרֹם יָצָתִי מִבֶּטֶן אִמִּי וְעָרֹם אָשׁוּב שָׁמָּה יְהוָה נָתַן וַיהוָה
לָקָח יְהִי שֵׁם יְהוָה מְבֹרָךְ:

Approximate pronunciation:

*va-YŌ-mer ā-RŌM yā-TSĀ-tee mi-BE-ten im-MEE vᵃ-ā-RŌM
ā-SHOOV SHĀ-mā ā-dō-NĪ nā-TAN vā-dō-NĪ lā-KACH ya-HEE
shaym ā-dō-NĪ mᵃ-bō-RĀCH*

Write the words you know beneath the words in the text, and
match the others to the words in the vocabulary.

Notes

וַיֹּאמֶר

We have seen this before in 2 Samuel 12:7a (see section 5.6). It
means *and he said*.

יָצָתִי

This is a verb in the Perfect. The א has dropped out, which can
happen sometimes with verbs that end in א, and this can make
it difficult to guess what the root is . However, it may have been
possible to guess from the vocabulary above! The verb is first
person singular, so it means *I went out* or *I was born*.

מִבֶּטֶן

The preposition מִן shortened to מִ and prefixed to בֶּטֶן, which
is in construct relationship to the following word. There is no
special construct form of בֶּטֶן. The word means *from the belly of*
or *from the womb of*.

אָשׁוּב

This is a verbal form we have not encountered yet. The word
means *I shall return*.

שָׁמָּה

This is the word שָׁם with a ה attached to it. It is known as a ה
of direction because it indicates movement towards a place or
thing. So this word means *towards there*, although often it is
better English to translate it simply *there*.

נָתַן

A verb in the Perfect: it is third person masculine singular, so it means *he has given* or *he gave*.

לָקַח

Another verb in the Perfect, also third person masculine singular, meaning *he has taken* or *he took*. If you are wondering why there are two long vowels, it is because this word comes at a natural pause in the verse (if reading aloud). There are usually two pause points in a verse: one about halfway through, and another at the end. This sometimes results in a lengthening of a vowel of the word in pause. So we could say that לָקָח is the pausal form of לָקַח.

יְהִי

This is a verb form we have not looked at yet. The word means *may it be* or *it will be*.

מְבֹרָךְ

Another verb we have not yet encountered. This word means *blessed*.

Possible translation

And he said, 'Naked I was born from my mother's womb, and naked I shall return. Yhwh has given and Yhwh has taken. May Yhwh's name be blessed.'

10.6 Suggestions

- Learn the Perfect of קָטַל thoroughly. The most effective ways are usually writing it out repeatedly and reading it out loud repeatedly. These are not necessarily exciting ways to learn, but they are usually useful.

- Make sure you know the usual word order (verb, subject, object) and understand the implications of changes in word order.

10.7 Summary

In this unit we have looked at

- forms of the Perfect

- usage of the Perfect, including use of different English tenses to translate the Perfect and use of word order as a device for emphasis

- the text of Job 1:21.

10.8 Self-assessment

The self-assessment is intended to test your knowledge and understanding of the points of grammar covered in Units 6 to 10.

Answer all the questions as fully as possible, if possible without looking up the answers.

1)

a) Write in English: קוֹלוֹ סוּסְךָ קוֹלָם סוּסֵנוּ

b) Write in English: קוֹלֵיהֶם סוּסָתָה פָּרוֹתֵינוּ סוּסוֹתֵיכֶן

c) Write in Hebrew: *my father, his princess, our voices.*

d) Translate into Hebrew: *The women are good.*

e) Translate: טוֹבִים פָּרֵינוּ וְרָעוֹת פָּרוֹתֵינוּ

2)

a) List the words for *this*, giving their gender and number.

b) List the words for *those*, giving their gender and number.

c) Write in Hebrew: *these horses, these mares.*

d) Translate: זֹאת אֵשֶׁת אָבִי וְהוּא סוּסוֹ

e) Translate: אֵלֶּה דִּבְרֵי כֹּהֲנֵי אֱלֹהֵי יִשְׂרָאֵל

3)

a) Write in Hebrew: *to, on, under, between.*

b) Translate into Hebrew: *He has a son.*

c) Translate: גָּדוֹל הַמֶּלֶךְ מִן־הָאֲנָשִׁים

d) Write in Hebrew, using בְּ and לְ: *to me, in her, to them* (m), *in us*.

e) Write in English: כַּעֲבָדִי בָּעִיר לְנַעַר

4)

a) Write the object marker both with and without *maqqef*.

b) Write in English: עָלֶיךָ מִמֶּנִּי בֵּינֵיהֶם כָּמוֹהוּ

c) Translate: הֲבֵל הַבָּלִים

d) Translate: וְדָוִד הוּא הַקָּטָן (1 Samuel 17:14)

e) Translate: גָּדוֹל בָּנָיו עִם אִמִּי

5)

a) Write out the whole of קָטַל in Hebrew.

b) Write in Hebrew: *he has ruled, she has eaten, I have walked, they have guarded*

c) Translate: הָלְכָה עַד הָעִיר

d) Translate: אָכְלוּ דָוִד וְדָנִאֵל אֵת הַלֶּחֶם

e) Translate: מָשַׁל הַמֶּלֶךְ בְּכָל־אֶרֶץ יְהוּדָה הוּא וּבָנָיו

The answers to the self-assessment are in the Key to the exercises.

Scoring: Each correct answer gets one mark. You lose a mark if you make a mistake. A mistake means a missing letter or a missing vowel, or other missing or incorrect information. The final score will be a number out of 25. Multiply by 4 to find your percentage.

At this stage it is almost inevitable that you will make a few mistakes. The important thing about mistakes is that they show the areas where you need to do a little more work. Whether you forget to write in some of the vowels, or confuse similar-sounding (or similar-looking) letters, or there are words in your vocabulary book that just don't seem to stick in your memory, it is helpful if you can see your mistakes as an opportunity to focus on the things you find particularly challenging. Make sure you understand your mistakes before you continue with Unit 11.

It can be very discouraging to make a lot of little mistakes; it is of course possible to make mistakes in every answer. If this happens, it is not a reason to worry too much. If you are able to answer the questions at all, that is evidence of how much you have learned.

This is a point in language learning where motivation can become a struggle. If you have reached this point, you have put in many hours of study. And yet it seems there is still so much to learn: another ten units in this book and then perhaps some higher-level Hebrew if you remain interested. If you are finding motivation to be a problem, it might be worth reminding yourself that you have learned a great deal. You can now recognize approximately 200 words (maybe more if you count words with pronominal suffixes), simple sentences, a number of common Hebrew constructions and even a few idioms. The kinds of things you have learned up to this point are the kinds of things you will find on every page of the Hebrew Bible.

verb: *to long for*	עָרַג used with אֶל	ā-RAG
verb: *to pass over, to go*	עָבַר used with בְּ	ā-VAR
noun m: *crowd*	סָךְ	sāk
noun f: *sin*	חַטָּאת	cha-TĀT

11.1 Verbs: Imperfect

The Imperfect in Hebrew used to be called the Future because it can be translated by the English future tense. And in fact it is commonly used to describe an incomplete action in the future. But, like the Perfect, it is impossible to map the Imperfect to a single English tense. Hebrew verbs really do not correspond directly to English verbs. Nevertheless, for now we will translate the Hebrew Imperfect with an English future.

When we learned the Perfect, we saw that the root קטל acquired endings in order to indicate who was doing the acting, e.g.:

| *I have guarded* | קָטַלְתִּי |
| *you have guarded* | קְטַלְתֶּם |

But in the Imperfect we find that the root acquires additional letters at the beginning and in some cases at the end as well. This is how it works, using קטל again as a demonstration verb:

| *he will kill* | יִקְטֹל | yik-TŌL |
| *she will kill* | תִּקְטֹל | tik-TŌL |

you will kill (ms)	תִּקְטֹל	tik-TŌL
you will kill (fs)	תִּקְטְלִי	tik-t^a-LEE
I will kill	אֶקְטֹל	ek-TŌL
they will kill (mp)	יִקְטְלוּ	yik-t^a-LOO
they will kill (fp)	תִּקְטֹלְנָה	tik-TŌL-nā
you will kill (mp)	תִּקְטְלוּ	tik-t^a-LOO
you will kill (fp)	תִּקְטֹלְנָה	tik-TŌL-nā
we will kill	נִקְטֹל	nik-TŌL

Note the identical forms: 2fs is identical to 3ms, and 2fp is identical to 3fp. Context should help with translation. Note also: unlike the Perfect, the third person plural is divided into masculine and feminine.

By this point you are probably more confident about reading the Hebrew aloud and less dependent on approximate pronunciations (if indeed you used them). It should now be possible to attempt to pronounce most new Hebrew words; you have probably begun to develop an ear for the language. Remember that the stress usually goes at the end (e.g. *da-VAR*, *yik-t^a-LOO*); exceptions will be noted. There will still be a little help with pronunciation, but it will diminish over the next few units.

Here are some more examples to help to get a sense of the form of the Imperfect. Use the model above to figure out how they are pronounced.

to rule מָשַׁל

he will rule	יִמְשֹׁל
she will rule	תִּמְשֹׁל
you will rule (ms)	תִּמְשֹׁל
you will rule (fs)	תִּמְשְׁלִי
I will rule	אֶמְשֹׁל
they will rule (mp)	יִמְשְׁלוּ
they will rule (fp)	תִּמְשֹׁלְנָה
you will rule (mp)	תִּמְשְׁלוּ
you will rule (fp)	תִּמְשֹׁלְנָה
we will rule	נִמְשֹׁל

to keep, to guard שָׁמַר

he will guard	יִשְׁמֹר
she will guard	תִּשְׁמֹר
you will guard (ms)	תִּשְׁמֹר
you will guard (fs)	תִּשְׁמְרִי
I will guard	אֶשְׁמֹר
they will guard (mp)	יִשְׁמְרוּ
they will guard (fp)	תִּשְׁמֹרְנָה
you will guard (mp)	תִּשְׁמְרוּ
you will guard (fp)	תִּשְׁמֹרְנָה
we will guard	נִשְׁמֹר

In Unit 10, we noted that the Perfect is sometimes known as the Qatal. In a similar way, the Imperfect is sometimes known as the Yiqtol. For example, the Qatal of שָׁמַר is שָׁמַר and the Yiqtol of שָׁמַר is יִשְׁמֹר.

Here is another example verb:

to stand עָמַד

he will stand	יַעֲמֹד
she will stand	תַּעֲמֹד
you will stand (ms)	תַּעֲמֹד
you will stand (fs)	תַּעֲמְדִי
I will stand	אֶעֱמֹד
they will stand (mp)	יַעֲמְדוּ
they will stand (fp)	תַּעֲמֹדְנָה
you will stand (mp)	תַּעֲמְדוּ
you will stand (fp)	תַּעֲמֹדְנָה
we will stand	נַעֲמֹד

Note: the vowels differ somewhat from קָטַל. This is because of the guttural at the beginning of עָמַד. If you look above at the Imperfect of קָטַל you will see that beneath the first root letter

(ק) there is always a *sheva*. Gutturals cannot take a simple *sheva* and so the vowel changes to a composite *sheva* or a full vowel. This attracts an *a* vowel in the prefix. However, at this stage it is usually possible to make a good translation from Hebrew into English without knowing all the rules about how vowels behave in verbal forms.

We have encountered one Imperfect form already, in Unit 7. The word is יָשִׁיר and is usually translated with a past tense: *he sang*. The word יְהִי in Job 1:21 (Unit 10) is also an Imperfect form meaning *it will be*. As you can see, neither of these follows the pattern we have just learned. This is because of the changes to the pattern that occur when the verbal root contains ו or י or gutturals. We will explore these changes in more detail in Unit 13.

11.2 Exercise 1

Write out the Imperfect of the following verbs, on the model of קָטַל. These are the same verbs you learned in the Perfect. Remember that the *dagesh* in the פ will not be necessary when פָּקַד has the Imperfect prefixes, since פ will no longer be the first letter of the word. The same applies to כָּתַב.

	to visit פָּקַד	*to write* כָּתַב	*to remember* זָכַר
3ms	_____	_____	_____
3fs	_____	_____	_____
2ms	_____	_____	_____
2fs	_____	_____	_____
1s	_____	_____	_____
3p	_____	_____	_____
2mp	_____	_____	_____
2fp	_____	_____	_____
1p	_____	_____	_____

11.3 Usage of the Imperfect

Like the Perfect, the Imperfect cannot be translated by a single English tense. Although we usually translate it with a future tense, there are times when it can be translated by a present or a past.

Future tense:

and your sins I will not remember וְחַטֹּאתֶיךָ לֹא אֶזְכֹּר
(Isaiah 43:25)

Note the change from the usual word order in this phrase. We might have expected לֹא אֶזְכֹּר to come before חַטֹּאתֶיךָ. This can have the effect of emphasizing חַטֹּאתֶיךָ and it is also a poetic device, but thorough discussion would require us to look more closely at the context.

Present tense:

My soul longs for you. נַפְשִׁי תַעֲרֹג אֵלֶיךָ
(Psalm 42:2; Engl 42:1)

Past tense:

I used to go with the crowd. אֶעֱבֹר בַּסָּךְ
(Psalm 42:5; Engl. 42:4)

The circumstances in which we would translate the Hebrew Imperfect with a present or a past tense in English can be complicated and a Hebrew grammar should provide a more detailed explanation. For now, we will translate the Imperfect with an English future tense.

11.4 Exercise 2

Match the Hebrew to the English:

You will rule over all the land of Israel.

נִשְׁפֹּט אֶת־הֶעָרִים הָאֵלֶּה

I will remember this day.

תִּשְׁבַּתְנָה תַּחַת הָעֵץ אֲשֶׁר בְּשָׂדֶה

We will judge those cities.

יְהִי מְבֹרָךְ

He/it will be blessed.

תִּמְשֹׁל בְּכָל־אֶרֶץ יִשְׂרָאֵל

They will keep the law.

תַּעַמְדוּ לִפְנֵי הַמֶּלֶךְ וְלִפְנֵי עֲבָדָיו

They will remember the name of Yhwh the God of gods.

יִשְׁמְרוּ אֶת־הַתּוֹרָה

She will visit the women of Judah.

אֶזְכֹּר הַיּוֹם הַזֶּה

You will stand before the king and his servants.

תִּכְתְּבִי בְּסִפְרֵיכֶן

You will rest under the tree which is in the field.

תִּזְכֹּרְנָה שֵׁם יְהוָה אֱלֹהֵי הָאֱלֹהִים

You will write in your books.

תִּפְקֹד אֶת־נָשֵׁי יְהוּדָה

11.5 Text: Judges 8:22–3

Points to look out for in this text:

- words we have already encountered
- verbs in the Imperfect

name: Gideon	גִּדְעוֹן	gid-ŌN
adverb: also	גַּם	gam
verb: to deliver, save	יָשַׁע	yā-SHA
name: Midian	מִדְיָן	mid-YĀN

Text

Read the verses aloud a few times to be sure of the pronunciation.

וַיֹּאמְרוּ אִישׁ־יִשְׂרָאֵל אֶל־גִּדְעוֹן מְשָׁל־בָּנוּ גַּם־אַתָּה גַּם־בִּנְךָ גַּם בֶּן־
בְּנֶךָ כִּי הוֹשַׁעְתָּנוּ מִיַּד מִדְיָן: וַיֹּאמֶר אֲלֵהֶם גִּדְעוֹן לֹא־אֶמְשֹׁל אֲנִי
בָּכֶם וְלֹא־יִמְשֹׁל בְּנִי בָּכֶם יְהוָה יִמְשֹׁל בָּכֶם:

Approximate pronunciation:

*va-yō-mª-ROO eesh yis-rā-AYL el gid-ŌN, mª-SHĀL bā-NOO gam
at-TĀ gam bin-CHĀ gam bayn bª-NAY-chā, kee hō-sha-TĀ-noo mi-
YAD mid-YĀN. va-YŌ-mer a-lay-HEM gid-ŌN lō em-SHŌL a-NEE
bā-CHEM, vª-lō yim-SHŌL bª-NEE bā-CHEM; a-dō-NĪ yim-SHŌL
bā-CHEM.*

Write the words you know beneath the words in the text, and
match the others to the words in the vocabulary.

Notes

וַיֹּאמְרוּ

This is similar to the word וַיֹּאמֶר which we have already
encountered. While וַיֹּאמֶר means *and he said*, וַיֹּאמְרוּ means *and
they said*. If you look carefully, you will see that both וַיֹּאמֶר
and וַיֹּאמְרוּ look rather like the Imperfect forms we have been
learning. And so you might wonder why they are translated with
a past tense instead of a future tense. There is a good reason why
they are translated with a past tense, and it will be explained in
Unit 12.

אִישׁ־יִשְׂרָאֵל

As you probably realized, this means literally *the man of Israel*.
However, the verb is plural: *they said*. So this is usually translated
with a plural in English: *the men of Israel*.

מְשָׁל־בָּנוּ

You should recognize the verbal root מָשַׁל but this is not a form
we have looked at yet. It is known as an imperative and is used
as an instruction. So we would translate it simply *rule!*. The word
בָּנוּ when used with מָשַׁל means *over us*. Thus the phrase means
the people of Israel are saying to Gideon, '*Rule over us.*'

גַּם־אַתָּה

This means *also you*. The word in Hebrew is used in a slightly different way from the English *also*; in idiomatic English we would not use the word *also* here, and so it is usually omitted.

גַּם־בִּנְךָ

Also your son

גַּם בֶּן־בִּנְךָ

Also the son of your son (your grandson). In English it might be more idiomatic to translate *and also your son and your grandson*.

הוֹשַׁעְתָּנוּ

This is a verbal form we have not yet learned. The word means *you have saved us*.

מִיַּד

The first letter here is the preposition מ attached to the word יַד which is the construct form of יָד. So it means *from the hand of*. We might also translate *from the people of Midian* or *from the Midianites*.

אֲלֵהֶם

This is the preposition אֶל with the third person masculine plural suffix. Sometimes you might see this kind of construction represented in grammars as: אֶל with suff 3mp. So it is important that you are able to remember what 3mp means, and of course the other abbreviations.

לֹא־אֶמְשֹׁל

The particle means *not* and the verb here is an Imperfect, 1s. So: *I shall not rule*.

אֲנִי בָּכֶם

The pronoun אֲנִי is not strictly necessary for the verb to be understood, but here it is being used for emphasis, meaning something like *It is not I who shall rule over you*.

וְלֹא־יִמְשֹׁל בְּנִי

Another Imperfect here, this time 3ms. Literally *and not he shall rule my son*.

יְהוָה יִמְשֹׁל

Here we discover who will in fact rule over the people of Israel: it will be יהוה. Again the verb is an Imperfect 3ms. In English we could insert the word *but* or *rather* or *instead* since the contrast is so strongly implied in the Hebrew, or we could simply use a semicolon.

Possible translation

Here are two possible translations: one more literal and the other freer. Which appeals most, and why? What would you change?

And the men of Israel said to Gideon, 'Rule over us: you and also your son and also your son's son, because you have delivered us from the hand of Midian.' And Gideon said to them, 'I will not rule over you and my son will not rule over you; the LORD will rule over you.'

The people of Israel said to Gideon, 'Rule over us: you and your son and your grandson, because you have saved us from the Midianites.' But Gideon said to them, 'It it not I who will rule over you, nor my son; instead Yhwh will rule over you.'

11.6 Suggestions

• Write out the Imperfect of קָטַל and שָׁמַר every day for a week.

• Make sure you have learned all the new vocabulary both in the units and in the texts we have looked at.

11.7 Summary

In this unit we have looked at

• the forms of the Imperfect

• usage of the Imperfect

• the text of Judges 8:22–3.

12.1 Vav Consecutive Imperfect

noun m: *book*	סֵפֶר	*SAY-fer*

The verbal forms we have learned so far are the most straightforward forms. But they are not necessarily the most common forms. The form we are going to learn in this unit is more common in biblical narrative than the less complex forms we have learned so far. In order to read the Bible in Hebrew it is necessary to grasp a concept that can be a little difficult to get used to: adding the conjunction *and* to the beginning of a verb can change the way we translate it.

This is how it works. We have learned that the Perfect is usually translated with a past tense:

he has killed   קָטַל

and the Imperfect is usually translated with a future tense:

he will kill   יִקְטֹל

However, if we attach the conjunction ו to the verb:

and he will kill   וְקָטַל

and he killed   וַיִּקְטֹל

The first is a Perfect with the prefix וְ. The second is an Imperfect with the prefix וַ.

Here are some more examples:

PERFECT	VC PERFECT	IMPERFECT	VC IMPERFECT
שָׁמַר	וְשָׁמַר	יִשְׁמֹר	וַיִּשְׁמֹר
he has guarded	*and he will guard*	*he will guard*	*and he guarded*
שָׁמַרְתִּי	וְשָׁמַרְתִּי	אֶשְׁמֹר	וָאֶשְׁמֹר
I have guarded	*and I will guard*	*I will guard*	*and I guarded*
זָכַר	וְזָכַר	יִזְכֹּר	וַיִּזְכֹּר
he has remembered	*and he will remember*	*he will remember*	*and he remembered*
זָכְרוּ	וְזָכְרוּ	יִזְכְּרוּ	וַיִּזְכְּרוּ
they have remembered	*and they will remember*	*they will remember*	*and they remembered*

These forms are called Vav Consecutive Perfect and Vav Consecutive Imperfect, though there is some scholarly debate about the use of the term 'consecutive'. A good Hebrew grammar should explain further, including the reason why it is called 'consecutive' at all. An alternative term for VC Imperfect is Vayyiqtol and an alternative term for VC Perfect is Veqatal, just as the Perfect and Imperfect are sometimes known as Qatal and Yiqtol. However, the term 'consecutive' is widely used and may be the most accessible term for the time being. We will look at the Vav Consecutive (VC or, in some grammars, WC) Imperfect first because it is extremely common in biblical narrative. In fact we have already seen examples of it in 2 Samuel 12:7a and in Judges 8:23: וַיֹּאמֶר means *and he said*, which comes from אָמַר *to say*. This form is actually a little unusual, but the word וַיֹּאמֶר is so common in the Hebrew Bible that you will become familiar with it very quickly. The form וַיֹּאמְרוּ also occurs in Judges 8:23, and is also VC Imperfect.

The וֹ in the VC Imperfect is pointed with a short *a* vowel, and the next letter takes *dagesh*: וַיִּכְתֹּב. If the next letter is a guttural it cannot take *dagesh* and so the vowel under the וֹ is lengthened: וָאֶזְכֹּר (see also וָאֶשְׁמֹר above).

Here are some examples from the Hebrew text:

And he wrote in the book וַיִּכְתֹּב בַּסֵּפֶר
(1 Samuel 10:25)

And I will remember my covenant וְאָזְכֹּר אֶת־בְּרִיתִי
(Exodus 6:5)

12.2 Exercise 1

Give English forms.

3ms	יִשְׁמֹר	*he has guarded*	וַיִּשְׁמֹר	*and he will guard*
3fs	תִּשְׁמֹר	_____	וַתִּשְׁמֹר	_____
2ms	תִּשְׁמֹר	_____	וַתִּשְׁמֹר	_____
2fs	תִּשְׁמְרִי	_____	וַתִּשְׁמְרִי	_____
1s	אֶשְׁמֹר	_____	וָאֶשְׁמֹר	_____
3mp	יִשְׁמְרוּ	_____	וַיִּשְׁמְרוּ	_____
3fp	תִּשְׁמֹרְנָה	_____	וַתִּשְׁמֹרְנָה	_____
2mp	תִּשְׁמְרוּ	_____	וַתִּשְׁמְרוּ	_____
2fp	תִּשְׁמֹרְנָה	_____	וַתִּשְׁמֹרְנָה	_____
1p	נִשְׁמֹר	_____	וַנִּשְׁמֹר	_____

Some very common verbs have unusual forms in the Imperfect, and they occur frequently in the VC Imperfect. Two such words are:

to walk, go	הָלַךְ	*he will walk/go*	יֵלֵךְ	*and he walked/went*	וַיֵּלֶךְ
to take	לָקַח	*he will take*	יִקַּח	*and he took*	וַיִּקַּח

12.3 Vav Consecutive Perfect

The Perfect can also change meaning when prefixed by וּ. However, it is vocalized differently. The וּ in the VC Perfect is pointed with a *sheva*, for example:

and you will take a wife for my son   וְלָקַחְתָּ אִשָּׁה לִבְנִי
(Genesis 24:7)

This usage is less common that the VC Imperfect, but worth knowing about.

Compare the sentence above (VC Perfect) with the same sentence in the VC Imperfect:

and you will take a wife for my son   וְלָקַחְתָּ אִשָּׁה לִבְנִי

and you took a wife for my son   וַיִּקַּח אִשָּׁה לִבְנִי

You may read elsewhere that the Vav Consecutive changes the Imperfect into a Perfect or the Perfect into an Imperfect; or that the Vav Consecutive changes a future tense into a past tense and vice versa. In my view this is an oversimplification; the sense of reversal relates to the *English* tense with which we translate these different forms. However, for now it may be helpful to think of the VC as a transformative *vav*. And if these ideas sound difficult, that is because they *are* difficult. The VC should become clearer when you are more familiar with the Hebrew text.

However difficult it may be to learn about Hebrew verbs by reading grammatical descriptions, the fact remains that with some practice and experience it is not too difficult to understand them. The best way to come to understand Hebrew verbs is probably to read as much Hebrew as possible.

For now, while you are learning to read Hebrew, it can be helpful to think of the Perfect and VC Imperfect as past tenses, and the Imperfect and VC Perfect as future tenses, all the while keeping in mind that the idea of tense in biblical Hebrew can be rather provisional.

12.4 Exercise 2

Write out the VC Perfect of זָכַר and give meanings.

Translate:

וַיִּזְכֹּר אֶת־בְּרִיתְכֶם:

וְתִּכְתֹּב דִּבְרֵיכֶם בְּסֵפֶר:

וָאֶמְשֹׁל בָּהֶם:

וַתֵּלַכְנָה בְּדַרְכֵי צְדָקָה:

וַתֹּאכְלוּ הַלֶּחֶם:

וַיִּשְׁמְרוּ אֶת־תּוֹרַת יְהוָה:

וַתִּקְטֹל אִישׁ:

וַיִּקְרָא שֵׁם בְּנוֹ שְׁלֹמֹה:

וַיֹּאמֶר אֶשְׁפֹּט אֶת־כָּל־אֶרֶץ יְהוּדָה:

וַיֹּאמְרוּ נִשְׁמֹר אֵת בֵּית הַמֶּלֶךְ:

12.5 Text: Isaiah 12:1–2

Points to look out for in this text:

- Words we have already encountered.
- Occurrences of the VC with Imperfect and Perfect forms.

name: God	אֵל	ayl
verb: to be angry	אָנַף	ā-NAF
noun m: nose, anger	אַף	af
verb: to cling to, trust, rely on	בָּטַח	bā-TACH
noun f: song, praise, music	זִמְרָה	zim-RĀ
verb: to thank, praise	יָדָה	yah-DĀ
name: abbreviation of יְהוָה	יָהּ	yāch
noun f: help, salvation	יְשׁוּעָה	yªshoo-Ā
verb: to comfort, console	נָחַם	nā-cham
noun m: strength, power	עֹז	ōz
verb: to tremble, be afraid	פָּחַד	pā-CHAD (Be careful not to confuse this with פָּקַד meaning to visit)

Text

Read the verses aloud a few times to be sure of the pronunciation.

וְאָמַרְתָּ בַּיּוֹם הַהוּא אוֹדְךָ יְהוָה כִּי אָנַפְתָּ בִּי יָשֹׁב אַפְּךָ וּתְנַחֲמֵנִי: הִנֵּה אֵל יְשׁוּעָתִי אֶבְטַח וְלֹא אֶפְחָד כִּי־עָזִּי וְזִמְרָת יָהּ וַיְהִי־לִי לִישׁוּעָה:

Approximate pronunciation:

vᵃ-ā-mar-TĀ bā-YŌM ha-HOO ōd-CHĀ ā-dō-NĪ kee ā-NAF-tā bee yā-SHŌV af-CHĀ oot-na-cha-MAY-nee. hin-NAY ayl yᵃ-shoo-ā-TEE ev-TACH vᵃ-LŌ ef-CHĀD; kee ā-ZEE vᵃ-zim-RĀTH yāch ā-dō-NĪ va-yᵃ-hee-LEE lee-shoo-Ā.

Write the words you know beneath the words in the text, and match the others to the words in the vocabulary.

Notes

וְאָמַרְתָּ

This is a VC Perfect. It comes from the verb אמר. Notice that when we discuss verbal roots we can write them without the vowels, though out loud we would still say *ā-MAR*. Without the ו this word would be אָמַרְתָּ meaning *you have said*. However, with the ו we translate with an English future tense, so we get *and you will say*.

בַּיּוֹם הַהוּא

The phrase *in that day* should have been fairly easy to translate. In English, we might be more likely to say *on that day*.

אוֹדְךָ

This is an Imperfect, though not one of the forms we have learned. (It is a form called Hifil, which will we learn about in Unit 18.) It comes from ידה meaning *to praise* or *to give thanks*. It also has a pronominal suffix: an ending associated with a pronoun. In this case the ending is ךָ, which means *you*. It is the same as the ending on סוּסְךָ *your horse* so it should be easy to recognise. The initial א should provide a clue that it is first person. So although we do not yet know what a Hifil is, we can understand that it means *I will praise you*. It is translated with an English future tense because it is an Imperfect *without* the VC.

אָנַפְתָּ

A fairly straightforward Perfect from the verb אנף meaning *to be angry*. Since it begins with א, it might be easily mistaken for an Imperfect, presumably from a hypothetical verb נפת. However, the תָּ ending should indicate that it is a Perfect, which should save you the time it takes to look up the non-existent נפת in the dictionary. Since it is a Perfect without the VC, we will translate with a past tense: *you were angry* or *you have been angry*. The preposition בְּ is used to indicate *with* as in *angry with* someone or something; here with the 1s suffix it means *with me*. The word כִּי can sometimes be translated *although*, which might make sense here.

יָשֹׁב

This is an Imperfect, from the verb שׁוב *to turn*, *return*, or *turn back*. It is not formed in the same way as the Imperfect of קטל because it is spelled with a ו in the middle. Confusingly, it looks like a 3ms Perfect form, from a verbal root יָשַׁב. And indeed there is a verbal root יָשַׁב which means *to sit*. However, the 3ms of יָשַׁב is יָשַׁב (*he has sat*) whereas this is יָשֹׁב (*he has turned back*). It is not a big difference in spelling, but enough to make a difference in meaning. And since the subject of the verb is *your anger* it makes sense to use the pronoun *it* rather than *he*: *it will turn back*. However, many English translations use a past tense to translate this word.

אַפְּךָ

The noun אַף *nose* with a 2ms suffix; hence: *your anger*. (The connection with the nose is that when people are angry they sometimes blow air through their nostrils. Thus the word for nose also indicates anger.)

וּתְנַחֲמֵנִי

This is another Imperfect form but again a version we have not yet learned about (this one is called Piel). It is 2ms (notice the ת at the beginning), comes from the verbal root נחם, and has a pronominal suffix. We have not yet learned much about suffixes on verbs (though nouns and prepositions with suffixes should be familiar by now). This suffix is first person singular. The verb is VC but notice that the ו is pointed as a vowel (וּ) rather than the more common וַ. This is because it comes before a letter that is pointed with *sheva* (תְּ); we saw examples of the same kind of thing in Unit 3 (remember וּדְבוֹרָה *and Deborah*). Thus the whole word means *and you comforted me*. Incidentally, this root is the origin of the name of the prophet Nahum, in Hebrew נַחוּם.

הִנֵּה

This word is often translated *behold*. Perhaps in today's English we might translate it *look* or *notice*.

אֵל

This is another word, or name, for God. We have seen it already in Unit 9. Be sure to distinguish it from אֶל meaning *to*.

יְשׁוּעָתִי

The noun יְשׁוּעָה with a first person singular suffix, so it means *my help* or *my deliverance*.

אֶבְטַח

Another Imperfect 1s from בטח. It is not VC, so it means *I will trust*.

אֶפְחָד

Imperfect 1s from פחד. It is not VC so we translate it with a future tense: *I will be afraid*. Of course, the phrase וְלֹא אֶפְחָד means *I will* not *be afraid*.

עָזִּי

This is עֹז with 1s suffix. Be sure to distinguish it from אָז, which means *therefore*. The word עָזִּי means *my strength*.

וְזִמְרָת

The construct singular form of זִמְרָה so it means *song of*.

יָהּ

An abbreviation of יְהוָה

We have seen this noun above: יְשׁוּעָה but this time it is found with the preposition לְ. It means literally *for a deliverance*, and this construction is common in Hebrew and is often translated as an idiomatic expression of becoming. So the phrase וַיְהִי־לִי לִישׁוּעָה is often rendered *Yhwh has become my salvation*.

After reading through these notes, you should have something like:

And you will say in that day I will praise/thank you LORD because/although you were/have been angry with me your anger will turn away and you comforted me. Look, God is my salvation I will trust and I will not fear because my strength and the song of the LORD, the LORD is to me for salvation.

This is a good start, but needs to be polished. However, there are some decisions to be made. How will we decide where the sentences begin and end? What will we do with that Imperfect יָשֹׁב which seems to be anomalous? Do we simply translate it with a past tense or should we leave it as a future? How do we deal with the construct form וְזִמְרָת in verse 2? Can we translate it *my song* as if it weren't construct? These kinds of questions are discussed in good commentaries, and it can be very helpful to read some commentaries while translating a passage so that you can come to your own conclusions about the most appropriate way to translate difficult passages. However, each decision may involve matters of theology as well as matters of language, and theology is beyond the scope of this book. It is probably impossible to be theologically neutral, but the possible translation below is an attempt to deal with some of the difficulties in the language and is not intended to provide any theological solutions!

Possible translation

And you will say on that day, 'I will thank you, Yhwh, although you were angry with me. Your anger will turn away, and you have comforted me.' Look, God is my salvation; I will trust and I will not be afraid, because Yhwh is my strength and my song. Yhwh has become my salvation.

One solution to the difficulty posed by יָשֹׁב is to translate both יָשֹׁב and וּתְנַחֲמֵנִי with English verbs in the present tense: *your anger turns away and you comfort me*. The other common solution is to translate יֵשֹׁב as a past tense, and then it fits in more easily with the other English past tenses: *your anger has turned away and you have comforted me*. Meanwhile, most translations render וְזִמְרָת *my song*.

Translation is partly a science and partly an art. There can be no perfection, but some solutions may seem more suitable than others. Sometimes it may seem as if very little is at stake; other times it may seem as if a fundamental principle depends on correctly understanding the meaning of the Hebrew. This can be difficult, but it can also be very rewarding.

12.6 Suggestions

- Look up Isaiah 12:1–2 in several translations and compare the English tenses used to render the Hebrew Perfects and Imperfects. If you look at a range of translations you will probably find some variety of past, present and future tenses.

- Write out the Perfect, Imperfect, VC Perfect and WC Imperfect of the 3ms forms of קָטַל and שָׁמַר every day for a week. Give English translations. Check them against this unit.

12.7 Summary

In this unit we have looked at

- the effect that placing a ו before a verb can have on the English tense used to translate it.

- the text of Isaiah 12:1–2, with particular reference to difficulties in deciding which English tense to use.

By now you should no longer be having much difficulty with pronunciation. If you find you are still struggling a little, it might be a good idea to practise with passages from previous units until you feel confident.

verb: *to come*	בּוֹא
verb: *to build*	בָּנָה
verb: *to reveal*	גָּלָה
verb: *to bear children*	יָלַד
verb: *to give birth*	יָלַד
verb: *to suck*	יָנַק
verb: *to go down* (e.g. to Egypt)	יָרַד
verb: *to sit*	יָשַׁב
verb: *to find*	מָצָא
verb: *to approach*	נָגַשׁ
verb: *to fall*	נָפַל
verb: *to turn*	סָבַב
verb: *to go up*	עָלָה
verb: *to arise*	קוּם
verb: *to see*	רָאָה
verb: *to kill, slaughter*	שָׁחַט
verb: *to put, place*	שִׂים
verb: *to stretch out*	שָׁלַח
verb: *to hear*	שָׁמַע

13.1 Weak verbs

Weak verbs are verbs that do not follow the patterns we have learned in Units 10 and 11. Most of them follow a very similar pattern but have slightly different vowels. Those are usually easy enough to translate. But other weak verbs change their spelling so that it is hard to guess the root unless you have seen the form before. The word 'weak' in this context tends to suggest that the vowels will be forced to change (e.g. if they occur under a guttural), or that some consonants in the word may disappear when prefixes and suffixes are added.

Verbs in English sometimes do similar things: for example, the verb *flee* becomes *fled* in the past tense: the vowel has reduced from a long *ee* sound to a short *e* sound. Meanwhile the verb *feed* becomes *fed* in the past tense: as well as vowel reduction the expected past tense ending is missing. We might expect the past tense of *feed* to be *feeded*, but in fact the *ed* ending close after the final *d* in the verb is a little uncomfortable to pronounce so it disappears. We see that same kind of pattern in many verbs that end in *d* or *t*: *lend/lent* (not *lended*), *put/put* (not *putted*).

We have already seen examples of weak verbs in Hebrew. One obvious example is the verb עָמַד. In Unit 11, we saw that its vowels are different from קָטַל:

VERB	IMPERFECT 3MS	MEANING
to kill קָטַל	יִקְטֹל	*he will kill*
to stand עָמַד	יַעֲמֹד	*he will stand*

We might have expected the Imperfect 3ms of עָמַד to be יַעְמֹד. However, the guttural ע cannot take a simple *sheva*. It has to take complex *sheva* instead: עֲ. The guttural also affects the vowel under the letter that comes before it, so instead of יִ we have יַ.

Verbs can be weak if:

the first letter of the root is a guttural	e.g.: עָמַד, אָכַל
the second letter is a guttural	e.g.: שָׁחַט
the third letter is a guttural	e.g.: שָׁלַח, מָצָא, גָּלָה
the first letter is a vowel (ו or י)	e.g.: יָשַׁב
the middle letter is a vowel (ו or י)	e.g.: קוּם

the first letter is נ   e.g.: נָגַשׁ

the middle letter is the same as the last letter   e.g.: סָבַב

In Hebrew grammars there is often a kind of shorthand for 'first letter', 'second letter' and so on.

The first letter is the פ letter.

The second letter is the ע letter

The third letter is the ל letter

If we want to say *the first letter of the verbal root is* alef, we say the verb is פ״א (*pe alef*). The mark that looks like an apostrophe, ' , is called a *geresh* (pl *gershayim* or *gerashayim*). It can be used singly or doubled, depending on context, e.g. פ״י or ק׳. The mark means 'not a word' and is used for abbreviations.

If we want to say *the second letter of the verbal root is* vav we say the verb is ע״ו (*ayin vav*).

If we want to say *the third letter of the verbal root is* he we say the verb is ל״ה (*lamed he*).

The letters ע, פ and ל are not random; in fact פָּעַל means *to make* or *to form*, which is quite an appropriate verb in the circumstances. As a noun, it can mean *verb* (פֹּעַל). In fact, if it weren't for the weakness in פָּעַל (it is, of course, *ayin* guttural), it might be more appropriate as a demonstration verb than קָטַל.

The weaknesses have various effects, and the effects can be found in the Perfect or Imperfect or other forms. Here are the most likely departures from the regular verb:

פ guttural (e.g. עָמַד): changes to the vowel patterns

ע guttural (e.g. שָׁחַט): changes to the vowel patterns

ל guttural (e.g. שָׁלַח): changes to the vowel patterns

פ״ו and פ״י (e.g. יָשַׁב): disappearing י or ו

ע״ו and ע״י (e.g. קוּם): disappearing י or ו

פ״נ (e.g. נָגַשׁ): disappearing נ

ע״ע (e.g. סָבַב): disappearing second letter

We have already seen some weak verbs in Units 10 and 11 and they were very similar to the קָטַל pattern. The weak verbs we have already encountered are: עָמַד אָכַל הָלַךְ לָקַח נָתַן שׁוּב הָיָה and others have appeared in the examples. Some verbs can be doubly weak; for example הָיָה is both *pe* guttural and *lamed* guttural.

13.2 Weak verbs in the Perfect

ע״ו and ע״י verbs

One thing to note about these verbs is that the form found in the dictionary is not the Perfect 3ms but a form called the Infinitive Construct, which we will learn about later.

to arise קוּם

he has arisen	קָם
she has arisen	קָמָה
you have arisen	קַמְתָּ
you have arisen	קַמְתְּ
I have arisen	קַמְתִּי
they have arisen	קָמוּ
you have arisen	קַמְתֶּם
you have arisen	קַמְתֶּן
we have arisen	קַמְנוּ

Verbs with a middle י follow the same pattern as קוּם. These are sometimes called 'hollow' verbs, and they are very common indeed, so it is worth learning them.

ל״ה verbs

These verbs drop the ה in the Perfect. The ה is replaced by י in most of the forms, but notice the 3fs where the ה is replaced by ת; and the 3rd person plural form, where the ה is simply absent.

to reveal גָּלָה

he has revealed	גָּלָה
she has revealed	גָּלְתָה
you have revealed	גָּלִיתָ
you have revealed	גָּלִית
I have revealed	גָּלִיתִי
they have revealed	גָּלוּ
you have revealed	גְּלִיתֶם
you have revealed	גְּלִיתֶן
we have revealed	גָּלִינוּ

פ"נ verbs

Most פ"נ verbs are straightforward enough in the Perfect. However, the verb נָתַן is slightly different and is worth learning because it is so common.

to give נָתַן

he has given	נָתַן
she has given	נָתְנָה
you have given	נָתַתָּ
you have given	נָתַתְּ
I have given	נָתַתִּי
they have given	נָתְנוּ
you have given	נְתַתֶּם
you have given	נְתַתֶּן
we have given	נָתַנּוּ

ע"ע verbs

The only other category in which weak verbs are significantly different in the Perfect is double *ayin* verbs. These are also known as reduplicated verbs or geminate verbs: think *gemini* = twins, and remember that there is a twinning of the *ayin* letter in these verbs. The second and third letters of the root are the same, and instead of being written out twice the *ayin* letter tends to be written only once (though it is written twice in some forms). This is the pattern:

to turn סָבַב

he has turned	סָבַב
she has turned	סָבְבָה
you have turned	סַבּוֹתָ
you have turned	סַבּוֹת
I have turned	סַבּוֹתִי
they have turned	סָבְבוּ
you have turned	סַבּוֹתֶם
you have turned	סַבּוֹתֶן
we have turned	סַבּוֹנוּ

Although it might seem as if these are yet more verbal forms to learn, it is worth remembering that the endings are always the same. So you should always be able to see that you are dealing with a verb in the Perfect.

13.3 Exercise 1

This exercise has two goals: to become familiar with the different kinds of weak verbs and to practise parsing (analysing) verbs. To parse a verbal form, you need to give the aspect (e.g. Perfect), person, gender, number and meaning; at a later stage there will be other things to add, but these will suffice at this stage. See below for an example.

VERB	WEAKNESS	EXAMPLE FORM	PARSED
to stand עָמַד	pe guttural	תַּעַמְדוּ	Impf 2mp *you will stand*
to send, stretch out שָׁלַח	_____	שָׁלְחָה	_____
to put, place שִׂים	_____	שָׂמָה	_____
to see רָאָה	_____	רָאִינוּ	_____
to hear שָׁמַע	_____	שְׁמַעְתִּי	_____
to drink שָׁתָה	_____	שְׁתִיתֶם	_____
to go up עָלָה	_____	עָלְתָה	_____
to come בּוֹא	_____	בָּא	_____
to give birth יָלַד	_____	יָלַדְתְּ	_____
to go out יָצָא	_____	יָצָאת	_____
to go down יָרַד (e.g. to Egypt)	_____	יָרְדוּ	_____
to die מוּת	_____	מֵתָן	_____
to build בָּנָה	_____	בָּנוּ	_____

13.4 Weak verbs in the Imperfect

Verbs in the Imperfect have prefixes and some forms also have suffixes. This can make them easy to spot, so most weak verbs should pose no problems. There are a few differences in vowel patterns in verbs with gutturals, but nothing that should cause confusion. The important thing to remember is that gutturals attract *a* vowels, so if you see the word יִמְצָא you should be able to recognize it as the Imperfect 3ms of מָצָא (*to find*) even though it does not follow exactly the vowel pattern you are used to in יִקְטֹל.

פ״י and פ״ו verbs

The Imperfect forms of verbs such as יָנַק (*to suck*) should not be difficult to find in a dictionary, since they follow the pattern of יִקְטֹל except for a few vowel changes. The 3ms Imperfect is יִינַק.

A few verbs which begin with ' follow a different pattern in the Imperfect. Since they are common, it is useful to learn this pattern.

יָשַׁב *to sit*

he will sit	יֵשֵׁב
she will sit	תֵּשֵׁב
you will sit	תֵּשֵׁב
you will sit	תֵּשְׁבִי
I will sit	אֵשֵׁב
they will sit	יֵשְׁבוּ
they will sit	תֵּשַׁבְנָה
you will sit	תֵּשְׁבוּ
you will sit	תֵּשַׁבְנָה
we will sit	נֵשֵׁב

Other verbs that follow this pattern are: יָלַד (*to bear children*), יָצָא (*to go out*), and יָרַד (*to go down*). The verb יָדַע (*to know*) follows the same pattern except with an *a* vowel because of the guttural:

he will know	יֵדַע
she will know	תֵּדַע
you will know	תֵּדַע
you will know	תֵּדְעִי
I will know	אֵדַע
they will know	יֵדְעוּ
they will know	תֵּדַעְנָה
you will know	תֵּדְעוּ
you will know	תֵּדַעְנָה
we will know	נֵדַע

And the verb הָלַךְ (*to walk, go*) follows the same pattern even though it is spelled with ה in the Perfect.

he will go	יֵלֵךְ
she will go	תֵּלֵךְ
you will go	תֵּלֵךְ
you will go	תֵּלְכִי
I will go	אֵלֵךְ
they will go	יֵלְכוּ
they will go	תֵּלַכְנָה
you will go	תֵּלְכוּ
you will go	תֵּלַכְנָה
we will go	נֵלֵךְ

ע״ו and ע״י verbs

The hollow verbs do not lose their middle letter in the Imperfect, and so they are fairly similar to יִקְטֹל with slightly different vowels. For example, the 3ms of קוּם is יָקוּם.

ל״ה verbs

In the Perfect these verbs drop the final ה but in the Imperfect most forms retain the final ה, with the exception of:

You (fs) will reveal	תִּגְלִי
They (m) will reveal	יִגְלוּ
You (mp) will reveal	תִּגְלוּ

פ״ן verbs

These verbs lose their initial נ in the Imperfect. The letter נ in biblical Hebrew tends to be very readily assimilated into the next letter and when that happens it is represented by *dagesh*. For example:

נָפַל to fall

he will fall	יִפֹּל
she will fall	תִּפֹּל
you will fall (ms)	תִּפֹּל
you will fall (fs)	תִּפְּלִי

I will fall	אֶפֹּל
they will fall (mp)	יִפְּלוּ
they will fall (fp)	תִּפֹּלְנָה
you will fall (mp)	תִּפְּלוּ
you will fall (fp)	תִּפֹּלְנָה
we will fall	נִפֹּל

Some פ"נ verbs have *a* vowels where נָפַל has *o* vowels, for example the verb נָגַשׁ (*to approach*). The Imperfect 3ms is יִגַּשׁ, and all the other parts of the Imperfect are found with *a* vowels instead of *o* vowels.

ע"ע verbs

The double *ayin* verbs in the Imperfect, like the Perfect, tend to be found with the *ayin* letter written only once; some forms with *dagesh* and some without *dagesh*:

to turn סָבַב

he will turn	יָסֹב
she will turn	תָּסֹב
you will turn (ms)	תָּסֹב
you will turn (fs)	תָּסֹבִּי
I will turn	אָסֹב
they will turn (mp)	יָסֹבּוּ
they will turn (fp)	תְּסֻבֶּינָה
you will turn (mp)	תָּסֹבּוּ
you will turn (fp)	תְּסֻבֶּינָה
we will turn	נָסֹב

It is not usually necessary at this stage to memorize long lists of weak verbs. If you were planning to speak biblical Hebrew you would probably need to learn lists of verbs, but since most people learn biblical Hebrew in order to read the Bible, it is assumed that the main purpose of learning about weak verbs is to recognize patterns so that you will be able to look up unfamiliar verbs in a dictionary. Readers who enjoy learning lists of verbs can find such lists at the back of any good Hebrew grammar. Indeed, it may be necessary at a later stage to learn the vowel patterns of the verbs with gutturals.

13.5 Exercise 2

Write out the Imperfect of יָלַד and יָרַד on the pattern of יָשַׁב.

3ms	_____	_____
3fs	_____	_____
2ms	_____	_____
2fs	_____	_____
1s	_____	_____
3mp	_____	_____
3fp	_____	_____
2mp	_____	_____
2fp	_____	_____
1p	_____	_____

13.6 Text: Psalm 9:2–9 (Engl. 1–9)

Points to look out for in this text:

• Words we have already encountered.

• Weak verbs and how their forms differ from קטל.

There is a great deal of new vocabulary in this passage, but the last few units have been much lighter, and this vocabulary is particularly useful: there are many words in this passage which appear frequently in biblical Hebrew.

verb: *to wander, perish, be lost; destroy*	אבד
adverb: *back*	אָחוֹר
noun m: *nation*	גּוֹי
verb: *to rebuke*	גָּעַר
verb: *to govern, judge*	דוּן
noun m: *judgement, cause*	דִּין
noun m: *remembrance, memory*	זֵכֶר
verb: *to sing praises*	זָמַר
noun f: *desolation, ruin*	חָרְבָּה
verb: *to establish*	כוּן
noun m: *seat, throne*	כִּסֵּא
verb: *to stumble*	כָּשַׁל
noun m: *people, nation*	לְאֹם
noun m: *heart*	לֵב
adverb: *forever*	לָנֶצַח
verb: *to destroy*	מָחָה
noun m: *righteousness, justice, truth*	מֵישָׁר
noun m: *judgement*	מִשְׁפָּט
noun f: *great deeds, greatness*	נִפְלָאוֹת
verb: *to tear, destroy*	נָתַשׁ
verb: *to tell, count*	סָפַר
noun ms: *eternity*	עַד
noun ms: *a time hidden or unlimited*	עוֹלָם
adjective: *high, most high*	עֶלְיוֹן
verb: *to rejoice*	עָלַץ
verb: *to do, make, accomplish*	עָשָׂה
noun m: *justice*	צֶדֶק
adjective m: *wicked, guilty*	רָשָׁע
verb: *to be glad*	שָׂמַח
noun f: *world*	תֵּבֵל
verb: *to be completed, be finished, be gone*	תָּמַם

Text

Read the text aloud a few times. By this point you should no longer be too dependent on the approximate pronunciation, and of course pronunciation is not crucial for this level of Hebrew study. You might make occasional mistakes, but as long as you have a general sense of what the words sound like you will be able to understand them.

אֲסַפְּרָה כָּל־נִפְלְאוֹתֶיךָ׃	2 אוֹדֶה יְהוָה בְּכָל־לִבִּי
אֲזַמְּרָה שִׁמְךָ עֶלְיוֹן׃	3 אֶשְׂמְחָה וְאֶעֶלְצָה בָךְ
יִכָּשְׁלוּ וְיֹאבְדוּ מִפָּנֶיךָ׃	4 בְּשׁוּב־אוֹיְבַי אָחוֹר
יָשַׁבְתָּ לְכִסֵּא שׁוֹפֵט צֶדֶק׃	5 כִּי־עָשִׂיתָ מִשְׁפָּטִי וְדִינִי
שְׁמָם מָחִיתָ לְעוֹלָם וָעֶד׃	6 גָּעַרְתָּ גוֹיִם אִבַּדְתָּ רָשָׁע
וְעָרִים נָתַשְׁתָּ אָבַד זִכְרָם	7 הָאוֹיֵב תַּמּוּ חֳרָבוֹת לָנֶצַח הֵמָּה׃
כּוֹנֵן לַמִּשְׁפָּט כִּסְאוֹ׃	8 וַיהוָה לְעוֹלָם יֵשֵׁב
יָדִין לְאֻמִּים בְּמֵישָׁרִים׃	9 וְהוּא יִשְׁפֹּט־תֵּבֵל בְּצֶדֶק

Write the words you know beneath the words in the text, and match the others to the words in the vocabulary.

Notes

Now that the passages we are reading are more lengthy, the notes will be discussed one verse at a time and the grammatical analysis of the Hebrew will be in note form.

Verse 2

Many of the Psalms have a heading (e.g. 'A Psalm of David'), and these headings are left out of the verse structure in English translations. So verse 1 of the English is what we are calling verse 2 here. In the Hebrew text, verse 1 is a heading that says: *To the choirmaster, according to Muth-labben. A Psalm of David.*

אוֹדֶה

See Unit 12 for ידה. This form is similar except that it is first person singular (1s). As in Unit 12, this is a Hifil and we have not yet looked at the Hifil, but we will learn about it in Unit 18. This verb is doubly weak because it is פ״י and ל״ה.

לִבִּי

noun ms + suff 1s from noun ms לֵב *heart*. With the suffix it means *my heart*.

אֲסַפְּרָה

This is in another form we have not yet learned: the Piel. We will learn it in Unit 17. Piel Impf 1s סִפֵּר: *I will tell*.

נִפְלְאוֹתֶיךָ

Unfortunately this is another form we have not yet learned. This one is called Nifal and we will learn it in Unit 16. It can be frustrating to be told to wait until a later unit before we look at these forms, but it does facilitate reading the actual Hebrew text. This word means: your greatness, your great things, your wondrous deeds. It comes from a verb that is *pe* guttural.

Verse 3

אֶשְׂמְחָה וְאֶעֶלְצָה

Both these verbs mean *rejoice* and both are Imperfect. Both verbs are weak and both also have an extra ה at the end of the form. This addition of an extra letter is rather common in Hebrew and perhaps occurs to aid pronunciation. The second verb is not VC because it is pointed וְ instead of וַ. In cases like this, the conjunction ו simply means *and*; we do not translate וְאֶעֶלְצָה as a past tense.

אֲזַמְּרָה

This is another Piel form. The verb is in the Imperfect and like the other two verbs in this verse it has an extra ה at the end.

Verse 4

בְּשׁוּב־אוֹיְבַי אָחוֹר

The preposition בְּ attached to a verb in this way often means *when*. The word is the plural of אוֹיֵב with the suffix 1s. Thus: *when my enemies turned back*.

יִכָּשְׁלוּ

This is a further form we have not yet learned: Nifal. It doesn't matter too much at the moment if we do not understand these forms perfectly; seeing them as we move through the text will enable us to remember them when we come to learn them. This word is a Perfect 3mp and means *they will stumble*.

וְיֹאבְדוּ

This, like וְאֶעֱלֹצָה above, is not VC Imperfect, even though it looks as if it should be. Like the example above, the ו is pointed וְ instead of וַ so it simply means *and*. The verb is *pe alef* and follows the usual vowel pattern for *pe alef* verbs, with an initial *o* vowel instead of an *i* vowel (יֹאבְדוּ compared with יִשְׁמְרוּ).

מִפָּנֶיךָ

This means literally *from your face* but in idiomatic English we might leave out the *from*. Also, instead of translating *your face* we might remember that this word means *before*.

Verse 5

עָשִׂיתָ

Perfect 2ms from עָשָׂה which is *lamed he* and has the typically *lamed he* feature in which the ה is replaced by a י.

מִשְׁפָּטִי

the noun מִשְׁפָּט with a suffix 1s.

יָשַׁבְתָּ

is a Perfect 2ms from יָשַׁב, a *pe yod* verb. *Pe yod* verbs follow the same pattern in the Perfect as קָטַל.

שׁוֹפֵט

comes from the verb שׁפט and means *judging*. It can also be used as a noun, hence *judge*. It is difficult to translate the sense of it into English, so have a look at a few translations and see if you can understand how they made the decision to translate in that way.

Verse 6

גָּעַרְתָּ גוֹיִם אִבַּדְתָּ רָשָׁע

In English we would add a definite article: *you have rebuked* the *nations* and *you have destroyed* the *wicked*. The word גָּעַרְתָּ is a

Perfect 2ms from גער which is *ayin* guttural. The main feature of *ayin* guttural verbs in the Perfect is that in the places where we would expect to find simple *shevas* we find complex *shevas*. However, this is only relevant in the 3fs and the 3p (because they are the only forms of the Perfect in which there is usually a *sheva* under the *ayin* letter). So in this case the verb גָּעַרְתָּ looks exactly like the קָטַל pattern. The word אִבַּדְתָּ, although clearly from a *pe alef* root, is a Piel form, and so for now we will not analyse it.

שְׁמָם מָחִיתָ

The first word is שֵׁם with a 3mp suffix: *their name*. The second word is a Perf 2ms from מחה which is a *lamed he* verb. Like עָשִׂיתָ in verse 5, the ה of the root has been replaced by a י in this form.

לְעוֹלָם וָעֶד

Literally *for an unlimited time and eternity*. The expression *forever and ever* is a good idiomatic expression with which to render the Hebrew.

Verse 7

הָאוֹיֵב תַּמּוּ חֳרָבוֹת לָנֶצַח

The subject comes before the verb here, which is a departure from the commonest Hebrew word order. The word תַּמּוּ is from the double *ayin* root תמם; it is Perfect 3p and like other double *ayin* verbs, the *ayin* letter is written only once but with a *dagesh*: compare תַּמּוּ with the Perfect 3mp of קָטַל : קָטְלוּ. In case you are wondering why no gender is given, the third person plural of the Perfect is not divided into masculine and feminine. Some grammars use the term *common* to describe forms that can be applied to either gender.

נָתַשְׁתָּ

This verb should not be too difficult to understand: the תָּ ending indicates that it is a Perfect, and so the three remaining letters are the letters of the root. It is a weak verb: it is *pe nun*, but *pe nun* verbs generally follow the קָטַל pattern in the Perfect.

אָבַד זִכְרָם הֵמָּה

Literally *their memory of them is lost/has perished*. A more idiomatic translation might be: *the memory of them has perished.* אָבַד is a weak verb, but *pe alef* verbs are identical to the קָטַל pattern in the Perfect.

Verse 8

יֵשֵׁב

Notice this Imperfect 3ms of יָשַׁב: one of the weak verbs we have been looking at in this unit.

כּוֹנֵן

The word כּוֹנֵן is in a form that occurs only infrequently in biblical Hebrew, but the meaning is straightforward enough: *he has established.* It is a weak verb from the hollow root כּוּן, but the uncommon form puts it outside the scope of our analysis at this stage.

The word לַמִּשְׁפָּט is מִשְׁפָּט with the preposition לְ: *for justice.* And the word כִּסְאוֹ is simply כִּסֵּא with a suffix 3ms: *his throne.*

Verse 9

וְהוּא יִשְׁפֹּט

The use of the pronoun הוּא here serves to emphasize that it is Yhwh who judges.

יָדִין

comes from the hollow root דּוּן and is Imperfect 3ms. It follows the same pattern as the verb שִׂים *to place, to put* (Impf 3ms: יָשִׂים), which is like קוּם but with slightly different vowel patterns.

לְאֻמִּים

Another word for *people*; it is not as common as עַם.

Possible translation

2. *I will praise Yhwh with all my heart; I will tell of all your greatness.*

3. *I will be glad and I will rejoice in you; I will sing praises to your most high name.*

4. *When my enemies turned back they stumbled and they perished before you.*

5. *For you have accomplished my judgement and my cause; you have sat on the throne judging justly.*

6. *You have rebuked the nations; you have destroyed the wicked. You have destroyed their name forever and ever.*

7. *The enemy is gone in eternal ruins; you have destroyed their cities; the memory of them is lost.*

8. *And Yhwh will sit forever : he has established his throne for judgement.*

9. *It is he who judges the world with righteousness; he judges peoples with truth.*

13.7 Suggestion

- It is not immensely important to learn all the vowel patterns at this stage, though it is useful to have a reasonable grasp of them. However, it should prove useful to learn the large quantity of vocabulary in this unit. Most of the new words are very common and familiarity with them help you to recognize them in the biblical text.

13.8 Summary

In this unit we have looked at

- the traditional way of describing weak verbs: *pe* guttural etc.

- the changes that take place in the Perfect forms of weak verbs

- the changes that take place in the Imperfect forms of weak verbs

- the text of Psalm 9:2–9.

pronoun m: *them*	אַתֶּם
verb: *to weep, lament*	בָּכָה
verb: *to die*	מוּת
verb: *to mourn*	סָפַד
noun f: *time*	עֵת
verb: *to be fertile, fruitful*	פָּרָה
place name: *Zion*	צִיּוֹן
verb: *to become many*	רָבַב
verb: *to leap, dance*	רָקַד
verb: *to laugh*	שָׂחַק

14.1 Imperative

Grammar: Imperative

Imperatives are for telling people what to do. Since we usually
command people directly, imperatives are in the second person.
An example in English is *Look at the moon!* In this sentence, *look*
is in the Imperative.

In biblical Hebrew, if you tell a man to guard you say: שְׁמֹר
(ms).

If you were addressing one woman: שִׁמְרִי (fs).

If you were addressing a group of men or a mixed group you
would say: שִׁמְרוּ (mp).

And if you were addressing two or more women: שָׁמֹרְנָה (fp).

In each case we would translate the Hebrew with the English *Guard!*

Here is an example with the verb כָּתַב:

write! (ms)	כְּתֹב
write! (fs)	כִּתְבִי
write! (mp)	כִּתְבוּ
write! (fp)	כְּתֹבְנָה

Sometimes people issue commands, but other times they say *please*. The word in Hebrew for *please* is known as the particle of entreaty, נָא. It comes after the Imperative, to which it is joined with *maqqef*:

| *please guard* | שְׁמֹר־נָא |
| *please write* | כְּתֹב־נָא |

Notice that the masculine singular form of the Imperative is identical to the Infinitive Construct (see below, section 14.4). This is not the case for all weak verbs, however. Note particularly the following weak verbs: *ayin* gutturals, *lamed* gutturals, *lamed alef*, *pe vav*, *lamed he*, and *pe nun* on the נָגַשׁ model. These are irregular in the Imperative.

At a glance (masculine singular only):

	VERB	IMPERATIVE	
Regular (strong) verb	קָטַל	קְטֹל	*kill!*
Pe guttural	עָמַד	עֲמֹד	*stand!*
Pe alef	אָכַל	אֱכֹל	*eat!*
Ayin guttural	שָׁחַט	שְׁחַט	*kill!*
Lamed guttural	שָׁלַח	שְׁלַח	*send!*
Lamed alef	מָצָא	מְצָא	*find!*
Pe vav	יָשַׁב	שֵׁב	*sit!*
Ayin vav and *ayin yod*	קוּם	קוּם	*arise!*
Lamed he	גָּלָה	גְּלֵה	*reveal!*
Pe nun	נָפַל	נְפֹל	*fall!*
Pe nun	נָגַשׁ	גַּשׁ/גְּשָׁה	*approach!*
Double *ayin*	סָבַב	סֹב	*turn!*

4.2 Participles

Grammar: participles

A participle is a verbal form that functions as an adjective. In English we have two kinds of participle:

present participle	He is start*ing*, she was stopp*ing*; a runn*ing* river, a compell*ing* reason
past participle	He has start*ed*, she had stopp*ed*; a paint*ed* fence, an edit*ed* book

---

The form of the Participle in Hebrew is קֹטֵל, pronounced *kō-TAYL*. It can be used in a way that is quite like the English present participle, though there are some other uses. Hebrew participles are usually translated with English present participles or with nouns. Here are some examples of how it can work.

He was judging the people of the land.   הוּא שֹׁפֵט אֶת־עַם הָאָרֶץ
(2 Kings 15:5 adapted)

Note that in the absence of a verb, this phrase could also be translated *He is judging the people of the land*.

For God is a judge.   כִּי־אֱלֹהִים שֹׁפֵט הוּא (Psalm 50:6)

Literally *for God a judge is he*. This is often translated *for God himself is judge* with the pronoun הוּא understood as emphatic.

The participle in the weak verbs is very regular, with just a few exceptions to the שֹׁפֵט model. Notice the extra *a* vowel in the *lamed* guttural verbs, the hollow verbs (*pe yod* and *pe vav*), and the short-*e* vowel in the *lamed he* verbs.

At a glance:

	VERB	PARTICIPLE	
Regular (strong) verb	קָטַל	קֹטֵל	*killing*
Pe guttural	עָמַד	עֹמֵד	*standing*
Pe alef	אָכַל	אֹכֵל	*eating*
Ayin guttural	שָׁחַט	שֹׁחֵט	*killing*
Lamed guttural	שָׁלַח	שֹׁלֵחַ	*sending*
Lamed alef	מָצָא	מֹצֵא	*finding*
Pe vav	יָשַׁב	יֹשֵׁב	*sitting*
Ayin vav and *ayin yod*	קוּם	קָם	*arising*
Lamed he	גָּלָה	גֹּלֶה	*revealing*
Pe nun	נָפַל	נֹפֵל	*falling*
Pe nun	נָגַשׁ	נֹגֵשׁ	*approaching*
Double *ayin*	סָבַב	סוֹבֵב	*turning*

If you are wondering about how to pronounce יֹשֵׁב, it is *yō-SHAYV*. The dot on the שׁ doubles as a long-*o* vowel. Instead of writing יֹ שֵׁב, it is written with a single dot.

14.3 Exercise 1

Fill in the blanks

VERB	to eat	to reveal	to go down
ROOT	אָכַל	גָּלָה	יָרַד
PARTICIPLE	אֹכֵל	_____	_____
MEANING	eating	revealing	going down
IMPERATIVE	_____	גְּלֵה	רֵד
MEANING	eat!	reveal!	go down!

VERB	to sit	to die	to find
ROOT	יָשַׁב	מוּת	_____
PARTICIPLE	_____	מֵת	מֹצֵא
MEANING	sitting	dying	finding
IMPERATIVE	שֵׁב	_____	מְצָא
MEANING	sit!	die!	find!

VERB	to approach	to fall	to turn
ROOT	נָגַשׁ	נָפַל	סָבַב
PARTICIPLE	_____	נֹפֵל	_____
MEANING	approaching	falling	turning
IMPERATIVE	גַּשׁ/גְּשָׁה	נְפֹל	סֹב
MEANING	approach!	fall!	turn!

VERB	to stand	to visit	to arise
ROOT	עָמַד	פָּקַד	_____
PARTICIPLE	_____	פֹּקֵד	קָם
MEANING	standing	visiting	arising
IMPERATIVE	עֲמֹד	_____	קוּם
MEANING	stand!	visit!	arise!

VERB	to kill	to put	to send
ROOT	שָׁחַט	שִׂים	שָׁלַח
PARTICIPLE	שֹׁחֵט	_____	שֹׁלֵחַ
MEANING	killing	putting	sending
IMPERATIVE	_____	שִׂים	שְׁלַח
MEANING	kill!	put!	send!

VERB	to hear
ROOT	שָׁמַע
PARTICIPLE	שֹׁמֵעַ
MEANING	hearing
IMPERATIVE	_____
MEANING	hear!

14.4 Infinitive Construct

Grammar: infinitives

In English, an infinitive is a verbal form often preceded by *to*, e.g.: *to say*. It is infinitive because it could apply to anyone at any time. This is in contrast to verbal forms like *he said*, which applies specifically to a male who has spoken in the past, or *they will say*, which applies specifically to a group of people who will speak in the future. Such forms are finite. However, the form *to say* has no person, no number, no gender and no tense, and so it has an infinite quality about it.

In Hebrew, there are two infinitives. We will learn the Infinitive Construct first. The Infinitive Construct is formed like this:

קְטֹל

(pronounced k^a-TŌL) and it works rather like the English infinitive. It can be translated *to kill* or *killing*. For example:

a time to mourn and a time to dance   עֵת סְפוֹד וְעֵת רְקוֹד
(Ecclesiastes 3:4b)

This is sometimes translated *a time for mourning and a time for dancing*.

Notice that the Infinitive Construct forms in this example are written with a ו rather than just a dot for the *o* vowel. This is simply an alternative spelling.

The Infinitive Construct is often found with ל prefixed to it, and the ל usually takes a short-*i* vowel instead of a *sheva* because the first vowel of the Infinitive Construct takes a *sheva* and Hebrew tends to avoid placing two *shevas* together:

to kill	לִקְטֹל
to rule	לִמְשֹׁל
to guard	לִשְׁמֹר

Another example:

a time to weep and a time to laugh   עֵת לִבְכּוֹת וְעֵת לִשְׂחוֹק
(Ecclesiates 3:4a)

Again, these Infinitive Constructs are written with וֹ, as in the example above.

Gutturals cannot usually take a simple *sheva*, but a *sheva* is the first vowel of the Infinitive Construct. This means that verbs that begin with a guttural must take a complex *sheva* in the Infinitive Construct, so if they are prefixed with לֹ it will take the corresponding short vowel:

to stand   לַעֲמֹד

Sometimes the Infinitive Construct is found with the prefix כֹ or בֹ, in which case we can translate כֹ or בֹ as *when*. For example:

When the priest remembered my words he sang.
כִּזְכֹר הַכֹּהֵן אֶת־דְּבָרַי שָׁר

When the priest remembers my words he will sing.
כִּזְכֹר הַכֹּהֵן אֶת־דְּבָרַי יָשִׁיר

Notice the form of the verb שִׁיר, which is a hollow verb. In the first sentence it appears in the Perfect 3ms (שָׁר) and so we translate both it and the Infinitive Construct (כִּזְכֹר) with an English past tense (*he remembered, he sang*).

In the second sentence it appears in the Imperfect 3ms (יָשִׁיר) and so we translate both it and the Infinitive Construct (כִּזְכֹר) with an English future tense (*he will remember, he will sing*).

The Infinitive Construct can be found with both a preposition as a prefix and a pronominal suffix, for example בְּזָכְרֵנוּ in the following verse:

when we remembered Zion   בְּזָכְרֵנוּ אֶת־צִיּוֹן (Psalm 137:1)

The vowels in the Infinitive Construct have changed because the suffix has been added. It is important to distinguish it from זָכַרְנוּ (*we have remembered*), which would not make sense with the prefix בְּ.

A very common (and slightly irregular) word in the Infinitive Construct is לֵאמֹר from אָמַר (*to say*). It comes after words introducing speech and it means *saying*. For example:

And God blessed them, saying 'Be fruitful and multiply'
וַיְבָרֶךְ אֹתָם אֱלֹהִים לֵאמֹר פְּרוּ וּרְבוּ (Genesis 1:22)

Infinitive constructs of weak verbs can vary quite a bit from the קְטֹל model. It is worth looking at the table below to see how they work. Remember that the Infinitive Construct of the hollow verbs is the citation or dictionary form: קוּם is an Infinitive Construct (the Perfect 3ms is קָם).

At a glance:

	VERB	INFINITIVE CONSTRUCT	
Regular (strong) verb	קָטַל	קְטֹל	*to kill*
Pe guttural	עָמַד	עֲמֹד	*to stand*
Pe alef	אָכַל	אֱכֹל	*to eat*
Ayin guttural	שָׁחַט	שְׁחַט	*to kill*
Lamed guttural	שָׁלַח	שְׁלֹחַ	*to send*
Pe aav	יָשַׁב	שֶׁבֶת	*to sit*
Ayin aav and *ayin yod*	קוּם	קוּם	*to arise*
Lamed he	גָּלָה	גְּלוֹת	*to reveal*
Pe nun	נָפַל	נְפֹל	*to fall*
Pe nun	נָגַשׁ	גֶּשֶׁת	*to approach*
Double *ayin*	סָבַב	סֹב	*to turn*

It should be clear from this table that although there are a few forms that differ from the strong verbs, most forms are identifiable as Infinitive Constructs. The more unusual forms, such as שֶׁבֶת, should be learned.

14.5 Infinitive Absolute

The Infinitive Absolute is a second infinitive in Hebrew. It is formed like this: קָטוֹל (sometimes קָטֹל without the *vav*). Note the difference from the Infinitive Construct: the first vowel is a long-*a* vowel.

The Infinitive Absolute can be used in a manner similar to the Infinitive Construct, but is more frequently found in a particular idiomatic construction in Hebrew. It is often used in combination with a finite verb in order to intensify the idea contained in the verb. Here are some examples:

I did indeed rule over them.   מָשׁוֹל מָשַׁלְתִּי בָּהֶם
(Literally *Ruling I ruled over them.*)

Know that you will certainly die. דַּע כִּי־מוֹת תָּמוּת
(Genesis 20:7) (Literally *Know that dying you will die.*)

Notice that the tense we use in English depends on whether the Hebrew finite verb is Perfect or Imperfect. In the examples above, the Perfect מָשַׁלְתִּי is translated with a past tense (*I did indeed rule*) and the Imperfect תָּמוּת with a future tense (*you will die*). This is what we would expect.

The Infinitive Absolute can be used in other ways (less frequently) and a Hebrew grammar should explain all the possibilities.

Happily, there are very few variations in form among the weak verbs. *Lamed* gutturals take an extra vowel, just like in the other infinitive: the Infinitive Absolute of שָׁלַח is שָׁלוֹחַ (pronounced *shā-LŌ-ach*). The other exception is the hollow verbs: their Infinitive Absolute is formed קוֹם.

Here is a table of the Infinitive Absolute.

	VERB	INFINITIVE ABSOLUTE	
Regular (strong) verb	קָטַל	קָטוֹל	*killing*
Pe guttural	עָמַד	עָמוֹד	*standing*
Pe alef	אָכַל	אָכוֹל	*eating*
Ayin guttural	שָׁחַט	שָׁחוֹט	*killing*
Lamed guttural	שָׁלַח	שָׁלוֹחַ	*sending*
Lamed alef	מָצָא	מָצוֹא	*finding*
Pe vav	יָשַׁב	יָשׁוֹב	*sitting*
Ayin vav and ayin yod	קוּם	קוֹם	*arising*
Lamed he	גָּלָה	גָּלֹה	*revealing*
Pe nun	נָפַל	נָפוֹל	*falling*
Pe nun	נָגַשׁ	נָגוֹשׁ	*approaching*
Double ayin	סָבַב	סָבוֹב	*turning*

Notice that all the examples of the infinitive absolute render the Hebrew infinitive with an English participle (guard*ing*) rather than with an English infinitive (to *guard*). It is usually more appropriate to translate a Hebrew Infinitive Absolute with a finite verb in English, though not always.

14.6 Exercise 2

Find in the text below: an imperative, a participle, an Infinitive Construct, a verb in the Perfect, and a verb in the Imperfect. You may find more than one in a single verse but you will not find all five forms in a single verse.

Translations are not provided here; you will need to find the words purely by their forms without the clues that translations can give. However, references are given so that you can look them up after you have completed the exercise.

a) Exodus 3:5b

הַמָּקוֹם אֲשֶׁר אַתָּה עוֹמֵד עָלָיו אַדְמַת־קֹדֶשׁ הוּא:

b) Jeremiah 24:7a

וְנָתַתִּי לָהֶם לֵב לָדַעַת אֹתִי כִּי אֲנִי יְהוָה

c) Deuteronomy 6:4

שְׁמַע יִשְׂרָאֵל יְהוָה אֱלֹהֵינוּ יְהוָה אֶחָד

d) 1 Samuel 26:25

גַּם עָשֹׂה תַעֲשֶׂה וְגַם יָכֹל תּוּכָל

14.7 Text: Genesis 3:1–5

Points to look out for in this text:

- Words we have already encountered.
- Participles.
- Infinitives.

conjunction: *indeed*	אַף
prep + noun ms: *in the middle of*	בְּתוֹךְ
noun fs: *living thing*	חַיָּה
verb: *to touch*	נָגַע
noun ms: *serpent*	נָחָשׁ
adj m: *clever, cunning, prudent*	עָרוּם
conjunction: *lest*	פֶּן
verb: *to open*	פָּקַח
noun ms: *fruit*	פְּרִי

Text

Read the text aloud a few times to be sure of the pronunciation. Then write the words you know beneath the words in the text, and match the others to the words in the vocabulary.

1 וְהַנָּחָשׁ הָיָה עָרוּם מִכֹּל חַיַּת הַשָּׂדֶה אֲשֶׁר עָשָׂה יְהוָה אֱלֹהִים
וַיֹּאמֶר אֶל־הָאִשָּׁה אַף כִּי־אָמַר אֱלֹהִים לֹא תֹאכְלוּ מִכֹּל עֵץ הַגָּן :

2 וַתֹּאמֶר הָאִשָּׁה אֶל־הַנָּחָשׁ מִפְּרִי עֵץ־הַגָּן נֹאכֵל :

3 וּמִפְּרִי הָעֵץ אֲשֶׁר בְּתוֹךְ־הַגָּן אָמַר אֱלֹהִים לֹא תֹאכְלוּ מִמֶּנּוּ וְלֹא
תִגְּעוּ בּוֹ פֶּן־תְּמֻתוּן :

4 וַיֹּאמֶר הַנָּחָשׁ אֶל־הָאִשָּׁה לֹא־מוֹת תְּמֻתוּן :

5 כִּי יֹדֵעַ אֱלֹהִים כִּי בְּיוֹם אֲכָלְכֶם מִמֶּנּוּ וְנִפְקְחוּ עֵינֵיכֶם וִהְיִיתֶם
כֵּאלֹהִים יֹדְעֵי טוֹב וָרָע :

Notes

Verse 1

הָיָה

the Perf 3ms of הָיָה, so *it was* or *he was*.

עָרוּם מִכֹּל חַיַּת הַשָּׂדֶה

This is the comparative structure we learned in Unit 8: *wiser than all the living creatures*. The word חַיַּת is in construct relationship to הַשָּׂדֶה.

אֲשֶׁר עָשָׂה יְהוָה

Typically, the verb comes before the subject: *which God made*.

אַף כִּי־אָמַר אֱלֹהִים

This phrase is difficult to translate into English. Many translations include some form of words to indicate that the serpent is asking a question, e.g. *'is it true that God said ... ?'*

לֹא תֹאכְלוּ

This could be understood as *you will not eat*, but the word לֹא followed by an Imperfect is usually a Hebrew way of saying *do not ...* in this case *do not eat*.

Possible translation of Verse 1

And the serpent was wiser than all the living things of the field which Yhwh God had made. And he said to the woman, 'Indeed, for God said, "Do not eat from all the trees of the garden"?'

Verse 2

מִפְּרִי עֵץ־הַגָּן נֹאכֵל

Notice the construct chain: *from the fruit of the trees of the garden*. The word is Imperfect 1p (first person plural) and can mean *we will eat*, but is usually translated here as *we may eat*.

Possible translation of Verse 2

And the woman said to the serpent, 'We may eat the fruit of the trees of the garden.'

Verse 3

הָעֵץ אֲשֶׁר בְּתוֹךְ־הַגָּן

Notice the use of אֲשֶׁר in this verbless clause. The word *is* does not need to be written: *the tree which is in the middle of the garden*.

לֹא תֹאכְלוּ מִמֶּנּוּ וְלֹא תִגְּעוּ בּוֹ

These two verbs are used in the same way as לֹא תֹאכְלוּ in verse 1: *do not eat* and *do not touch*. Both verbs are used with prepositions to indicate the object: *do not eat from it* (מִמֶּנּוּ), where מִמֶּנּוּ is the preposition מִן with the 3ms suffix (see Unit 9); and similarly *do not touch it* (בּוֹ), where בּוֹ is the preposition בְּ with the 3ms suffix (see Unit 8).

פֶּן־תְּמֻתוּן

This means *lest you die*. The verb is an Imperfect 2mp with an extra letter ן at the end (the technical term is a paragogic ן). This kind of feature is unusual in English, but perhaps the extra *y* in *scaredy cat* might be considered paragogic.

Possible translation of Verse 3

But [concerning] the fruit of the tree which is in the middle of the garden God said, 'Do not eat of it and do not touch it or you will die.'

Verse 4

לֹא־מוֹת תְּמֻתוּן

The serpent says literally, *Dying you will not die*. This is an example of an infinitive absolute (מוֹת) used with a finite form (תְּמֻתוּן) of the same verb (מוּת). We translate *you will not die* because the word תְּמֻתוּן is Imperfect; if it were Perfect we would probably use an English past tense.

Possible translation of Verse 4

And the serpent said to the woman, 'You certainly will not die.'

Verse 5

יֹדֵעַ אֱלֹהִים

Notice the participle here. Literally this means *God is knowing* but a more idiomatic English translation would be *God knows*.

בְּיוֹם אֲכָלְכֶם מִמֶּנּוּ

The verb here is a Perfect 2mp from אכל. Although we generally translate the Perfect with an English past tense, it makes more sense to use an English present tense here: *on the day you eat it* rather than *on the day you ate it*.

וְנִפְקְחוּ עֵינֵיכֶם

This means *and your eyes will be opened*. In English we would not use a conjunction (*and*) here, but in Hebrew it is quite common. Notice the shift from past tense to future tense in English translation: the ו is not VC because it is not pointed וַ. It is far more common for a ו prefixed to an Imperfect to be a VC Imperfect, but sometimes this form is also found. The word עֵינֵיכֶם is the dual form of עַיִן with a 2mp suffix.

וִהְיִיתֶם כֵּאלֹהִים יֹדְעֵי טוֹב וָרָע

The verb is a VC Perfect 2mp. Notice that the ו is pointed וִ instead of the usual VC Perfect pointing וְ. This is because the first vowel in הְיִיתֶם is a *sheva* and so the vowel under the ו changes. If the idea of the Vav Consecutive is still confusing, review Unit 12.

Possible translation of Verse 5

'For God knows that in the day that you eat of it your eyes will be opened and you will be like God, knowing good and evil.'

14.8 Suggestion

- Make your own verb table of the forms of the regular verb (use קטל or שמר) including: Perfect (3ms, 3fs etc.), Imperfect (3ms, 3fs etc), Imperative, Participle, Infinitive Construct and Infinitive Absolute.

14.9 Summary

In this unit we have looked at

- the Imperative (*guard!*)

- the Participle (*guarding*)

- the Infinitive Construct (*to guard*), which is often found with the prefix לְ and acts as an infinitive or as a verbal noun

- the Infinitive Absolute (*guarding*), which is often used to intensify the meaning of the verb

- the text of Genesis 3:1–5.

The remaining units will focus more strongly on the use of Hebrew text. We will read through a substantial portion of text in order to get a better idea of how the context can be important in biblical Hebrew.

to try, test	בָּחַן
to swallow	בָּלַע
to cut	כָּרַת
to add	יָסַף
to fear	יָרֵא
to answer	עָנָה
name: *Sarah*	שָׂרָה

15.1 Object pronouns

In Unit 5, we learned the subject pronouns: words such as הוּא, הִיא meaning *he*, *she* and so on, which are used to indicate the subject of a verb. There are different pronouns which are used to indicate the object of a verb.

Grammar: object pronouns

Consider these sentences:

He gave a hammer to Mark.

Mark gave a saw to him.

In the first sentence, the pronoun is the subject of the verb: the person who is doing the action. We do not know the subject's name; only that he is male. The pronoun *he* is the subject of the verb *gave*, and *Mark* is the object.

In the second sentence, *Mark* is the subject, the one who is doing the giving. The object of the verb *gave* is the pronoun *him*.

Similarly:

SUBJECT	VERB	OBJECT
My friend	*likes*	*me.*
The cat	*climbed*	*it.*
The computer	*will calculate*	*them.*
Newspapers	*popularized*	*her.*
Nobody	*saw*	*us.*

Hebrew object pronouns are formed by adding a pronominal suffix to the object marker. The object pronouns are:

him	אֹתוֹ	*them* (mp)	אֹתָם
her	אֹתָהּ	*them* (fp)	אֹתָן
you (ms)	אֹתְךָ	*you* (mp)	אֹתְכֶם
you (fs)	אֹתָךְ	*you* (fp)	אֹתְכֶן
me	אֹתִי	*us*	אֹתָנוּ

Here are some examples of Hebrew object pronouns used in sentences:

Yhwh has created it.	בָּרָא יְהוָה אֹתוֹ
The king has feared her.	יָרֵא הַמֶּלֶךְ אֹתָהּ
David has not tested you.	לֹא בָּחַן דָּוִד אֹתְךָ
My mother has seen you.	רָאֲתָה אִמִּי אֹתָן

The sword has cut me.	כָּרְתָה הַחֶרֶב אֹתִי
We have swallowed them.	בָּלַעְנוּ אֹתָם
The women have taken them.	לָקְחוּ הַנָּשִׁים אֹתָן
I have sent you.	שָׁלַחְתִּי אֶתְכֶם
Gideon has found you.	מָצָא גִדְעוֹן אֶתְכֶן
He has answered us.	עָנָה אֹתָנוּ

15.2 Exercise 1

Translate into Hebrew the following variations on the above sentences, using verbs in the Imperfect. The verbs you will need are given below.

יִבְרָא יִירָא יִבְחַן תִּרְאֶה תִּכְרֹת נִבְלַע תִּקַּחְנָה אֶשְׁלַח יִמְצָא יַעֲנֶה

Yhwh will create them.

The king will fear you.

David will not test me.

My mother will see them.

The sword will cut you.

We will swallow it.

The women will take you.

I will send her.

Gideon will find us.

He will answer you.

15.3 Relative pronouns and interrogative pronouns

We have already encountered the relative pronoun אֲשֶׁר in Unit 9, where we learned simply that it means *that*, *which* or *who*. There is nothing particularly difficult about the meaning of אֲשֶׁר but when we translate it into English we need to choose the most appropriate word.

In English we need different relative pronouns (or adverbs) in the following sentences:

*This is my covenant **which** you will keep.* (Genesis 17:10)
זֹאת בְּרִיתִי אֲשֶׁר תִּשְׁמְרוּ

*This is the man **who** will keep the covenant.*
זֶה הָאִישׁ אֲשֶׁר יִשְׁמֹר אֶת־הַבְּרִית
(Literally *this is the man which he will keep the covenant.*)

*This is the man **whom** you will guard.*
זֶה הָאִישׁאֲשֶׁר תִּשְׁמְרוּ
(Literally *this is the man which you will guard.*)

*This is the man **whose** servants you will guard.*
זֶה הָאִישׁאֲשֶׁר תִּשְׁמְרוּ אֶת־עֲבָדָיו
(Literally *this is the man which you will guard his servants.*)

Notice that אֲשֶׁר does not have masculine, feminine or plural forms: it is used with בְּרִיתִי (feminine) and with הָאִישׁ (masculine) without changing its spelling. Similarly, עֲבָדָיו is plural but אֲשֶׁר remains the same.

Other pronouns that do not have masculine or feminine forms are the interrogative pronouns. Just like English, Hebrew has special words for questions: pronouns, known as interrogative pronouns. Here are the commonest:

Who ...?	מִי
What ...?	מֶה or מַה
Why ...?	לְמֶה or לָמָּה
Where ...?	אֵי or אִי
When ...?	מָתַי
How ...?	אֵיךְ

Here are examples of how they are used:

Who am I? (Exodus 3:11)	מִי אָנֹכִי
What have I done? (Jeremiah 8:6)	מֶה עָשִׂיתִי
Why have you deserted me? (Psalm 22:2 [Engl 22:1])	לָמָה עֲזַבְתָּנִי

(The *dagesh* in the מ of לָמָה can be absent before gutturals.)

Where is Abel your brother? (Genesis 4:9)	אֵי הֶבֶל אָחִיךָ
You fools, when will you be wise? (Psalm 94:8)	וּכְסִילִים מָתַי תַּשְׂכִּילוּ
How can you say, 'I love you'? (Judges 16:15)	אֵיךְ תֹּאמַר אֲהַבְתִּיךְ

It is important to remember that each of the above phrases is asking a question. The interrogative pronouns are always used in contexts where a question is implied. For example, the word מִי only means *who?* as in *who am I?*. It never means *who* as in *You are the man who wrote that book*. In that case אֲשֶׁר would be used: אַתָּה הָאִישׁ אֲשֶׁר כָּתַב הַסֵּפֶר הַהוּא.

15.4 Exercise 2

Fill in the blanks with the appropriate interrogative or relative pronoun. Choose from

אֲשֶׁר מִי מַה לָמָה אֵי

Note: in the paragraph below there are two words which you have not previously seen. They are וַיַּרְא and וַיַּעַן. The word וַיַּרְא is VC Imperfect 3ms from רָאָה and the word וַיַּעַן is VC Imperfect 3ms from עָנָה. In both cases the final ה of the root is missing. This is very common in VC Imperfect forms of verbs that end in ה. The technical term for a shortened form like this is *apocopated*.

בּוֹא דָּוִד אֶל־הַבַּיִת _____ בֵּין הֶהָרִים וַיַּרְא אֶלְהַנַּעַר _____ שָׁמַר הַבַּיִת: וַיֹּאמֶר אֵלָיו _____ הָאִשָּׁה _____ אָבָה יָשַׁב בְּבַיִת הַזֶּה: וַיֹּאמֶר הַנַּעַר _____ אַתָּה _____ וַיַּעַן דָּוִד אֲנִי הַמֶּלֶךְ וַיֹּאמֶר הַנַּעַר _____ בָּאתָ וַיֹּאמֶר דָּוִד בָּאתִי לִפְקֹד שָׂרָה _____ שְׁמֶךָ:

Hint: it might be easier if you translate it first.

15.5 *Patach* furtive

We have seen already how in some verbal forms that end in a guttural an extra *a* vowel (*patach*) creeps in underneath the guttural. For example, in Unit 14 we saw that the Participle

of שָׁלַח is not שָׁלַח but rather שֹׁלֵחַ, pronounced *shō-LAY-ach*.
Similarly, the Infinitive Construct of שָׁלַח is not שְׁלֹח as we
might expect, but rather שְׁלֹחַ, pronounced *shᵃ-LŌ-ach*, and
the Infinitive Absolute is not שָׁלֹח but rather שָׁלֹחַ, pronounced
shā-LŌ-ach. The likely function of *patach* furtive is to make the
guttural easier to pronounce. The rule generally applies to verbs
ending in ח or ע rather than in א or ה.

Here are some more examples:

VERB	*to hear*	שָׁמַע	*to know*	יָדַע
PARTICIPLE	שֹׁמֵעַ	*hearing*	יוֹדֵעַ	*knowing*
INFINITIVE CONSTRUCT	שְׁמֹעַ	*to hear*	דַּעַת	*to know*
INFINITIVE ABSOLUTE	שָׁמֹעַ	*hearing*	יָדוֹעַ	*knowing*

VERB	*to take*	לָקַח	*to touch*	נָגַע
PARTICIPLE	לֹקֵחַ	*taking*	נוֹגֵעַ	*touching*
INFINITIVE CONSTRUCT	קַחַת	*to take*	נְגֹעַ	*to touch*
INFINITIVE ABSOLUTE	לָקֹחַ	*taking*	נָגוֹעַ	*touching*

VERB	*to rejoice*	שָׂמַח	*to forget*	שָׁכַח
PARTICIPLE	שָׂמֵחַ	*rejoicing*	שֹׁכֵחַ	*forgetting*
INFINITIVE CONSTRUCT	שְׂמֹחַ	*to rejoice*	שְׁכֹחַ	*to forget*
INFINITIVE ABSOLUTE	שָׂמוֹחַ	*rejoicing*	שָׁכוֹחַ	*forgetting*

Notice that the Infinitive Construct of יָדַע is דַּעַת. This is because
it is *pe yod* (or, some might argue, *pe vav*) as well as *lamed*
guttural. Remember that the Infinitive Construct of יָשַׁב is שֶׁבֶת;
so similarly the Infinitive Construct of יָדַע is דַּעַת, which is also
the word for *knowledge*. And likewise the verb לָקַח, although
it begins with *lamed* in the Perfect, behaves like a *pe yod* verb
in the Imperfect and other forms, and so its Infinitive Construct
follows the *pe yod* pattern.

159

unit 15

15

15.6 Text: Genesis 21:1–6

We are going to begin to work on a larger piece of Hebrew narrative (Genesis 21 and 22), which will occupy us throughout the remaining units. It might be helpful to put this in context if you read Genesis chapters 12 to 20 in English.

Points to look out for in this text:

- Words we have already encountered.

- Object pronouns.

- Relative and interrogative pronouns.

- Examples of *patach* furtive.

pronoun + prefix: *as, when*	כַּאֲשֶׁר
verb: *to speak, promise*	דָּבַר
verb: *to conceive, to be pregnant*	הָרָה
noun mp: *old age*	זְקֻנִים
noun m: *time*	מוֹעֵד
verb: *to cut off, to circumcise*	מוּל
number: *eight*	שְׁמֹנֶה
verb: *to command*	צָוָה
number: *one hundred*	מֵאָה
noun f: *year*	שָׁנָה
verb: *to laugh*	צָחַק
noun m: *laughter, ridicule*	צְחֹק

Text

Read the text aloud a few times to be sure of the pronunciation. Then write the words you know beneath the words in the text, and match the others to the words in the vocabulary.

אֵ בֵּלְדָה
1 וַיהוָה פָּקַד אֶת־שָׂרָה כַּאֲשֶׁר אָמָר וַיַּעַשׂ יְהוָה לְשָׂרָה כַּאֲשֶׁר דִּבֵּר׃
2 וַתַּהַר וַתֵּלֶד שָׂרָה לְאַבְרָהָם בֵּן לִזְקֻנָיו לַמּוֹעֵד אֲשֶׁר־דִּבֶּר אֹתוֹ אֱלֹהִים׃
3 וַיִּקְרָא אַבְרָהָם אֶת־שֶׁם־בְּנוֹ הַנּוֹלַד־לוֹ אֲשֶׁר־יָלְדָה־לּוֹ שָׂרָה יִצְחָק׃
4 וַיָּמָל אַבְרָהָם אֶת־יִצְחָק בְּנוֹ בֶּן־שְׁמֹנַת יָמִים כַּאֲשֶׁר צִוָּה אֹתוֹ אֱלֹהִים׃
5 וְאַבְרָהָם בֶּן־מְאַת שָׁנָה בְּהִוָּלֶד לוֹ אֵת יִצְחָק בְּנוֹ׃
6 וַתֹּאמֶר שָׂרָה צְחֹק עָשָׂה לִי אֱלֹהִים כָּל־הַשֹּׁמֵעַ יִצְחַק־לִי׃

Notes

Verse 1

כַּאֲשֶׁר

This is the relative pronoun with the preposition כ. It can mean *when* in the sense of *when it happened*, or it can mean *as*.

וַיַּעַשׂ

VC Imperfect 3ms from עָשָׂה: *and he did*. Notice that it is apocopated: the final ה is missing, as in וַיִּרְא and וַיַּעַן above.

לְשָׂרָה

This could be *to Sarah* or *for Sarah*.

דִּבֵּר

You have already encountered דָּבָר meaning *word*. דִּבֵּר is a verbal form from the same root and it means *he said*. It can also mean *he promised*. It is Piel, which we will learn about in Unit 17.

Possible translation of Verse 1

And Yhwh visited Sarah as he said, and Yhwh did for Sarah what he promised.

Verse 2

וַתַּהַר

VC Imperfect 3fs of הָרָה. This is another example of an apocopated (shortened) form.

לְאַבְרָהָם

Remember that the preposition ל can mean *for* as well as *to*. It is probably better translated *for* in this context, since Sarah does not give birth to Abraham.

לִזְקֻנָיו

Literally *for his old age*. The idea is that the child is born when the father is old.

לַמּוֹעֵד אֲשֶׁר־דִּבֶּר אֹתוֹ אֱלֹהִים

Notice the relative pronoun and the object pronoun in this phrase. Also, the subject of the verb דִּבֶּר is אֱלֹהִים, which comes after the object. The usual word order in biblical Hebrew is verb, subject, object. Here the relative pronoun can be translated *when*.

Possible translation of Verse 2

And Sarah conceived and she bore a son for Abraham in his old age at the time when God promised him.

Verse 3

וַיִּקְרָא אַבְרָהָם אֶת־שֶׁם־בְּנוֹ

This is a common formula following the birth of a child in Hebrew narrative: one of the parents will name the baby. Literally this is: *And he called Abraham the name of his son ...* but in idiomatic English it might be more appropriate to say that Abraham named him.

הַנּוֹלַד־לוֹ

The word is simply the preposition ל with the 3ms pronominal suffix, so it means *to him*. The word הַנּוֹלַד is from יָלַד but it is a form we have not encountered before. This form is called Nifal and we will learn about it in Unit 16.

אֲשֶׁר־יָלְדָה־לּוֹ שָׂרָה

Notice the relative pronoun again. The word יָלְדָה is a simple Perfect 3fs from יָלַד. The word לּוֹ is spelled with *dagesh* here, but it means the same as the earlier לוֹ.

The name of the child is withheld until the end of the verse, which perhaps creates some suspense. The name itself is from the verb צחק: *to laugh*.

Possible translation of Verse 3

And Abraham named his son, whom Sarah bore for him, Isaac.

Verse 4

בֶּן־שְׁמֹנַת יָמִים

Literally *the son of eight days*. This is an idiomatic expression meaning *when he was eight days old*.

כַּאֲשֶׁר צִוָּה אֹתוֹ אֱלֹהִים

Notice the object pronoun. The verb צִוָּה is in Piel form, and we will find out more about Piel in Unit 16.

Possible translation of Verse 4

And Abraham circumcised Isaac his son when he was eight days old as God commanded him.

Verse 5

וְאַבְרָהָם בֶּן־מְאַת שָׁנָה

Just as in the previous verse, this is a way of indicating a person's age. Literally *And Abraham was the son of one hundred years*. The word שָׁנָה remains singular in this construction, even though we are talking about more than one year; the word usually remains singular when it comes after a number.

בְּהִוָּלֶד

The preposition בְּ is sometimes used to mean *when*, as it does here. The verb is another Nifal form and means *was born*.

Possible translation of Verse 5

And Abraham was one hundred years old when Isaac his son was born.

Verse 6

צְחֹק עָשָׂה לִי אֱלֹהִים

Literally *laughter he has made for me God.*

כָּל־הַשֹּׁמֵעַ

The word הַשֹּׁמֵעַ is a Participle being used as a noun, with the
definite article. Literally *all the hearing ones*; we might prefer
to translate: *everyone who hears*. Since this is the Participle of a
lamed guttural verb, there is a *patach* furtive.

יִצְחַק־לִי

The verb is an Imperfect 3mp: *they will laugh*. When צָחַק is used
with ל it can mean *to mock* or *to laugh at*.

Possible translation of Verse 6

*And Sarah said, 'God has made laughter for me; all who hear
will laugh for me.'*

Or:

*And Sarah said, 'God has made me an object of ridicule; all who
hear will mock me.'*

15.7 Suggestion

• Make a table of Hebrew pronouns. Include subject pronouns,
object pronouns, interrogative pronouns, and the relative
pronoun.

15.8 Summary

In this unit we have looked at

• object pronouns, which are formed by adding pronominal
suffixes to the object marker

• the relative pronoun, which can be translated *that, which,
who, whom* or *whose* depending on context

• interrogative pronouns, which only occur in questions

- *patach* furtive, which occurs in some forms of the *lamed* guttural verbs.

- the text of genesis 21:1–6.

15.9 Self-assessment

The self-assessment is intended to test your knowledge and understanding of the points of grammar covered in Units 11 to 15.

Answer all questions as fully as possible. Try to answer the questions without looking up the answers.

1)

a) Write out all the forms of the Imperfect of פָּקַד.

b) Translate: זָכַר אָבִי אֶת־דְּבָרִים הַכֹּהֵן אֲשֶׁר כָּתַבְתָּ בְּסֵפֶר

c) Translate: יְהוָה יִמְשֹׁל בָּכֶם (Judges 8:23).

d) Which English tenses can be used to translate the Imperfect?

e) Why is the Imperfect 3ms of עָמַד written יַעֲמֹד instead of יִעְמֹד?

2)

a) Which English tense do we usually use to translate a VC Imperfect?

b) What vowel would we usually find underneath the ו in a VC Perfect?

c) Translate: וַיֵּלֶךְ עַד יְהוּדָה

d) Translate: אָנַף וַיִּקַּח חַרְבּוֹ וָאֶפְחַד

e) Parse this verbal form. Give the stem, tense, person, gender, number, root and meaning of וַיָּקָם.

3)

a) How would we describe a verbal root whose third letter is ה?

b) The Perfect 3ms is not used as the citation (or dictionary) form of hollow verbs. Which form is used instead?

c) Parse יָדְעוּ.

d) What happens to *pe nun* verbs in the Imperfect? Give an example.

e) Explain the ה at the end of אֶשְׂמְחָה and וְאֶעֶלְצָה.

4)

a) Look at this verse (Deuteronomy 6:4). What kind of word is שְׁמַע?

שְׁמַע יִשְׂרָאֵל יְהוָה אֱלֹהֵינוּ יְהוָה אֶחָד

b) Translate: כְּתֹב סְפָרִים

c) Why does the form שֹׁלֵחַ differ from other Participle forms such as נֹפֵל and אֹכֵל?

d) Translate: וַיַּעַן דָּנִאֵל אוֹתִי לֵאמֹר שֵׁב־נָא וֶאֱכָל־נָא

e) How can an Infinitive Absolute be used to intensify the verbal idea?

5)

a) Write out the object pronouns.

b) Write out the Hebrew words for *why?*, *what?* and *who?*

c) We have learned five ways that אֲשֶׁר can be translated into English. Which one would you use in the following sentence?

אֵלֶּה הָאֲנָשִׁים אֲשֶׁר קוֹלֵיהֶם יָשִׁירוּ שִׁירוֹת

d) Give the Participle, the Infinitive Construct and the Infinitive Absolute of שָׁמַע.

e) Translate: בֶּן־שְׁמֹנַת שָׁנָה

The answers to the self-assessment are in the Key to the exercises. Check your score as before and use your results to determine whether there is anything you need to focus on or learn thoroughly before proceeding to the next unit.

At this stage you have learned a substantial amount of Hebrew. Although the verbal forms can be complicated, they can usually be found in a lexicon, and being aware of the possibilities should be useful. Your vocabulary now includes many of the words found most frequently in the biblical text, and you have encountered many Hebrew idiomatic devices that are necessary in order to understand the text. The grammar may seem increasingly complicated as you work through the units, but you are able to understand and translate more and more of the text, which is, after all, the point of learning the language.

In the remaining units we will read two chapters of the book of Genesis and the grammatical work will be dictated by the features of the text. Therefore the grammatical work will become less structured and will centre around the text. It may seem, therefore, as if the grammatical work is less orderly than in the first 15 units, but it is to be hoped that the textual work will be stimulating enough that prioritizing it will seem worthwhile.

noun m: *morning*	בֹּקֶר
verb: *to be full, to fill*	מָלֵא
noun: *righteousness*	צְדָקָה
noun: *sanctuary, holiness*	קֹדֶשׁ

16.1 Verb stems: Qal and Nifal

Hebrew verbs are unlike English verbs in many respects, and one difference is that Hebrew verbs come in seven forms called stems. The different stems indicate different meanings which can be applied to the verb; for example, verbs can be made passive in certain stems. It is usually easiest to see how this works in practice.

Grammar: active and passive voice

In English we use the term *voice* to describe whether the subject of the verb is doing the action or whether the subject is having something done to them. An example:

SUBJECT	VERB		OBJECT
I	sent		*the present.*
The present	was sent	by	*me.*

Notice that the object of the first sentence is the subject of the second sentence. Other examples of sentences in the passive voice are:

SUBJECT	VERB		OBJECT
The movie	*was praised*	*by*	*the critics.*
The donations	*will be given*	*to*	*charity.*
Results of surveys	*are published*	*in*	*magazines.*

These are the stems of the verb:

HIFIL	Causative active	הִקְטִיל	*to cause to kill*
HOFAL	Causative passive	הָקְטַל	*to be caused to kill*
PIEL	Intensive active	קִטֵּל	*to slaughter*
PUAL	Intensive passive	קֻטַּל	*to be slaughtered*
HITPAEL	Reflexive	הִתְקַטֵּל	*to kill oneself*
NIFAL	Passive	נִקְטַל	*to be killed*
QAL	'Light'	קָטַל	*to kill*

The word Qal (קַל), as we learned in Unit 1, means *light*. Qal forms are light because they are not encumbered by the verb stem changes caused by Nifal, Piel and so on.

The names of the other stems are taken from their forms according to the root פָּעַל. So for פָּעַל the Nifal is נִפְעַל, and the Hifil is הִפְעִיל. The names of the stems describe what happens to the root to change its meaning. As you can see, Nifal changes the root by adding a נ prefix in the Perfect tense and changing the first vowel to a *sheva*.

Here is the complete Perfect of the Nifal of קָטַל:

3ms	נִקְטַל	*he has been killed*	3p	נִקְטְלוּ	*they have been killed*
3fs	נִקְטְלָה	*she has been killed*			
2ms	נִקְטַלְתָּ	*you have been killed*	2mp	נִקְטַלְתֶּם	*you have been killed*
2fs	נִקְטַלְתְּ	*you have been killed*	2fp	נִקְטַלְתֶּן	*you have been killed*
1s	נִקְטַלְתִּי	*I have been killed*	1p	נִקְטַלְנוּ	*we have been killed*

Here is the complete Imperfect of the Nifal of קָטַל. The נ prefix
of the Nifal disappears; it is assimilated into the first root letter,
which is therefore written with *dagesh*, probably because it is
easier to say *yi-ka-tayl* than *yin-ka-tayl*. If you try to say *yin-ka-
tayl* quickly, you may find yourself 'swallowing' the *n* sound.

3ms	יִקָּטֵל	*he will be killed*	3mp	יִקָּטְלוּ	*they will be killed*
3fs	תִּקָּטֵל	*she will be killed*	3fp	תִּקָּטַלְנָה	*they will be killed*
2ms	תִּקָּטֵל	*you will be killed*	2mp	תִּקָּטְלוּ	*they will be killed*
2fs	תִּקָּטְלִי	*you will be killed*	2fp	תִּקָּטַלְנָה	*they will be killed*
1s	אֶקָּטֵל	*I will be killed*	1p	נִקָּטֵל	*we will be killed*

Each stem comes in all the forms: Perfect, Imperfect, Imperative,
Infinitive, Participle. So we will encounter Nifal Perfects, Nifal
Imperfects, Nifal Infinitives and so on.

However, not every *root* occurs in every form of every stem.
Some roots occur almost exclusively in Qal, others occur almost
exclusively in Piel or Hifil. So although the system is complicated,
the Hebrew vocabulary itself is not necessarily so complicated.
Very few verbal roots occur in all the stems, and most of those
are weak verbs. The only strong verb that occurs in all the stems
is פקד and so we will use this as a model for further examples.

In this unit we will concentrate on Nifal; the other stems will be
addressed in later units. From the table above we see that Nifal is
described as passive. Essentially this means that with the addition
of prefixes that indicate Nifal, the verb is usually translated with
an English passive tense.

This is how we usually translate Qal and Nifal:

	PERFECT 3ms	IMPERFECT 3ms	INFINITIVE CONSTRUCT
QAL	*he has visited* פָּקַד	*he will visit* יִפְקֹד	*to visit* פְּקֹד

	INFINITIVE ABSOLUTE	PARTICIPLE
	visiting פָּקוֹד	*visiting* פֹּקֵד

	PERFECT 3ms	IMPERFECT 3ms	INFINITIVE CONSTRUCT
NIFAL	he has been visited נִפְקַד	he will be visited יִפָּקֵד	to be visited הִפָּקֵד

	INFINITIVE ABSOLUTE	PARTICIPLE
	being visited הִפָּקֹד	being visited נִפְקָד

Although we have learned that the verb פָּקַד means *to visit*, it can be translated in a variety of other ways (*to attend, to take care of, to number, to appoint*). Furthermore, the infinitives can be translated in other ways (see Unit 14). So the table above is an example rather than a comprehensive analysis of the root פָּקַד in Qal and Nifal.

Here are some examples of how the Nifal is used, compared with examples in Qal to demonstrate the difference.

QAL PERFECT: *Yhwh visited the sons of Israel.*
פָּקַד יְהוָה אֶת־בְּנֵי יִשְׂרָאֵל (Exodus 4:31)

NIFAL PERFECT: *And you will be missed because your seat will be empty.* וְנִפְקַדְתָּ כִּי יִפָּקֵד מוֹשָׁבֶךָ (1 Samuel 20:18)

(Note: the first word is a Nifal VC Perfect and the third word is a Nifal Imperfect.)

QAL IMPERFECT: *And when he visits, what shall I answer him?* וְכִי־יִפְקֹד מָה אֲשִׁיבֶנּוּ (Job 31:14)

NIFAL IMPERFECT: *He shall not be visited with evil.*
בַּל־יִפָּקֵד רָע (Proverbs 19:23)

Recognizing the Nifal (most verbs)

PERFECT: נ prefixed to the root, Perfect suffixes, *sheva* under the first root letter

IMPERFECT: *Dagesh* in first letter of root, Imperfect prefixes and suffixes

IMPERATIVE / INFINITIVE CONSTRUCT: הִ prefix, *dagesh* in first letter of root

INFINITIVE ABSOLUTE: נִ prefixed to the root

PARTICIPLE: נִ prefixed to the root

Weak verbs and the Nifal

As we have already seen when learning the Perfect and Imperfect, the weak verbs often undergo some departures from the pattern of the strong verbs. This is also true for verbs in the Nifal and other stems. Most of the differences are vowel changes, such as complex *shevas* instead of simple *shevas* under gutturals, and *patach* furtives in *lamed* guttural verbs. These should not present many problems in translation.

The basic patterns in Nifal forms of weak verbs are outlined here, although it is probably not necessary at this stage to learn them all. It is more important to learn the Qal forms. However, it can be useful to have an overview of the changes in other stems in the weak verbs so that they can be recognized.

If you remember from Unit 13, some of the *pe yod* verbs behave as if they were *pe vav* verbs. The model we looked at was the verb יָשַׁב. In the Nifal, the *pe* verbs that follow the יָשַׁב model regain their putative initial ו. So the Nifal Perfect 3ms of יָשַׁב is נוֹשַׁב (we might have expected נִיְשַׁב if we had expected them to follow the קָטַל model) and the Nifal Imperfect 3ms is יִוָּשֵׁב (we might have expected יִיְשֵׁב). Notice that the ו has *dagesh* in the places one might expect in the first root letter of Nifal forms. It is pronounced *v* rather than *oo* in these circumstances, so יִוָּשֵׁב is pronounced *yi-vā-SHAYV*. The Imperative, Infinitives and Participle of these *pe yod* verbs are similarly written with ו instead of י.

Ayin yod and *ayin vav* verbs in the Nifal are also noticeably different from the strong verb pattern. The prefix נִ becomes נָ or נַ in the Perfect (3ms of קוּם is נָקוֹם rather than נִקַם). However, despite vowel changes in the Imperfect and other forms, they follow the קָטַל pattern closely enough to be recognizable.

The Nifal forms of *lamed he* verbs should cause no problems to anyone familiar with the Qal patterns of *lamed he* verbs. The Nifal forms are simply the usual signs of the Nifal combined with the usual patterns of *lamed he* verbs (e.g. the loss of the final ה).

We have already encountered several examples of an initial נ dropping out, so it should come as no surprise that the Nifal Perfects of *pe nun* verbs are generally written with one נ instead

of two (Nifal Perfect 3ms of נָגַשׁ is נִגַּשׁ rather than נִנְגַּשׁ).
Similarly, the Participle is נִגָּשׁ rather than נִנְגָּשׁ. However, the
Imperfects follow the קָטַל pattern.

The Nifal forms of double *ayin* verbs are similar to *pe vav* and
pe yod verbs, in that the Perfect forms begin with נָ or נִ rather
than נִ. The Nifal Perfect 3ms of סָבַב is נָסַב rather than נָסַב or
נִסְבַב. The Nifal Imperfects are recognizable by the *dagesh* in the
first root letter, just like Nifal Imperfects in the strong verbs. And
likewise the Nifal Imperative, Infinitives and Participle should be
recognizable if you are familiar with the double *ayin* patterns in
the Qal (notably the use of a *dagesh* in the *ayin* letter).

16.2 Gentilic adjectives

When we discuss nationality in English we might refer to
ourselves or others as Australian, or Scottish, or Chinese or
Israeli. In Hebrew those words that describe nationality are
called *gentilic* adjectives; 'gentilic' means *of the nations*. They
are formed by adding particular endings, as the examples below
should demonstrate:

Moabite (ms)	מוֹאָבִי	*Egyptian* (ms)	מִצְרִי
Moabite (fs)	מוֹאָבִית	*Egyptian* (fs)	מִצְרִית
Moabite (mp)	מוֹאָבִים	*Egyptian* (mp)	מִצְרִים
Moabite (fp)	מוֹאָבִיּוֹת	*Egyptian* (fp)	מִצְרִיּוֹת

In English we sometimes use the gentilic adjectives as nouns: *an
Israeli, the Australians* (although it is not possible with adjectives
like Scottish: we need to say *the Scots*). A similar thing happens
in Hebrew: for example, the word מִצְרִי (*Egyptian*) can be used
as an adjective or a noun. Hence:

Adjective: *He was the son of an Egyptian man.*
הוּא בֶּן־אִישׁ מִצְרִי (Leviticus 24:10)

Noun: *And he was in the house of his master the Egyptian.*
וַיְהִי בְּבֵית אֲדֹנָיו הַמִּצְרִי (Genesis 29:2)

16.3 Exercise 1

Here is a list of verb forms in Qal. Work out the corresponding
Nifal forms.

	QAL	MEANING	NIFAL	MEANING
PERFECT				
3ms	פָּקַד	he has visited	_____	_____
3fs	פָּקְדָה	she has visited	_____	_____
2ms	פָּקַדְתָּ	you have visited	_____	_____
2fs	פָּקַדְתְּ	you have visited	_____	_____
1s	פָּקַדְתִּי	I have visited	_____	_____
3p	פָּקְדוּ	they have visited	_____	_____
2mp	פְּקַדְתֶּם	you have visited	_____	_____
2fp	פְּקַדְתֶּן	you have visited	_____	_____
1p	פָּקַדְנוּ	we have visited	_____	_____
IMPERFECT				
3ms	יִפְקֹד	he will visit	_____	_____
3fs	תִּפְקֹד	she will visit	_____	_____
2ms	תִּפְקֹד	you will visit	_____	_____
2fs	תִּפְקְדִי	you will visit	_____	_____
1s	אֶפְקֹד	I will visit	_____	_____
3mp	יִפְקְדוּ	they will visit	_____	_____
3fp	תִּפְקֹדְנָה	they will visit	_____	_____
2mp	תִּפְקְדוּ	they will visit	_____	_____
2fp	תִּפְקֹדְנָה	they will visit	_____	_____
1p	נִפְקֹד	we will visit	_____	_____

16.4 Jussive

We have already looked at a number of forms related to the Imperfect, but there are still a couple that we have not yet learned about. One of these is the Jussive. However, we have seen an example of it in section 14.7: לֹא תֹאכְלוּ and וְלֹא תִגְּעוּ in Genesis 3:3.

Like the Imperative, the Jussive can be used for expressing commands. In Hebrew the Imperative is usually used when the commands are in the second person; the Jussive is used when the commands are in the third person. Here are some examples:

2nd person command	*Go away.*
3rd person command	*Let him leave.*
2nd person command	*Wiggle your tongues.*
3rd person command	*Let them eat cake.*

In Hebrew the Jussive is almost always identical in form to the Imperfect:

IMPERFECT		JUSSIVE	
he will kill	יִקְטֹל	*let him kill*	יִקְטֹל

The only way to determine how to translate a jussive is by examining the context.

Jussive in weak verbs

The exceptions are in the hollow verbs and the *lamed he* verbs, in which the Jussive differs from the Imperfect:

Hollow verb	*he will arise*	יָקוּם	*let him arise*	יָקֹם
Lamed he verb	*he will reveal*	יִגְלֶה	*let him reveal*	יִגֶל

Jussive in Nifal

Jussives occur not just in Qal but in the other verb stems as well. Here are the examples in Nifal:

Regular verb	*he will be killed*	יִקָּטֵל	*let him be killed*	יִקָּטֵל
Lamed he verb	*it will be revealed*	יִגָּלֶה	*let it be revealed*	יִגָּל

Jussive in VC Imperfect: Qal

Strictly speaking, the VC Imperfect is really formed by adding וַ to the Jussive form. This causes no difficulties in the majority of verbs, where the Imperfect is identical to the Jussive. However, in hollow verbs and *lamed he* verbs the VC Imperfect is formed differently from the Imperfect.

Regular verb

IMPERFECT	JUSSIVE	VC IMPERFECT
he will kill יִקְטֹל	*let him kill* יִקְטֹל	*and he killed* וַיִּקְטֹל

Hollow verb

IMPERFECT	JUSSIVE	VC IMPERFECT
he will arise יָקוּם	*let him arise* יָקֹם	*and he arose* וַיָּקָם (the last vowel is a short o: *vay-YĀ-kom*)

Lamed he verb

IMPERFECT	JUSSIVE	VC IMPERFECT
he will reveal יִגְלֶה	*let him reveal* יִגֶל	*and he revealed* וַיִּגֶל

Jussive in VC Imperfect: Nifal

Regular verb

IMPERFECT	JUSSIVE	VC IMPERFECT
he will be killed יִקָטֵל	*let him be killed* יִקָטֵל	*and he was killed* וַיִּקָטֵל

Lamed he verb

IMPERFECT	JUSSIVE	VC IMPERFECT
it will be revealed יִגָלֶה	*let it be revealed* יִגָל	*and it was revealed* וַיִּגָל

Negative commands

There is one feature of the Jussive that is particularly important, and that is its usage in negative commands (prohibitions). Consider these phrases:

Kill them	קְטֹל אוֹתָם	Imperative 2ms
Do not kill them	אַל תִּקְטֹל אוֹתָם	Jussive 2ms + negative particle אַל
You absolutely must not kill them	לֹא תִקְטֹל אוֹתָם	Jussive 2ms + negative particle לֹא
He will kill them	יִקְטֹל אוֹתָם	Imperfect 3ms
Let him kill them	יִקְטֹל אוֹתָם	Jussive 3ms
Let him not kill them	אַל יִקְטֹל אוֹתָם	Jussive 3ms + negative particle אַל

Note that:

- All the above phrases except two are commands or prohibitions. The exceptions are the Imperfects. Neither commands nor prohibitions are Imperfect.

- All the prohibitions are Jussive with a negative particle (either אַל or לֹא).

- Second-person commands are Imperative, but second-person prohibitions are Jussive.

- Third-person commands are Jussive, and third-person prohibitions are Jussive.

- Third-person prohibitions use the particle אַל.

- Second-person prohibitions come in two strengths: the regular strength prohibition used with the particle אַל and the stronger prohibition used with the particle לֹא. This second formula is the same as the formula used in the ten commandments (e.g. 'you must not covet your neighbour's house': לֹא תַחְמֹד בֵּית רֵעֶךָ Exodus 20:17).

16.5 Noun declensions

> **Grammar: declensions**
>
> Declensions are different patterns that nouns can have. In English, it is difficult to categorize nouns according to declension, but in other languages declension categories are common. For example, Latin nouns can be grouped according to how they behave. At the risk of over-simplifying, here are some examples of Latin nouns of various declensions that have retained some of their characteristics in English:
>
> | | SINGULAR | PLURAL |
> | ---------------------- | --------- | -------- |
> | DECLENSION 1 feminine | antenna | antennae |
> | DECLENSION 2 masculine | focus | foci |
> | DECLENSION 2 neuter | medium | media |
> | DECLENSION 3 masculine | crisis | crises |
> | DECLENSION 3 neuter | criterion | criteria |
>
> From the example above it should be possible to see that nouns can be grouped according to form. Latin nouns include words like

The number of Hebrew declensions is somewhat disputed. Some grammars list as many as 13; others list as few as four. It is worth being aware of some of the patterns because it will be easier to idenitify plural nouns or nouns with pronominal suffixes if you are aware of some of the basic patterns.

Nouns with a long-*a* vowels (most nouns containing a long-*a* vowel follow this pattern)

SINGULAR ABSOLUTE	*word* דָּבָר	*prophet* נָבִיא
PLURAL ABSOLUTE	*words* דְּבָרִים	*prophets* נְבִיאִים
SINGULAR CONSTRUCT	*word of* דְּבַר	*prophet of* נְבִיא
PLURAL CONSTRUCT	*words of* דִּבְרֵי	*prophets of* נְבִיאֵי
SING WITH 1s SUFFIX	*my word* דְּבָרִי	*my prophet* נְבִיאִי

Notice that the first vowel becomes shorter (reducing to *sheva* or an *i* vowel) in all the forms except the singular absolute.

Nouns with short-*e* vowels (some nouns without short-*e* vowels follow the same pattern)

SINGULAR ABSOLUTE	*king* מֶלֶךְ	*book* סֵפֶר
PLURAL ABSOLUTE	*kings* מְלָכִים	*books* סְפָרִים
SINGULAR CONSTRUCT	*king of* מֶלֶךְ	*book of* סֵפֶר
PLURAL CONSTRUCT	*kings of* מַלְכֵי	*books of* סִפְרֵי
SING WITH 1s SUFFIX	*my king* מַלְכִּי	*my books* סְפָרַי

SINGULAR ABSOLUTE	*morning* בֹּקֶר	*young man* נַעַר
PLURAL ABSOLUTE	*mornings* בְּקָרִים	*young men* נְעָרִים
SINGULAR CONSTRUCT	*morning of* בֹּקֶר	*young man of* נַעַר
PLURAL CONSTRUCT	*mornings of* בָּקְרֵי	*young men of* נַעֲרֵי
SING WITH 1s SUFFIX	*my morning* בָּקְרִי	*my young man* נַעֲרִי

These nouns are sometimes called *segolates* because they often contain a *segol* vowel (short-*e* vowel). The singular absolute and the singular construct forms are always accented on the first syllable: *ME-lech, NA-ar, SAY-fer, BŌ-ker*. Notice also that their vowels do not shorten in the singular construct: the construct is the same as the absolute. Notice also that several of them lose their *e* vowel in favour of an *a* vowel, *i* vowel or short-*o* vowel when they become construct plural or gain a suffix. Thus בָּקְרֵי is pronounced *bok-RAY* and בָּקְרִי is pronounced *bok-REE*: the ָ is a short *o* rather than a long *a* (if you have an accent that can distinguish the two).

Nouns with participle-type vowels (the קֹטֵל pattern of the Qal Participle: see Unit 14) are another category:

SINGULAR ABSOLUTE	*enemy* אֹיֵב	*priest* כֹּהֵן
PLURAL ABSOLUTE	*enemies* אֹיְבִים	*priests* כֹּהֲנִים
SINGULAR CONSTRUCT	*enemy of* אֹיֵב	*priest of* כֹּהֵן
PLURAL CONSTRUCT	*enemies of* אֹיְבֵי	*priests of* כֹּהֲנֵי
SING WITH 1s SUFFIX	*my enemy* אֹיְבִי	*my priest* כֹּהֲנִי

In these nouns the singular construct is the same as the singular absolute (like מֶלֶךְ type nouns) but the second vowel reduces in the plural absolute and construct, and with the addition of a suffix.

Some single syllable nouns double their second consonant when they form plurals or acquire suffixes:

SINGULAR ABSOLUTE	sea יָם	people עַם
PLURAL ABSOLUTE	seas יַמִּים	peoples עַמִּים
SINGULAR CONSTRUCT	sea of יַם	people of עַם
PLURAL CONSTRUCT	seas of יַמֵּי	peoples of עַמֵּי
SING WITH 1s SUFFIX	my sea יַמִּי	my people עַמִּי

All the nouns above, in all types, are masculine. Feminine nouns tend to match the patterns of the masculine nouns.

It should be noted that adjectives decline just like nouns, and so they follow one of the above patterns. For example רָשָׁע (wicked) follows the דָּבָר model:

SINGULAR ABSOLUTE	wicked רָשָׁע
PLURAL ABSOLUTE	wicked רְשָׁעִים
SINGULAR CONSTRUCT	wicked רְשַׁע
PLURAL CONSTRUCT	wicked רִשְׁעֵי

16.6 Exercise 2

Translate the sentences below with either commands or prohibitions as appropriate. Categorize the nouns according to whether they are formed like יָם or אֹיֵב or מֶלֶךְ or דָּבָר.

a) גּוּר־נָא בְּאַרְצִי

b) לֹא תִּקְטְלוּ אֶת־הַשֹּׁמְרִים

c) יִמְלָא לְבַב מֹשֶׁה

d) אַל תִּגַּע אֶת־אַפִּי

e) זְכֹר צִדְקַת שְׁלֹמֹה

f) יִשְׂמְחוּ שֹׁפְטֵי יִשְׂרָאֵל

g) אַל תִּתּשׁ אֶת־קָדְשֵׁי יְהוּדָה
(Hint: the word תִּתּשׁ comes from the verb נָתַשׁ)

h) יִפְקֹד אוֹתִי גּוֹאֲלִי
(Hint: the א in גּוֹאֲלִי needs a complex *sheva* because it cannot take a simple *sheva*.)

i) לֹא תִשְׁכַּח אֶת־אֵמוֹת בְּנֵי־יִשְׂרָאֵל

j) לֹא תִּרָא מִן דַּעְתִּי
(Hint: מִן can be translated *of* when it is used with the verb יָרֵא.)

16.7 Text: Genesis 21:7–13

Points to look out for in this text:

- words we have already encountered.
- Nifal forms.
- Gentilic adjectives.
- Jussive forms.
- Segolate nouns

noun f: *handmaid*	אָמָה
verb: *to grow, become big*	גָּדַל
noun m: *nation*	גּוֹי
verb: *to wean*	גָּמַל
verb: *to drive away, expel*	גָּרַשׁ
noun m: *seed, progeny, family*	זֶרַע
noun m: *child*	יֶלֶד
verb: *to suck*	יָנַק
verb: *to inherit*	יָרַשׁ
adverb: *very*	מְאֹד
verb: *to say, speak*	מָלַל
noun m: *feast, banquet*	מִשְׁתֶּה
adverb: *on account of, because of*	עַל אוֹדֹת
verb: *to be bad*	רָעַע

Text

Read the text aloud a few times to be sure of the pronunciation. Then write the words you know beneath the words in the text, and match the others to the words in the vocabulary.

7 וַתֹּאמֶר מִי מִלֵּל לְאַבְרָהָם הֵינִיקָה בָנִים שָׂרָה כִּי־יָלַדְתִּי בֵן לִזְקֻנָיו :

8 וַיִּגְדַּל הַיֶּלֶד וַיִּגָּמַל וַיַּעַשׂ אַבְרָהָם מִשְׁתֶּה גָדוֹל בְּיוֹם הִגָּמֵל אֶת־יִצְחָק :

9 וַתֵּרֶא שָׂרָה אֶת־בֶּן־הָגָר הַמִּצְרִית אֲשֶׁר־יָלְדָה לְאַבְרָהָם מְצַחֵק :

10 וַתֹּאמֶר לְאַבְרָהָם גָּרֵשׁ הָאָמָה הַזֹּאת וְאֶת־בְּנָהּ כִּי לֹא יִירַשׁ בֶּן־הָאָמָה הַזֹּאת עִם־בְּנִי עִם־יִצְחָק :

11 וַיֵּרַע הַדָּבָר מְאֹד בְּעֵינֵי אַבְרָהָם עַל אוֹדֹת בְּנוֹ :

12 וַיֹּאמֶר אֱלֹהִים אֶל־אַבְרָהָם אַל־יֵרַע בְּעֵינֶיךָ עַל־הַנַּעַר וְעַל־אֲמָתֶךָ כֹּל אֲשֶׁר תֹּאמַר אֵלֶיךָ שָׂרָה שְׁמַע בְּקֹלָהּ כִּי בְיִצְחָק יִקָּרֵא לְךָ זָרַע :

13 וְגַם אֶת־בֶּן־הָאָמָה לְגוֹי אֲשִׂימֶנּוּ כִּי זַרְעֲךָ הוּא :

Notes

Verse 7

מִלֵּל

This is a Piel form, and we will learn about the Piel in the next unit. It means *he has said*.

הֵינִיקָה

This is a Hifil form. We will learn about the Hifil in Unit 19. This word comes from the verb יָנַק and means *she breastfed*.

The phrase מִי מִלֵּל לְאַבְרָהָם הֵינִיקָה ... שָׂרָה is usually translated: *Who* would have said *to Abraham that Sarah* would breastfeed *sons*. The reasons are too complicated to explain at this stage, but any good book about Hebrew syntax will explain it once you are more familiar with verb stems.

Possible translation of Verse 7

And she said, 'Who would have said to Abraham that Sarah would breastfeed sons? For I have given birth to a son in his old age.'

Verse 8

וַיִּגָּמַל

The verb גָּמַל means *to wean*, so the Nifal means *to be weaned*. This is VC Imperfect 3ms so it means *and he was weaned*.

וַיַּעַשׂ

This is a very common word and you may recognize it from previous texts. It is VC Imperfect 3ms apocopated (shortened) from the verb עָשָׂה and it means *and he made*.

בְּיוֹם הִגָּמֵל אֶת־יִצְחָק

The word הִגָּמֵל is a Nifal infinitive construct, and could perhaps be translated as a noun (*on the day of the weaning*) or as a verb (*on the day he was weaned*).

Possible translation of Verse 8

And the child grew and was weaned and Abraham made a big feast on the day that Isaac was weaned.

Verse 9

וַתֵּרֶא

This is VC Imperfect 3fs of רָאָה (*to see*).

אֶת־בֶּן־הָגָר הַמִּצְרִית

The word הַמִּצְרִית is a gentilic adjective, so this phrase means *the son of Hagar the Egyptian*.

אֲשֶׁר־יָלְדָה לְאַבְרָהָם

This is a reference to Ishmael, the son Hagar bore for Abraham before Sarah gave birth to Isaac.

מְצַחֵק

Another Piel form; this time a participle. It can mean *playing* or *laughing*, or possibly *teasing* or *mocking*. It is difficult to kow exactly what is meant, though an early Greek translation of the biblical text (called the Septuagint) includes the words *with Isaac*. So perhaps Ishmael is playing with Isaac or teasing Isaac.

Possible translation of Verse 9

And Sarah saw the son of Hagar the Egyptian, whom she bore to Abraham, playing [with Isaac].

Verse 10

גָּרֵשׁ

This is a Piel Imperative. It means *expel* or *drive away*.

לֹא יִירַשׁ בֶּן־הָאָמָה הַזֹּאת עִם־בְּנִי

The verb is Imperfect 3ms from יָרַשׁ, so *he will not inherit*. The subject of the verb is *the son of the handmaid* and עִם־בְּנִי is *with my son*.

Possible translation of Verse 10

And she said to Abraham, 'Drive away this handmaid and her son, because the son of this handmaid will not inherit with my son, with Isaac.'

Verse 11

וַיֵּרַע

This is VC Imperfect of רָעַע *to be bad*. The word דָּבָר can mean *word*, but it can also mean *thing* or *matter*. So *the matter was very bad in Abraham's eyes*. This is a common Hebrew expression indicating a person's distress or displeasure.

Possible translation of Verse 11

And Abraham was distressed because of his son.

Verse 12

אַל־יֵרַע בְּעֵינֶיךָ עַל־הַנַּעַר

This is a prohibition with the negative particle used with the
Jussive 3ms of רָעַע. The Jussive is identical in form to the
Imperfect, but it is translated differently. This phrase means
literally *Let it not be bad in your eyes on account of the young
man*. If we were translating as Imperfect instead of Jussive we
would get *It is not bad in your eyes on account of the boy*, so it
really needs to be Jussive to make sense.

כֹּל אֲשֶׁר תֹּאמַר אֵלֶיךָ שָׂרָה שְׁמַע בְּקֹלָהּ

Literally *all which she said to you Sarah listen to her voice*. To
listen to someone's voice is often associated with obeying them
or doing as they suggest. So this phrase is an exhortation to
Abraham to do as Sarah has requested despite his misgivings.

כִּי בְיִצְחָק יִקָּרֵא לְךָ זָרַע

The verb יִקָּרֵא is Nifal Imperfect 3ms. In Qal the verb קָרָא means
to call and in Nifal it means *to be called*. So literally *because in/by
Isaac will be called to/for you seed*. The idea is that Abraham's
descendants through Isaac will be particularly significant as
Abraham's progeny.

Possible translation of Verse 12

*And God said to Abraham, 'Do not be distressed about the
young man or about your handmaid. Listen to Sarah's voice in
all that she has said to you, because your descendants will be
recognized through Isaac.'*

Verse 13

וְגַם אֶת־בֶּן־הָאָמָה

This refers to Hagar's son.

לְגוֹי אֲשִׂימֶנּוּ

The word is an Imperfect 1s of שִׂים (*to put, place*) and the suffix
נוּ indicates the object of the verb, which is 3ms. We will learn
more about suffixes on verbs in the next unit. The whole word
means *I will place him* or *I will establish him*. And לְגוֹי means
as a nation.

Literally *because your seed is he*. Ishmael is also Abraham's progeny.

Possible translation of Verse 13

And I will also make the handmaiden's son into a nation because he is your progeny.

16.8 Suggestions

- Ensure you understand how Nifal works.

- Ensure you understand how the Jussive works.

Both Nifal and the Jussive are common in biblical Hebrew and it is important to understand how they function. It is probably not necessary at this stage to learn all the forms of the Nifal; a general understanding of its purpose is likely to be suffucient for now.

16.9 Summary

In this unit we have looked at

- the place of Nifal among the verb stems
- the use of gentilic adjectives
- different patterns of nouns
- uses of the Jussive
- the text of Genesis 21:7–13.

verb: *to break*	שָׁבַר
verb: *to tear away*	נָתַק
verb: *to be holy*	קָדַשׁ
verb: *to command* (Piel)	צִוָּה
verb: *to praise* (Piel)	הָלַל
verb: to *abandon, forsake*	עָזַב

17.1 Verbs with object suffixes

So far we have learned about pronominal suffixes on nouns (e.g. סוּסוֹ) and on prepositions (e.g. לָהֶם) but we have not yet looked at how these suffixes are attached to verbs, although we have encountered a few examples.

With nouns and prepositions it was a fairly straightforward process of adding the appropriate endings. If the ending was 3fs, it was usually ה. Some of the prepositions acquired a few extra letters (e.g. כְּ with 1s suffix became כָּמוֹנִי) but essentially it was somewhat predictable. Verbs are not so predictable: there is a variety of endings that can be applied to verbs and it is necessary to be aware of the possibilities in order to make sense of them. At this stage it is not necessary to learn the rules about the usage of particular suffixes; recognizing them is enough for now.

	SUFFIX ON ל (for comparison)	SUFFIXES ON VERB					MEANING
3ms	וֹ	נוּ	הוּ	תוֹ	תוּ	וֹ	*him*
3fs	הָ	נָּה	הָ	הָ	הָ		*her*
2ms	ךָ		וּךְ	ךָ	ךָ		*you*
2fs	ךְ		וּךְ	ךְ	ךְ		*you*
1s	יִ	בִּי	תּוּנִי	תְנִי	נִי		*me*
3mp	הֶם	ֵם	וּם	ָם	ָ֫ם	ָם	*them*
3fp	הֶן	ָ֫ן	וּן	ָ֫ן	ָ֫ן	ָ֫ן	*them*
2mp	כֶם				כֶם		*you*
2fp	כֶן				כֶן		*you*
1p	נוּ			תָנוּ	נוּ		*us*

When a suffix is added to a verb the vowels in the verb will often change. Sometimes extra vowels are added to make the word easier to pronounce. Here are some examples:

WITHOUT SUFFIX		WITH SUFFIX		
he has visited	פָּקַד	*he has visited me*	פְּקָדַנִי	*pᵃ-kā-DA-nee*
they have visited	פָּקְדוּ	*they have visited him*	פְּקָדוּהוּ	*pᵃ-kā-DOO-hoo*
he will visit	יִפְקוֹד	*he will visit me*	יִפְקְדַנִי	*yif-kᵃ-DAY-nee*
they will visit	יִפְקְדוּ	*they will visit him*	יִפְקְדוּהוּ	*yif-kᵃ-DOO-hoo*

Verbs with pronominal suffixes are very common in biblical Hebrew; much more common than using object pronouns such as אוֹתוֹ. Fortunately, despite the number of alternative suffixes for verbs there is not a great variety among them. The five possibilities for the 3mp, for example, are simply the letter ם with one of five vowels. The 3mp forms are the most important to learn, partly because they are very common, but also because they are less immediately recognizable than most of the others.

Verbs with pronominal suffixes can cause a little confusion at first. For example, פָּקַדְנוּ looks very like פְּקָדָנוּ but the two mean *we have visited* and *he has visited us* respectively. The 3ms pronominal suffix וֹ can also be tricky: it is easy to mistake it for the third person Perfect suffix. However, context usually provides some assistance.

17.2 Cohortative

We have already learned the Imperative and the Jussive. The Cohortative is another way of issuing commands, and this time they are commands to oneself. This means they are first person. (Remember, Imperatives are second person commands and Jussives can be second person or third person.) The Cohortative is formed by adding the ending הָ to the Imperfect form. This lengthens the word by one syllable, and so the long-*o* vowel of the Imperfect changes to a *sheva* in the Cohortative.

I will visit	אֶפְקֹד	*I will remember*	אֶזְכֹּר	*I will write*	אֶכְתֹּב
Let me visit	אֶפְקְדָה	*Let me remember*	אֶזְכְּרָה	*Let me write*	אֶכְתְּבָה
We will visit	נִפְקֹד	*We will remember*	נִזְכֹּר	*We will write*	נִכְתֹּב
Let us visit	נִפְקְדָה	*Let us remember*	נִזְכְּרָה	*Let us write*	נִכְתְּבָה

Here are some examples of how the Cohortative is used:

Let me remember your words.	אֶזְכְּרָה דְּבָרֶיךָ
Let us make a covenant.	נִכְרְתָה בְּרִית

(the verb used for making a covenant is כָּרַת *to cut*)

17.3 Exercise 1

Match the English to the Hebrew.

this great fire will consume us (Deuteronomy 5:25)

וַיֶּאֱהָבֵהוּ מְאֹד

and he took them from the middle of the tent (Joshua 7:3)

וַיִּזְכְּרֶהָ יְהוָה

and Yhwh remembered her (1 Samuel 1:19)

וְלֹא יְדַעְתָּם

and he loved him very much (1 Samuel 16:21)

בֶּרַכְנוּכֶם מִבֵּית יְהוָה

and you did not know them (Isaiah 48:6)

יְהוָה יִשְׁמָרְךָ מִכָּל־רָע

We bless you from the house of Yhwh. (Psalm 118:26)

אֵלִי אֵלִי לָמָה עֲזַבְתָּנִי

Yhwh will guard you from all evil. (Psalm 121:7)

תֹּאכְלֵנוּ הָאֵשׁ הַגְּדֹלָה הַזֹּאת

My God, my God, why have you abandoned me?
(Psalm 22:2; Engl. 22:1)

וַיִּקָּחוּם מִתּוֹךְ הָאֹהֶל

17.4 Verbs: Piel, Pual and Hitpael

We have seen a number of examples of verbs in the Piel in the biblical texts. The Piel is another of the verb stems, like the Nifal we learned in Unit 16. As you probably remember, Nifal forms are usually translated with an English passive, so Nifal can be thought of as a passive stem. Piel is slightly different: Piel is traditionally described as *intensive*: it intensifies the verbal idea. It is known as Piel because in the Perfect 3ms its vowels are a short *i* and a long *e*. Applied to the verb פָּעַל (formerly the model verb) the intensive form is פִּעֵל, pronounced *pee-ayl*.

QAL	PIEL	
to break	*to shatter*	שָׁבַר
to pull off, tear away	*to tear apart, tear to pieces*	נָתַק
to be holy	*to sanctify, consecrate*	קָדַשׁ

Other verbs have meanings in the Piel that are very similar to their Qal meanings:

QAL	PIEL	
to go, walk	*to go, walk*	הָלַךְ
to uncover, reveal	*to uncover, reveal*	גָּלָה

And some meanings appear to be less similar to the Qal meanings:

QAL	PIEL	
to visit, take care of	*to muster* (Isaiah 13:4)	פָּקַד

However, *to muster* is a possible meaning of the Qal of פָּקַד so it is not so dissimilar as it first appears.

Some verbs are never found in Qal in biblical Hebrew; they occur only in Piel form and their meanings are not necessarily inherently intensive.

QAL	PIEL	
—	*to command*	צִוָּה
—	*to praise*	הָלַל

The ו in the verb צִוָּה is not a vowel as it is in קוּם; it is a consonant, even with *dagesh* (וּ) which makes it look like a vowel. Therefore it is pronounced *v* and not *oo*.

Like Nifal, Piel occurs in Perfect, Imperfect and the other forms.

PIEL PERFECT

3ms	פִּקֵּד	*he has mustered*	3p	פִּקְּדוּ	*they have mustered*
3fs	פִּקְּדָה	*she has mustered*			
2ms	פִּקַּדְתָּ	*you have mustered*	2mp	פִּקַּדְתֶּם	*you have mustered*
2fs	פִּקַּדְתְּ	*you have mustered*	2fp	פִּקַּדְתֶּן	*you have mustered*
1s	פִּקַּדְתִּי	*I have mustered*	1p	פִּקַּדְנוּ	*we have mustered*

There is, of course, a *dagesh* in the initial פ because it is one of the letters that always takes *dagesh* at the beginning of a word.

However, the *dagesh* to notice is the *dagesh* in the middle root letter (ק). All Piel forms have this *dagesh*. And for that reason, פִּעֵל is not an ideal model verb, because its middle letter is a guttural and so cannot take *dagesh*.

PIEL IMPERFECT

3ms	יְפַקֵּד	*he will muster*	3p	יְפַקְּדוּ	*they have mustered*
3fs	תְּפַקֵּד	*she will muster*	3fp	תְּפַקֵּדְנָה	*they have mustered*
2ms	תְּפַקֵּד	*you have mustered*	2mp	תְּפַקְּדוּ	*you have mustered*
2fs	תְּפַקְּדִי	*you have mustered*	2fp	תְּפַקֵּדְנָה	*you have mustered*
1s	אֲפַקֵּד	*I have mustered*	1p	נְפַקֵּד	*we have mustered*

PIEL IMPERATIVE ms

muster! פַּקֵּד

PIEL INFINITIVE CONSTRUCT
(identical to the Imperative, as in Qal)

to muster פַּקֵּד

PIEL INFINITIVE ABSOLUTE

mustering פַּקֹד

PIEL PARTICIPLE
(Participles in all stems except Qal and Nifal begin with מ.)

mustering מְפַקֵּד

Piel and weak verbs

Ayin gutturals and verbs with a ר as the *ayin* letter are the most obviously likely to deviate from the strong verb pattern, since the Piel employs a *dagesh* in the *ayin* letter. With the absence of *dagesh* the vowel under the *pe* letter can change from a short *i* to a long *e*: for example בֵּרֵךְ (*he has blessed*) instead of the clearly wrong בֶּרֵךְ. Another possibility is that the long *e* changes to a short *a*, e.g. נִחַם (*he has comforted*). The word פִּעֵל itself, of course, is a weak verb. In fact, instead of pronouncing it *piel*, it should probably be written פִּעֵל and pronounced *pee-al*. However, the Piel of פָּעַל does not appear in biblical Hebrew so the correct spelling is only interesting as a point of grammar.

Lamed guttural verbs attract *a* vowels instead of the long-*e* vowel, thus שִׁלַּח is the Piel Perfect 3ms, and not שִׁלֵּח, and the same is true for any gender and number. For the same reason the Piel Imperfect 3ms of שָׁלַח is יְשַׁלַּח. Similarly, *lamed he* verbs replace the short *e* with short *a* in the Piel Perfect (e.g. גִּלָּה) and replace it with short *e* in the Piel Imperfect (e.g. יְגַלֶּה). Other vowel changes occur in other forms, but they are usually recognizable if you are familiar with the general pattern of the Piel.

Pual

In Unit 16 we learned that Nifal is usually translated with an English passive. The Pual is a passive stem that corresponds to the Piel. It is therefore both intensive and passive. It is formed in a similar way to Piel, with the *dagesh* in the *ayin* letter (with the exception of gutturals), but it is formed with *u* and *a* vowels, hence the name Pual. It is much less common than Piel, and there is no need at this stage to learn lists of verbal forms. Here are examples of how it is used:

QAL		PIEL		PUAL	
he has broken	שָׁבַר	he has shattered	שִׁבֵּר	he/it has been shattered	שֻׁבַּר
he has torn (something) away	נָתַק	he has torn (something) to pieces)	נִתֵּק	he/it has been torn to pieces	נֻתַּק
he is holy	קָדַשׁ	he has consecrated	קִדֵּשׁ	he/it has been consecrated	קֻדַּשׁ

Notice the irregular Piel form קִדֵּשׁ. We might have expected קִדַּשׁ.

Although it is not necessary to learn verb lists, it may be useful to be aware of the five basic forms of the verb in Pual, with Qal and Piel for comparison:

	QAL	PIEL	PUAL
PERFECT 3ms	קָטַל	קִטֵּל	קֻטַּל
IMPERFECT 3ms	יִקְטֹל	יְקַטֵּל	יְקֻטַּל
IMPERATIVE 2ms	קְטֹל	קַטֵּל	—
INFINITIVE CONSTRUCT	קְטֹל	קַטֵּל	קֻטַּל
PARTICIPLE	קֹטֵל	מְקַטֵּל	מְקֻטָּל

Hitpael

The Hitpael, like the Pual, is related to the Piel. It is frequently used as a reflexive form of the Piel although it can carry other meanings and is sometimes translated with the same meaning as the Qal or Piel. It is formed with the prefix הִת and with *dagesh* in the *ayin* letter and *a* and *e* vowels. Here are some examples:

QAL	*he is holy*	קָדַשׁ
PIEL	*he has consecrated*	קִדֵּשׁ
PUAL	*he/it has been consecrated*	קֻדַּשׁ
HITPAEL	*he has consecrated himself*	הִתְקַדֵּשׁ

QAL	*he has visited*	פָּקַד
PIEL	*he has mustered*	פִּקֵּד
PUAL	*he has been mustered*	פֻּקַד
HITPAEL	*he has mustered*	הִתְפַּקֵּד

In the Hitpael Imperfect the prefix changes according to the person and number, in a manner very similar to the Qal Imperfect prefix:

3ms	יִתְקַדֵּשׁ	*he will consecrate himself*
3fs	תִּתְקַדֵּשׁ	*she will consecrate herself*
2ms	תִּתְקַדֵּשׁ	*you* (ms) *will consecrate*
2fs	תִּתְקַדְּשִׁי	*you* (fs) *will consecrate*
1s	אֶתְקַדֵּשׁ	*I will consecrate myself*
3mp	יִתְקַדְּשׁוּ	*they* (m) *will consecrate themselves*
3fp	תִּתְקַדֵּשְׁנָה	*they* (f) *will consecrate themselves*

2mp	תִּתְקַדְּשׁוּ	you (mp) *will consecrate yourselves*
2fp	תִּתְקַדֵּשְׁנָה	you (fp) *will consecrate yourselves*
1p	נִתְקַדֵּשׁ	*we will consecrate ourselves*

Again, it is not necessary at this stage to learn lists of verbs in the Hitpael, but it may be useful to see how the five basic forms of the verb look in Hitpael with Qal for comparison:

	QAL	HITPAEL
PERFECT 3ms	קָטַל	הִתְקַטֵּל
IMPERFECT 3ms	יִקְטֹל	יִתְקַטֵּל
IMPERATIVE 2ms	קְטֹל	הִתְקַטֵּל
INFINITIVE CONSTRUCT	קְטֹל	הִתְקַטֵּל
PARTICIPLE	קֹטֵל	מִתְקַטֵּל

17.5 Identifying the stems

There are certain factors to look for if you want to determine whether a verb is Piel or Pual or another stem. Here are the factors that can help you recognize one of the intensives:

Recognizing the Piel

PERFECT: *Dagesh* in second root letter. E.g. קִטַּלְתִּי

IMPERFECT: *Dagesh* in second root letter, *sheva* under prefix (1s has a complex *sheva* because the prefix is א which cannot take a simple *sheva*). E.g. אֲקַטֵּד

IMPERATIVE and INFINITIVES: Short-*a* vowel under the first root letter. E.g. קַטֵּד

PARTICIPLE: Begins with מ *and* has short-*a* vowel under the first root letter. E.g. מְקַטֵּד

Recognizing the Pual

PERFECT: *Dagesh* in second root letter, ֻ vowel in first syllable. E.g קֻטַּלְתִּי

IMPERFECT: *Dagesh* in second root letter, *sheva* under prefix, ֻ vowel under first root letter. E.g. אֲקֻטַּל

IMPERATIVE: does not exist.

INFINITIVES: ˌvowel in first syllable. E.g. קַטֵּל

PARTICIPLE: Begins with מ *and* has ˌvowel under the first root letter. E.g. מְקַטֵּל

Recognizing the Hitpael

PERFECT: *Dagesh* in second root letter, prefix הִת. E.g. הִתְקַטַּלְתִּי

IMPERFECT: *Dagesh* in second root letter, prefix incorporates a ת. E.g. אֶתְקַטֵּל

IMPERATIVE and INFINITIVES: Prefix הִת. E.g. הִתְקַטֵּל

PARTICIPLE: Prefix מִת. E.g. מִתְקַטֵּל

17.6 Exercise 2

Complete the table below.

The meanings of the verbs used are as follows:

	קָדַשׁ	פָּקַד	אָסַף
QAL	*to be holy*	*to visit*	*to gather*
PIEL	*to consecrate*	*to muster*	*to gather*
PUAL	*to be consecrated*	*to be mustered*	*to be gathered*
HITPAEL	*to consecrate oneself*	*to muster*	*to be gathered together*

	בָּקַע	צָוָה
QAL	*to divide*	*to command*
PIEL	*to tear in pieces*	—
PUAL	*to be torn in pieces*	*to be commanded*
HITPAEL	*to be torn*	—

	Perf. 3ms	Perf. 1s	Impf. 3mp
QAL	קָדֵשׁ	פָּקַדְתִּי	יַאַסְפוּ
MEANING	*he is holy*	*I have visited*	_____
PIEL	קִדֵּשׁ	פִּקַּדְתִּי	יְאַסְּפוּ
MEANING	_____	*I have mustered*	*they will gather*
PUAL	קֻדַּשׁ	פֻּקַּדְתִּי	יְאֻסְּפוּ
MEANING	*he has been consecrated*	_____	*they will be gathered*
HITPAEL	הִתְקַדֵּשׁ	הִתְפַּקַּדְתִּי	יִתְאַסְּפוּ
MEANING	*he has consecrated himself*	_____	_____

	Impv.	Perf. 3mp	Impf. 1p
QAL	קְדַשׁ	בָּקְעוּ	נִבְקַע
MEANING	*be holy*	_____	*we will divide*
PIEL	קַדֵּשׁ	בִּקְּעוּ	נְבַקַּע
MEANING	_____	*they have torn in pieces*	_____
PUAL	—	בֻּקְּעוּ	נְבֻקַּע
MEANING	—	_____	*we will be torn in pieces*
HITPAEL	הִתְקַדֵּשׁ	הִתְבַּקְּעוּ	נִתְבַּקַּע
MEANING	_____	*they have been torn*	_____

	Impf. 3ms.	Impv.	Part.
QAL	—	פְּקֹד	אֹסֵף
MEANING	—	_____	*gathering*
PIEL	יְצַוֶּה	פַּקֵּד	מְאַסֵּף
MEANING	_____	*muster*	_____
PUAL	צֻוָּה	—	מְאֻסָּף
MEANING	*he has been commanded*	—	*being gathered*
HITPAEL	—	הִתְפַּקֵּד	מִתְאַסֵּף
MEANING	—	_____	_____

	Inf. Cstr.
QAL	בְּקֹעַ
MEANING	*to divide*
PIEL	בַּקֵּעַ
MEANING	*to tear in pieces*
PUAL	בֻּקַּע
MEANING	_____
HITPAEL	הִתְבַּקֵּעַ
MEANING	_____

17.7 Text: Genesis 21:14–21

Points to look out for in this text:

- Words we have already encountered.
- Verbs with object suffixes.
- Verbs in Intensive stems.

number : *one*	אֶחָד
noun f: *well*	בְּאֵר
place name: *Beersheba*	בְּאֵר שָׁבַע
verb: *to weep*	בָּכָה
verb (Hifil with בְּ): *to hold*	חָזַק

noun f: *container*	חֵמֶת pronounced CHAY-met
verb: *to shoot*	טָחָה
verb: *to be finished*	כָּלָה
noun m: *death*	מָוֶת pronounced MĀ-vet
noun dual: *water*	מַיִם
verb: *to be full* (Qal); *to fill* (Piel)	מָלֵא
noun m: *angel, messenger*	מַלְאָךְ
adverb: *in front of, opposite*	נֶגֶד
verb: *to lift, carry*	נָשָׂא
verb: *to open* (eyes)	פָּקַח
place name: *Paran*	פָּארָן
noun f: *bow*	קֶשֶׁת pronounced KE-shet
verb: *to shoot*	רָבָה
verb: *to be distant*	רָחַק
noun m: *shrub*	שִׂיחַ
verb: *to get up early*	שָׁכַם
noun m: *shoulder*	שְׁכֶם pronounced SHE-chem
verb: *to throw*	שָׁלַךְ
verb: *to give someone a drink* (Hifil)	שָׁקָה
verb: *to wander*	תָּעָה

Text and notes

Read each verse aloud a few times to be sure of the pronunciation. Then write the words you know beneath the words in the text, and match the others to the words in the vocabulary.

Verse 14

וַיַּשְׁכֵּם אַבְרָהָם בַּבֹּקֶר וַיִּקַּח־לֶחֶם וְחֵמַת מַיִם וַיִּתֵּן אֶל־הָגָר שָׂם עַל־
שִׁכְמָהּ וְאֶת־הַיֶּלֶד וַיְשַׁלְּחֶהָ וַתֵּלֶךְ וַתֵּתַע בְּמִדְבַּר בְּאֵר שָׁבַע :

וַיַּשְׁכֵּם אַבְרָהָם בַּבֹּקֶר

The verb וַיַּשְׁכֵּם is in the Hifil stem, which we will learn in the next unit. It is related to שְׁכֶם (*shoulder*). It is VC Imperfect 3ms. The word בַּבֹּקֶר is בֹּקֶר with the preposition בְּ.

וַיִּקַּח־לֶחֶם וְחֵמַת מַיִם

The word וַיִּקַּח is from לָקַח: VC Imperfect 3ms. חֵמַת is in the construct form, thus *a container of water*.

וַיִּתֵּן אֶל־הָגָר

The verb וַיִּתֵּן is VC Imperfect 3ms from נָתַן. The object pronoun (or pronominal suffix) that we might expect, i.e. a word for *them* referring to the bread and water, is absent. This is commonplace in Hebrew.

שָׂם עַל־שִׁכְמָהּ וְאֶת־הַיֶּלֶד וַיְשַׁלְּחֶהָ

The word שָׂם is either Perfect 3ms or Qal Participle from שִׂים. As שִׂים is a hollow verb, the Perfect 3ms is not the same as the citation form. Again, the pronoun or pronominal suffix is absent. The noun שִׁכְמָהּ has a pronominal suffix 3fs. וְאֶת־הַיֶּלֶד means *and the child*, and וַיְשַׁלְּחֶהָ is VC Imperfect of שָׁלַח with a pronominal suffix 3fs.

וַתֵּלֶךְ בְּמִדְבַּר בְּאֵר שָׁבַע

The verb וַתֵּלֶךְ is VC Imperfect 3fs from תָּעָה and is a shortened (or apocopated) form: the final ה is missing. בְּמִדְבַּר is מִדְבַּר with the preposition בְּ and is in construct relationship to בְּאֵר שָׁבַע.

Possible translation of Verse 14

And Abraham got up early in the morning and took bread and a water container and gave them to Hagar, putting them on her shoulder and the child, and he sent her away. And she went and wandered in the desert of Beersheba.

Verse 15

וַיִּכְלוּ הַמַּיִם מִן־הַחֵמֶת וַתַּשְׁלֵךְ אֶת־הַיֶּלֶד תַּחַת אַחַד הַשִּׂיחִם :

וַיִּכְלוּ הַמַּיִם מִן־הַחֵמֶת

The verb is VC Imperfect 3mp from כָּלָה. It is plural because the word מַיִם (*water*) is dual in form and therefore takes a plural verb. וַיִּכְלוּ is also shortened, like many VC Imperfect forms of verbs with a final ה.

וַתַּשְׁלֵךְ אֶת־הַיֶּלֶד

It is easy to confuse שָׁלַךְ with שָׁלַח but this is the former, meaning *to throw*, and only occurs in the Hifil. The form וַתַּשְׁלֵךְ is Hifil VC Imperfect 3fs.

תַּחַת אַחַד הַשִּׂיחִם

The word אַחַד is in construct relationship to הַשִּׂיחִם: *one of the shrubs*.

Possible translation of Verse 15

And the water in the container was finished and she threw the child under one of the shrubs.

Verse 16

וַתֵּלֶךְ וַתֵּשֶׁב לָהּ מִנֶּגֶד הַרְחֵק כִּמְטַחֲוֵי קֶשֶׁת כִּי אָמְרָה אַל־אֶרְאֶה בְּמוֹת הַיָּלֶד וַתֵּשֶׁב מִנֶּגֶד וַתִּשָּׂא אֶת־קֹלָהּ וַתֵּבְךְּ:

וַתֵּלֶךְ וַתֵּשֶׁב לָהּ

The verb הָלַךְ behaves like a *pe yod* verb in the Imperfect, so this form is VC Imperfect 3fs. וַתֵּשֶׁב לָהּ means *and she sat down*.

הַרְחֵק כִּמְטַחֲוֵי קֶשֶׁת

The word הַרְחֵק is a Hifil Infinitive Absolute from רָחַק and means *far away*. The word כִּמְטַחֲוֵי is an unusual form called Pilel, which you do not need to learn at this stage, although it is worth mentioning that it functions like the Piel stem. It is a Participle from טָחָה with the prefix כְּ so it means *like shooters* and is in construct relationship to קֶשֶׁת. Therefore the whole phrase means literally *far away like shooters of a bow*.

כִּי אָמְרָה אַל־אֶרְאֶה בְּמוֹת הַיָּלֶד

The verb usually means *to say*. However, it is also used in the sense of *to think*. אָמְרָה is Perfect 3fs. בְּמוֹת is the construct form of מָוֶת with the preposition בְּ.

וַתִּשָּׂא אֶת־קֹלָהּ וַתֵּבְךְּ

The verb is VC Imperfect of נָשָׂא; the initial נ is incorporated into the שׂ, which acquires a *dagesh*. קֹלָהּ is קוֹל with a pronominal suffix 3fs, and וַתֵּבְךְּ is VC Imperfect 3fs from בָּכָה. As we have seen frequently, the verb is shortened because the final ה is missing.

Possible translation of Verse 16

And she went and she sat down opposite, a bow-shot's distance, because she thought, 'Let me not see the death of the child.' And she sat opposite and she lifted her voice and wept.

Verse 17

וַיִּשְׁמַע אֱלֹהִים אֶת־קוֹל הַנַּעַר וַיִּקְרָא מַלְאַךְ אֱלֹהִים אֶל־הָגָר מִן־הַשָּׁמַיִם וַיֹּאמֶר לָהּ מַה־לָּךְ הָגָר אַל־תִּירְאִי כִּי־שָׁמַע אֱלֹהִים אֶל־קוֹל הַנַּעַר בַּאֲשֶׁר הוּא־שָׁם :

וַיִּשְׁמַע אֱלֹהִים אֶת־קוֹל הַנַּעַר

The verb וַיִּשְׁמַע is VC Imperfect 3ms from שָׁמַע. The word קוֹל is in construct relationship to הַנַּעַר. We have seen that נַעַר is often translated *young man* but in this passage it is used alongside יֶלֶד (*child*) to describe Hagar's son, and so we might better translate נַעַר as *boy* in this context.

וַיִּקְרָא מַלְאַךְ אֱלֹהִים

The verb וַיִּקְרָא is VC Imperfect 3ms from קָרָא. The word מַלְאַךְ is in construct relationship to אֱלֹהִים and is therefore definite: *the angel*, rather than an *angel*, because אֱלֹהִים is definite. All names are definite.

מַה־לָּךְ הָגָר

Literally '*What is to you, Hagar?*'

אַל־תִּירְאִי

This is a Jussive 2fs because it is a prohibition. It is the weaker kind of Jussive; a stronger prohibition would use the particle לֹא.

כִּי־שָׁמַע אֱלֹהִים אֶל־קוֹל הַנַּעַר

The verb שָׁמַע used with the preposition אֶל means *to listen to*.

בַּאֲשֶׁר הוּא־שָׁם

Literally *in which he was there*. A more fluent translation in English might be *where he was*.

Possible translation of Verse 17

And God heard the voice of the boy and the angel of God called to Hagar from heaven and he said to her, 'What is wrong with you, Hagar? Do not be afraid, for God has listened to the voice of the boy where he was.'

Verse 18

קוּמִי שְׂאִי אֶת־הַנַּעַר וְהַחֲזִיקִי אֶת־יָדֵךְ בּוֹ כִּי־לְגוֹי גָּדוֹל אֲשִׂימֶנּוּ :

קוּמִי שְׂאִי אֶת־הַנַּעַר

There are two Imperatives here: קוּמִי from קוּם and שְׂאִי from נָשָׂא. They are both feminine forms of the Imperative (see Unit 14) because Hagar is a woman.

וְהַחֲזִיקִי אֶת־יָדֵךְ בּוֹ

This verb is a Hifil Imperative (we will learn about the Hifil in Unit 18) and when used with the preposition בְּ it means *hold*. אֶת־ is the preposition meaning *with* and יָדֵךְ is יָד with a pronominal suffix 2fs.

כִּי־לְגוֹי גָּדוֹל אֲשִׂימֶנּוּ

Literally *because for a nation a great I will make him*. The word אֲשִׂימֶנּוּ was in verse 13.

Possible translation of Verse 18

Get up, lift up the boy and hold him with your hand, for I will make him a great nation.

Verse 19

וַיִּפְקַח אֱלֹהִים אֶת־עֵינֶיהָ וַתֵּרֶא בְּאֵר מָיִם וַתֵּלֶךְ וַתְּמַלֵּא אֶת־הַחֵמֶת מַיִם וַתַּשְׁקְ אֶת־הַנָּעַר :

וַיִּפְקַח אֱלֹהִים אֶת־עֵינֶיהָ

The verb וַיִּפְקַח is VC Imperfect 3ms from פָּקַח. The word עֵינֶיהָ is the f dual of עַיִן with a pronominal suffix 3fs.

וַתֵּרֶא בְּאֵר מָיִם וַתֵּלֶךְ

The verb is VC Imperfect 3fs from רָאָה and the verb וַתֵּלֶךְ is VC Imperfect 2fs from הָלַךְ.

וַתְּמַלֵּא אֶת־הַחֵמֶת מַיִם

The verb is Piel VC Imperfect 3fs from מָלֵא. This verb can have two objects: in this case the subject is *she* and the objects are *the container* and *water*. So we would not translate this phrase: *she filled the container of water* because חֵמֶת is *not* in construct relationship to מַיִם in this phrase. The only way to know this is to know that the construct form of חֵמֶת is הֵמַת. We can find this in a good dictionary. So we need to say *she filled the container with water*.

וַתַּשְׁקְ אֶת־הַנָּעַר

Another Hifil form, and we will learn more about it in the next unit. Literally *and she caused the boy to drink*.

Possible translation of Verse 19

And God opened her eyes and she saw a well of water and she went and she filled the container with water and she gave the boy a drink.

Verse 20

וַיְהִי אֱלֹהִים אֶת־הַנַּעַר וַיִּגְדָּל וַיֵּשֶׁב בַּמִּדְבָּר וַיְהִי רֹבֶה קַשָּׁת :

וַיְהִי אֱלֹהִים אֶת־הַנַּעַר

The verb וַיְהִי is VC Imperfect 3ms from הָיָה. It often introduces a new story, and a traditional translation is *and it came to pass*, although that particular phrase is not used in everyday English. However, the word also means simply *and it was* or *and he was*.

אֶת־ here is the preposition meaning *with* and not the object marker.

וַיִּגְדַּל וַיֵּשֶׁב בַּמִּדְבָּר

The first verb וַיִּגְדַּל is VC Imperfect 3ms from גָּדַל and the second verb וַיֵּשֶׁב is VC Imperfect 3ms from יָשַׁב (*to sit, to dwell*). It is easy to confuse יָשַׁב (*to return*) and שׁוּב, especially in Imperfect forms. For the record they are as follows:

Verb	VC Imperfect 3ms	
יָשַׁב	וַיֵּשֶׁב	*and he sat/lived*
שׁוּב	וַיָּשָׁב	*and he returned*

וַיְהִי רֹבֶה קַשָּׁת

Literally *and he became a shooter of bow*. The word רֹבֶה is a Participle.

Possible translation of Verse 20

And God was with the boy, and he grew and he lived in the desert, and he became an archer.

Verse 21

וַיֵּשֶׁב בְּמִדְבַּר פָּארָן וַתִּקַּח־לוֹ אִמּוֹ אִשָּׁה מֵאֶרֶץ מִצְרָיִם :

וַיֵּשֶׁב בְּמִדְבַּר פָּארָן

The word בְּמִדְבַּר is in construct relationship to the word פָּארָן.

וַתִּקַּח־לוֹ אִמּוֹ אִשָּׁה

Literally *and she took for him his mother a wife*.

מֵאֶרֶץ מִצְרָיִם

Simply *from the land of Egypt*. Remember that Hagar herself is described as an Egyptian.

Possible translation of Verse 21

And he lived in the desert of Paran and his mother chose a wife for him from the land of Egypt.

17.8 Suggestion

- Read a commentary on Genesis 21. There are many questions that you might have thought of. Perhaps you wonder whether Abraham actually puts the child on Hagar's shoulders, or why Hagar throws him under a shrub. A good commentary will address the kinds of questions readers often have when they encounter the biblical text.

17.9 Summary

In this unit we have looked at

- the various pronominal suffixes we can find on verbs

- the Cohortative as a means of expressing commands to oneself

- the Intensives: the Piel, Pual (passive of Piel) and Hitpael (reflexive of Piel)

- the text of Genesis 21:14–21.

18.1 Verbs: Hifil and Hofal

The last two stems of the verb are known as the *causatives*. Just as Nifal is often understood as a passive version of Qal, and Piel is understood to intensify the verbal idea, so Hifil and Hofal introduce the idea of cause to the verbal idea. And just as Puel was the passive form of Piel, Hofal is the passive form of Hifil. The names come, like most of the other verb stem names, from what the Perfect 3ms of פָּעַל does in that form. So the Hifil of פָּעַל is הִפְעִיל.

Here are some examples:

	QAL	HIFIL	HOFAL
בּוֹא	to come	to bring (to cause to come)	to be brought (to be caused to come)
יָלַד	to give birth	to beget (to cause to give birth) to be born	
פָּקַד	to visit	to appoint	to be appointed
רוּם	to be high	to raise, exalt (to cause to be high)	to be exalted (to be caused to be high)
שׁוּב	to return	to restore (to cause to return)	to be restored (to be caused to return)

Like the other stems, the Hifil and Hofal can be found in any form. The Hofal is much less common than Hifil, and there is no need to learn it thoroughly at this stage, but it may be helpful to have a short look at it. Hifil Perfects begin with הַ, while Hifil Imperfects have the usual prefixes, but pointed with ַ . In some (though not all) parts of the verb an extra **י** is inserted between the second and third root letters.

HIFIL PERFECT

3ms	הִפְקִיד	*he has appointed*	3p	הִפְקִידוּ	*they have appointed*
3fs	הִפְקִידָה	*she has appointed*			
2ms	הִפְקַדְתָּ	*you have appointed*	2mp	הִפְקַדְתֶּם	*you have appointed*
2fs	הִפְקַדְתְּ	*you have appointed*	2fp	הִפְקַדְתֶּן	*you have appointed*
1s	הִפְקַדְתִּי	*I have appointed*	1p	הִפְקַדְנוּ	*we have appointed*

HIFIL IMPERFECT

3ms	יַפְקִיד	*he will appoint*	3mp	יַפְקִידוּ	*they will appoint*
3fs	תַּפְקִיד	*she will appoint*	3fp	תַּפְקֵדְנָה	*they will appoint*
2ms	תַּפְקִיד	*you will appoint*	2mp	תַּפְקִידוּ	*you will appoint*
2fs	תַּפְקִידִי	*you will appoint*	2fp	תַּפְקֵדְנָה	*you will appoint*
1s	אַפְקִיד	*I will appoint*	1p	נַפְקִיל	*we will appoint*

HIFIL IMPERATIVE ms

appoint!   הַפְקֵד

HIFIL INFINITIVE CONSTRUCT
Differs from the Imperative, unlike Qal and Piel:

to appoint   הַפְקִיד

HIFIL INFINITIVE ABSOLUTE

appointing   הַפְקֵד

HIFIL PARTICIPLE

Participles in all stems except Qal and Nifal begin with מ.

appointing   מַפְקִיד

Hifil and weak verbs

Like the other stems, some changes can be found when weak verbs occur in Hifil stems. Roots with gutturals experience some vowel changes: for example the Hifil Perfect 3ms of the guttural verb עָמַד cannot be הֶעְמִיד because the ע cannot take a simple *sheva*. Instead it must take the complex *sheva*: עֲ. This *e*-type vowel attracts an *e* vowel underneath the ה of the Hifil. So the Hifil Perfect 3ms is הֶעֱמִיד. Similarly, in *lamed* guttural verbs we find a *patach* furtive in some forms: the Hifil Perfect 3ms of שָׁלַח is הִשְׁלִיחַ. The *pe yod* and *pe vav* verbs take a longer vowel than the usual ה of the Hifil, so the Hifil Perfect 3ms of יָשַׁב is הוֹשִׁיב and the Hifil Perfect 3ms יָנַק of is הֵינִיק. The נ of *pe nun* verbs is assimilated into the second root letter, which acquires a *dagesh*: the Hifil Perfect 3ms of נָגַשׁ is הִגִּישׁ. And the Hifil Perfects of the *ayin yod* and *ayin vav* (hollow) verbs and the double *ayin* (reduplicated) verbs are formed with הֵ instead of הֶ, while the Imperfects are formed with long-*a* vowels. So, for example the Hifil Perfect 3ms of קוּם is הֵקִים and of סָבַב is הֵסֵב. And the Hifil Imperfect 3ms of קוּם is יָקִים and of סָבַב is יָסֵב.

At a glance:

Pe gutturals; *lamed* gutturals	vowel changes (הֶ instead of הֲ; *patach* furtive)
Pe yod and *pe vav* verbs	vowel lengthening: הֵי or הוֹ instead of ה
Pe nun verbs	*nun* assimilated
Ayin yod and *ayin vav*; double *ayin*	vowel lengthening: הֵ instead of הֶ

Hofal

We have seen that the Hofal is the passive form of Hifil. So Hofal is both causative and passive. Where Hifil indicates that something causes something to happen, Hofal indicates that something is caused to happen. It is much less common than Hifil, and there is no need at this stage to learn lists of verbal forms. However, it may be useful to know the five basic forms of the Hofal, with Qal and Hifil for comparison:

	QAL	HIFIL	HOFAL
Perfect 3ms	קָטַל	הִקְטִיל	הָקְטַל
Imperfect 3ms	יִקְטֹל	יַקְטִיל	יָקְחַל
Imperative 2ms	קְטֹל	הַקְטֵל	–
Infinitive Construct	קְטֹל	הַקְטִיל	הָקְטַל
Participle	קֹטֵל	מַקְטִיל	מָקְטָל

Notice that the first vowel in the Hofal forms is ָ. This is a short-*o* vowel, rather than a long-*a* vowel, if your accent distinguishes between the two.

As with other stems, there are factors that help us determine whether a verb is Hifil or Hofal.

Recognizing the Hifil

PERFECT: Begins with הִ. Some forms have an extra י between the second and third root letters. E.g. הִקְטִילוּ

IMPERFECT: Vowel in prefix is ַ. E.g. אַקְטִיל

IMPERATIVE and INFINITIVES: Begin with הַ. E.g. הַקְטֵל (Imperative)

PARTICIPLE: Begins with מַ. E.g. מַקְטִיל

Recognizing the Hofal

PERFECT: Begins with הָ. E.g. הָקְטַלְתִּי

IMPERFECT: Vowel in prefix is ָ. E.g. אָקְטַל

IMPERATIVE: does not exist.

INFINITIVES: Begin with הָ. E.g. הָקְטַל (Infinitive Construct)

PARTICIPLE: Begins with מָ. E.g. מָקְטַל

18.2 Exercise 1

We have encountered a number of Hifil forms in previous units. Here is a list of those we have seen before, and parsed (analysed). Can you give meanings for them? If you have a good memory, you may be able to remember their meanings from previous units, but it may still be useful to look at them carefully in order to understand their meanings.

a) הוֹשַׁעְתָּנוּ (Unit 11) Hifil Perf 2ms + suffix 1p יָשַׁע

b) אוֹרְךָ (Unit 12) Hifil Impf 1s + suff 2mp from ידה

c) אוֹדֶה (Unit 13) Hifil Impf 1s from ידה

d) הֵינִיקָה (Unit 16) Hifil Perf 3fs from יָנַק

e) וְהַחֲזִיקִי (Unit 17) Hifil Impv 2fs from חָזַק with simple *vav*

f) וַתַּשְׁקְ (Unit 17) Hifil VC Imperfect apocopated 3fs from שָׁקָה

18.3 Recognizing the stems

Identifying the Perfect in the various stems is not too difficult; usually there is some change to the consonants in the root that makes the stem obvious. The table below explains this in more detail.

	DESCRIPTION	EXAMPLE
Qal	—	קָטַל
Nifal	begins with נ	נִקְטַל
Piel	*dagesh* in second root letter, first vowel ִ	קִטֵּל
Pual	*dagesh* in second root letter, first vowel ֻ	קֻטַּל
Hitpael	begins with הִת, *dagesh* in second root letter	הִתְקַטֵּל
Hifil	begins with ה	הִפְקִיד
Hofal	begins with הָ	הָקְטַל

The Imperfect is a very common form in biblical Hebrew, and yet it can be one of the most difficult to identify or parse because the differences between the forms are more often difference in vowels than in consonants. The following table gives the clues to look for.

	DESCRIPTION	EXAMPLE
Qal	. vowel under prefix; ִ vowel under first root letter	יִקְטֹל
Nifal	. vowel under prefix; ָ vowel under first root letter	יִקָּטֵל
Piel	ְ vowel under prefix; ַ vowel under first root letter	יְקַטֵּל
Pual	ְ vowel under prefix; ֻ vowel under first root letter	יְקֻטַּל
Hitpael	. vowel under prefix; ַ vowel under first root letter	יִתְקַטֵּל
Hifil	ַ vowel under prefix; ִ vowel under first root letter	יַקְטִיל
Hofal	ָ vowel under prefix; ָ vowel under first root letter	יָקְטַל

The tables above are not necessarily reliable for weak verbs, but once you know how to recognize verbs of the קָטַל type it will be easier to learn how and why the weak verbs deviate from the regular patterns.

18.4 Exercise 2

Look at the examples in the tables above and write out further examples using the verb פָּקַד.

18.5 Text: Genesis 22:1–6

Points to look out for in this text:

- Words we have already encountered.
- Hifil, Piel and Hitpael forms.

preposition: *after*	אַחַר
noun m and f: *fire*	אֵשׁ
verb: Piel: *to divide, split*	בָּקַע
verb: *to bind, saddle* (an animal)	חָבַשׁ
noun m: *donkey*	חֲמוֹר
adverb: *together*	יַחְדָּו pronounced *yach-DAV*
adjective: *only*	יָחִיד
noun f: *burnt offering*	עוֹלָה
noun f: *knife*	מַאֲכֶלֶת
adverb: *in the distance*	מֵרָחֹק
verb: Piel: *to test, try*	נסה Note: verbs that do not exist in Qal are sometimes written without vowels in dictionaries or vocabulary lists.
adverb: *as far as there, yonder*	עַד־כֹּה
verb: Qal: *to go up*; Hifil: to *offer*	עָלָה
adverb: *here*	פֹּה
verb: Hitpael: *to bow down, worship*	שׁחה
numeral: *three*	שָׁלוֹשׁ

Text

Read each verse aloud a few times to be sure of the pronunciation. Then write the words you know beneath the words in the text, and match the others to the words in the vocabulary.

Notes

Verse 1

וַיְהִי אַחַר הַדְּבָרִים הָאֵלֶּה וְהָאֱלֹהִים נִסָּה אֶת־אַבְרָהָם וַיֹּאמֶר אֵלָיו אַבְרָהָם וַיֹּאמֶר הִנֵּנִי :

וַיְהִי אַחַר הַדְּבָרִים הָאֵלֶּה

We saw the word וַיְהִי in Unit 8 and in Unit 17. It means *and it was* or *and it happened*. It is VC Imperfect 3ms apocopated (shortened) from הָיָה. The construction הַדְּבָרִים הָאֵלֶּה should be familiar from Unit 6.

וְהָאֱלֹהִים נִסָּה אֶת־אַבְרָהָם

The subject comes before the verb here, which is often an indication of emphasis in biblical Hebrew. The verb is a Piel Perfect 3ms from נסה.

וַיֹּאמֶר אֵלָיו אַבְרָהָם וַיֹּאמֶר הִנֵּנִי

The name אַבְרָהָם is the content of what is said: it is direct reported speech. The subject of the verb וַיֹּאמֶר is וְהָאֱלֹהִים. If Abraham were the subject we would expect to see his name directly after the verb, and if he were the object we would expect to see the object marker. However, in this context Abraham is being addressed by God. The word הִנֵּנִי is הִנֵּה with a pronominal suffix 1s. It can be translated *behold me* but in contemporary English we would probably say *Here I am*.

Possible translation of Verse 1

And it came to pass (it happened) after these events (these things) God tested Abraham and he said to him, 'Abraham.' And he said, 'Behold me (Here I am).'

Verse 2

וַיֹּאמֶר קַח־נָא אֶת־בִּנְךָ אֶת־יְחִידְךָ אֲשֶׁר־אָהַבְתָּ אֶת־יִצְחָק וְלֶךְ־לְךָ
אֶל־אֶרֶץ הַמֹּרִיָּה וְהַעֲלֵהוּ שָׁם לְעֹלָה עַל אַחַד הֶהָרִים אֲשֶׁר אֹמַר אֵלֶיךָ :

וַיֹּאמֶר קַח־נָא אֶת־בִּנְךָ אֶת־יְחִידְךָ

The Imperative of לָקַח is קַח which is found here with the particle of entreaty נָא (the word for *please*). The ל is absent in the Imperative because לָקַח behaves like a *pe yod* verb in the Imperfect, Imperative, Participle and Infinitives; for example the Imperative of יְשַׁב is שֵׁב: it loses its first root letter. The word בִּנְךָ is בֵּן with a pronominal suffix 2ms. There is a pronominal suffix 2ms on יָחִיד.

אֲשֶׁר־אָהַבְתָּ אֶת־יִצְחָק

The verb here is Perfect 3ms from אָהַב. The relative pronoun אֲשֶׁר is probably best translated *whom*.

The expression וְלֶךְ־לְךָ is similar to the phrase וַתֵּשֶׁב לָהּ which
we saw in Genesis 21:16. לֵךְ is the Imperative of הָלַךְ, which
behaves like a *pe yod* verb in the Imperfect, Imperative, Participle
and Infinitives, just like לָקַח above. Therefore it loses its first
root letter in the Imperative. The phrase means literally *go
yourself*. The verb וְהַעֲלֵהוּ is a Hifil Imperative ms from עָלָה with
a pronominal suffix 3ms, so the whole word means *and offer
him*. The noun עוֹלָה is related to the verb עָלָה, and with the
preposition לְ it means *as a burnt offering*.

עַל אַחַד הֶהָרִים אֲשֶׁר אֹמַר אֵלֶיךָ

We have seen the number אֶחָד before: it means *one*. Here it
is in construct form: *one of*. We saw the word הַר in Unit 2
and הָרִים is the plural. Notice that the definite article is pointed
with ֶ rather than with an *a* vowel as we might have expected.
This is common when the definite article comes before a הָ sound.
אֹמַר is the Imperfect 3ms of אָמַר, so it means *will say*. We are
more used to seeing the VC Imperfect, which is slightly different
in form.

Possible translation of Verse 2

*And he said, 'Please take your only son Isaac, whom you
love, and go to the land of Moriah and offer him up there as a
burnt offering upon one of the mountains which I will tell you
about.'*

Verse 3

וַיַּשְׁכֵּם אַבְרָהָם בַּבֹּקֶר וַיַּחֲבֹשׁ אֶת־חֲמֹרוֹ וַיִּקַּח אֶת־שְׁנֵי נְעָרָיו אִתּוֹ
וְאֵת יִצְחָק בְּנוֹ וַיְבַקַּע עֲצֵי עֹלָה וַיָּקָם וַיֵּלֶךְ אֶל־הַמָּקוֹם אֲשֶׁר־אָמַר־לוֹ
הָאֱלֹהִים :

וַיַּשְׁכֵּם אַבְרָהָם בַּבֹּקֶר וַיַּחֲבֹשׁ אֶת־חֲמֹרוֹ

The first three words of this verse are identical to Genesis 21:14:
Abraham got up early in the morning. The verb וַיַּשְׁכֵּם is Hifil VC
Imperfect 3ms from שָׁכַם. The verb וַיַּחֲבֹשׁ is VC Imperfect 3ms
from חָבַשׁ. The noun חֲמֹרוֹ has a pronominal suffix 3ms.

וַיִּקַּח אֶת־שְׁנֵי נְעָרָיו אִתּוֹ וְאֵת יִצְחָק בְּנוֹ

The first word here is the VC Imperfect of לָקַח which, as
mentioned above, behaves like a *pe yod* verb in the Imperfect.
שְׁנֵי is the construct form of the dual word שְׁנַיִם meaning *two*

(see Unit 8), so it means *two of.* נְעָרָיו is the plural of נַעַר with a pronominal suffix 3ms. אִתּוֹ is the preposition אֵת with a pronominal suffix and should not be confused with אֹתוֹ meaning *him.* The doubling of the ת in the preposition should help you to distinguish them (see Unit 9).

וַיְבַקַּע עֲצֵי עֹלָה

We saw the verb בָּקַע in Unit 17, where we translated it *to divide,* but it can also mean to split, as here where it refers to Abraham's chopping the firewood. It is Piel VC Imperfect 3ms. עֲצֵי is a plural construct form from עֵץ.

וַיָּקָם וַיֵּלֶךְ אֶל־הַמָּקוֹם אֲשֶׁר־אָמַר־לוֹ הָאֱלֹהִים

The first word is from קוּם and is VC Imperfect. Note that the last is pronounced as a short *o,* so the whole word is pronounced *va-YĀ-kom,* although some accents do not distinguish between long *a* and short *o.* וַיֵּלֶךְ is the VC Imperfect 3ms of הָלַךְ, again acting as a *pe yod* verb in the Imperfect. The subject of אָמַר is הָאֱלֹהִים so the phrase means literally *which he said to him God.*

Possible translation of Verse 3

And Abraham got up early in the morning and saddled his donkey and he took two of his young men with him, and Isaac his son. And he chopped wood for the sacrifice and he got up and went to the place about which God had told him.

Verse 4

בַּיּוֹם הַשְּׁלִישִׁי וַיִּשָּׂא אַבְרָהָם אֶת־עֵינָיו וַיַּרְא אֶת־הַמָּקוֹם מֵרָחֹק :

בַּיּוֹם הַשְּׁלִישִׁי

Literally *in the day the third.*

וַיִּשָּׂא אַבְרָהָם אֶת־עֵינָיו

In Genesis 21: *Hagar lifted up her voice and wept,* which is an idiomatic expression in biblical Hebrew. Similarly, in biblical Hebrew people *lift their eyes and see,* which we could also understand as *looking up.* The verb here is VC Imperfect 3ms of נָשָׂא and the noun is the dual form of עַיִן with a pronominal suffix 3ms.

וַיַּרְא אֶת־הַמָּקוֹם מֵרָחֹק

The verb here is VC Imperfect 3ms from רָאָה.

Possible translation of Verse 4

On the third day Abraham looked up and he saw the place in the distance.

Verse 5

וַיֹּאמֶר אַבְרָהָם אֶל־נְעָרָיו שְׁבוּ־לָכֶם פֹּה עִם־הַחֲמוֹר וַאֲנִי וְהַנַּעַר נֵלְכָה
עַד־כֹּה וְנִשְׁתַּחֲוֶה וְנָשׁוּבָה אֲלֵיכֶם :

וַיֹּאמֶר אַבְרָהָם אֶל־נְעָרָיו

This phrase should be simple enough to translate. Remember that נְעָרָיו is a plural form with a pronominal suffix.

שְׁבוּ־לָכֶם פֹּה עִם־הַחֲמוֹר

This is direct speech. As you may have noticed, biblical Hebrew does not have punctuation equivalents to our quotation marks. The phrase שְׁבוּ־לָכֶם is very similar to וַתֵּשֶׁב לָהּ (Genesis 21:16) and לָךְ־לֶךְ (above, verse 2). שְׁבוּ is a masculine plural Imperative from יָשַׁב; we have looked mainly at masculine singular Imperatives but feminine and plural forms were addressed in Unit 14. However, since יָשַׁב is a weak verb the י drops out in the Imperative: it has an Imperative formed like קַח and לֵךְ, from לָקַח and הָלַךְ respectively.

וַאֲנִי וְהַנַּעַר נֵלְכָה עַד־כֹּה

The verb נֵלְכָה is an Imperfect 1p from הָלַךְ. We might have expected נֵלֵךְ (since הָלַךְ behaves like a *pe yod* verb in the Imperfect). This word, however, has an extra ה (sometimes called a paragogic ה), which may have made it easier to pronounce before עַד־כֹּה.

וְנִשְׁתַּחֲוֶה וְנָשׁוּבָה אֲלֵיכֶם

These two verbs are Imperfects. The first is Hitpael Imperfect 1p from שׁחה (see the paragraph below for why it looks strange) and the second is Qal Impf 1p with an extra (paragogic) ה, from שׁוּב. Notice the pointing on each ו; it is a *sheva* rather than an *a* vowel. This means the verbs are not Vav Consecutive and should probably be translated with English future tense verbs rather than past tense verbs.

The first verb, וַֽנִּשְׁתַּחֲוֶה, demonstrates an interesting phenomenon of the Hitpael: in verbs that begin with an *s* sound (ס or שׁ/שׂ) the Hitpael *reverses the* ת *of* הִת *and the first root letter*. This is the case in all verb stems: Perfect, Imperfect, Infinitives and so on. So if you thought the letters were in the wrong order, you noticed something very important. Here are further examples of the same phenomenon:

QAL PERFECT 3ms		HITPAEL PERFECT	
שָׁמַר	he guarded	הִשְׁתַּמֵּר	he guarded himself
סָתַר	he hid (something)	הִסְתַּתֵּר	he hid himself

Possible translation of Verse 5

And Abraham said to his young men, 'Sit you down here (stay here) with the donkey and (whilst) I and the boy go further on that we might worship (lit. and we will worship) and we will return to you.

Verse 6

וַיִּקַּח אַבְרָהָם אֶת־עֲצֵי הָעֹלָה וַיָּשֶׂם עַל־יִצְחָק בְּנוֹ וַיִּקַּח בְּיָדוֹ אֶת־הָאֵשׁ
וְאֶת־הַמַּאֲכֶלֶת וַיֵּלְכוּ שְׁנֵיהֶם יַחְדָּו :

וַיִּקַּח אַבְרָהָם אֶת־עֲצֵי הָעֹלָה

This phrase should be fairly simple to translate. The verb is VC Imperfect 3ms.

וַיָּשֶׂם עַל־יִצְחָק בְּנוֹ

The verb is VC Imperfect 3ms from שִׂים. The word עַל is a preposition and בְּנוֹ is the noun בֵּן with a pronominal suffix 3ms.

וַיִּקַּח בְּיָדוֹ אֶת־הָאֵשׁ וְאֶת־הַמַּאֲכֶלֶת

The subject of the verb is still Abraham. בְּיָדוֹ is the preposition בְּ, the noun יָד and the pronominal suffix 3ms.

וַיֵּלְכוּ שְׁנֵיהֶם יַחְדָּו

The verb is VC Imperfect 3mp. שְׁנֵיהֶם is the number שְׁנַיִם with a pronominal suffix 3mp and means *both*.

Possible translation of Verse 6

And Abraham took the wood for the burnt offering and he put it on Isaac his son but he himself carried the fire and the knife, and the two of them went on together.

18.6 Suggestion

- Read a commentary on Genesis 22:1–8. We are looking almost exclusively at matters of biblical Hebrew grammar in this book, but there are many other interesting features of the text that are addressed in commentaries. Ideally you should read two or three commentaries on Genesis that discuss the Hebrew; some commentaries discuss only an English translation. It is highly likely that as you read you will find points at which other scholars translate substantially differently from the way we have been translating in this book. There are reasons why some ways of translating may be considered more appropriate than others (it often depends on the purpose of the translation), and you may find you have a preference for a particular style of translating. The advantage of becoming familiar with the Hebrew text is that you will be able to understand nuances of language that were previously out of reach. The purpose of this book is to give you the tools to go forward towards a more in-depth exploration of the biblical texts, and as you learn more you will find your own interpretive voice.

18.7 Summary

In this unit we have looked at

- the Hifil and Hofal stems, which are causative
- ways of recognizing verbs in the various stems
- the text of Genesis 22:1–6.

19.1 Dictionaries and lexicons

The work we have done on texts so far has included vocabulary lists, but of course when you come to read other passages in the Bible you will need to look up unknown words yourself. There are two kinds of books for looking up words in biblical Hebrew: lexicons and dictionaries. Anyone who wishes to read the biblical texts in Hebrew will need to be able to use a dictionary or lexicon. Since using a Hebrew–English dictionary is rather more complicated than using, say, a Spanish–English dictionary, we will do a bit of practising.

Dictionaries tend to give plenty of information about a word, such as examples of usage. Lexicons tend simply to give definitions. Having said that, some books that call themselves lexicons give a great deal of information about the words they list, and some books that call themselves dictionaries are lists of equivalent words, which can actually be very useful if the word you want is listed and if you do not need to have the forms analysed.

Obviously it helps if you can remember the order of the alphabet. If you have forgotten (and admittedly we have not looked at it since the beginning of the book), now might be a good time to refresh your memory.

Another problem that might have occurred to you is this: how can we speak of 'alphabetical order' when we are talking about a language whose alphabet consists only of consonants? What happens to the vowels? Do we look for שָׁמֹר before or after שָׁמַר?

In fact this is not as big a problem as we might imagine. There are only a few words in biblical Hebrew that use exactly the same consonants as other words. And since vowels are used in dictionaries and lexicons of biblical Hebrew, there is an order to the vowels as well. So if you look up שְׁמֹר (Qal Impv ms or Qal Inf Cstr) you will find it somewhere between שָׁמֹר (Qal Inf Abs) and שֹׁמֵר (Qal Ptc ms). But if you look up אֶשְׁמָר there will be no such problem because no other word in biblical Hebrew is spelled with the consonants אשמר. The majority of words in biblical Hebrew have unique consonantal spellings, so the task is simpler than we might have expected. So in a dictionary you might see:

שְׁמִקְרֶה

שָׁמַר

שָׁמֵר

שָׁמֵר

שָׁמֹר

שְׁמֹר

שְׁמֵר

שֹׁמֵר

שְׁמָרָה

There are seven words here with the same consonants but different vowels. You are unlikely to encounter a set of consonants with more than seven vowel possibilities. If you are looking up שְׁמֹר you should be able to find it without problems. Can you find it in the list above?

Although the order of the vowels in a lexicon is not usually a problem, it is important to remember that some vowels are written with consonants: י and יִ and ו and וּ. In a dictionary or lexicon these consonants are treated as full consonants rather than as mere vowel-placers. For example, in words with a ו vowel (e.g. שָׁמוֹר), the *vav* will be treated as a consonant, but where long *o* is written without *vav* (e.g. שָׁמֹר) it will be treated as a vowel. This means that you will not find שָׁמוֹר next to שָׁמֹר even though they are essentially the same word: they are pronounced the same way and mean the same thing (they are both Qal Inf Abs from שָׁמַר). Instead you will find שָׁמוֹר between שְׁמוּעָה and שָׁמוֹת, which are both spelled with ו:

שְׁמוּעָה

שָׁמוֹר

שָׁמוֹת

How do you choose a dictionary? It can depend on what you need. Some dictionaries and lexicons have the majority of words listed after the root they come from. For example:

שָׁמַר

QAL Impf 3ms יִשְׁמֹר, Inf שְׁמֹר, Impv ms שְׁמֹר, Ptc שֹׁמֵר: *to hedge about, to guard, to watch, to keep*. NIFAL Perf נִשְׁמַר, Impf הִשָּׁמֵר: *to be kept*. PIEL Ptc מְשַׁמֵּר: *to worship, to honour*. HITPAEL הִשְׁתַּמֵּר: *to observe*.

This is a good basic indication of the meanings of שָׁמַר in the various verbal stems that you might encounter in biblical Hebrew. This is fine if you are good at working out which root a word comes from, and often it is straightforward enough. If you want to look up the word יִקְטֹל you can probably guess that it is an imperfect from קָטַל and look up קָטַל to find the meaning.

But it might be less obvious in other cases. Which roots do the following words come from? Can you guess? Or perhaps remember? These words can be found in previous units of this book, so they might be familiar.

וַיִּשָּׂא

וַיָּשֶׂם

נָתַתִּי

וַיַּעַשׂ

קַח

Clearly, the kind of arrangement described above is ideal for those with advanced Hebrew but can be a little difficult for beginners to use. For example, if you are working on Micah 6:16 and you see the word וְיִשְׁתַּמֵּר, you may recognize it as a Hitpael form, and remember the letter-swapping that occurs in Hitpael forms of roots that begin with *s* sounds. So you would know that you should look up the word under שָׁמַר to see if it has a special meaning in the Hitpael. But what if you didn't remember? How would you find out what וְיִשְׁתַּמֵּר meant?

In my view, the easiest kind of book for beginners to use is a lexicon that lists all the words in the Hebrew Bible in order. This kind of book is sometimes called an analytical lexicon. In an analytical lexicon you will be able to look up any word in exactly the form in which it appears in the text. Note, however, that a great many words begin with the definite article ה or the conjunction ו, or even both. It is generally assumed that you can recognize these and that you do not need to look up הַמֶּלֶךְ under ה or וַיִּשְׁמֹר under ו. Look them up under מ and י respectively.

There are some disadvantages to using an analytical lexicon. Meanings are not usually given for each and every form; it usually points you to the root instead, so you may need to look up the root to understand the meaning.

For example

יִשְׁתַּמֵּר   Hit Impf 3ms שָׁמַר

The explanation means: Hitpael Imperfect 3rd person masculine singular from the root שָׁמַר.

If you look up שָׁמַר you will see that the Hitpael means *to observe*. Next, you need to determine how to translate Impf 3ms. 3ms is effectively *he*, and Imperfect is frequently translated with an English future tense. So the Hit Impf 3ms is likely to mean *he will observe*. But of course the form in the text of Micah is *Vav Consecutive*, so you would probably translate *he observed*.

Here are the five words above for which you were asked to guess the root:

וַיִּשָּׂא	Qal VC Impf 3ms	נָשָׂא
וַיָּשֶׂם	Qal VC Impf 3ms	שִׂים
נָתַתִּי	Qal Perf 1s	נָתַן
וַיַּעַשׂ	Qal VC Impf apoc	עָשָׂה
קַח	Qal Impv 2ms	לָקַח

There is a lexicon at the back of this book that you can use for practice. It has far fewer words in it that a full-size lexicon of biblical Hebrew. Most of the words found in this book can be found in the lexicon at the back. Once you get used to the way it works you will be ready to use a full lexicon.

Look at the abbreviations on the first page of the lexicon to ensure you understand the analysis of the forms. Bear in mind that there can sometimes be grey areas. For example, some dictionaries might say that שֹׁמֵר is a noun; others might say it is a Qal Participle. Participles are often used as nouns (see Unit 14), so it could be either.

In addition to listing all forms in alphabetical order, analytical lexicons will often list some of the most common forms under a main entry. Here is an example:

אָנֵשׁ	verb	*to be mortal*
אֲנָשִׁים	noun mp	*men*
אַנְשֵׁי	noun mp cstr	*men of*
אִשָּׁה	noun fs	*woman*
אֵשֶׁת	noun fs cstr	*woman of, wife of*
נָשִׁים	noun fp	*women*
נְשֵׁי	noun fp cstr	*women of*
אִשְׁתּוֹ	noun fs + suff 3ms	*his wife*

The words will usually be listed separately in alphabetical order, so that for example you could find נָשִׁים and נְשֵׁי under נ.

19.2 Exercise 1

There are still a number of words we have encountered in biblical texts whose form we have not identified. Here is a list of the words. Using the lexicon at the back of this book, identify them and give suggested meanings. A few examples are given: look these up first to ensure you know how to find things. Remember that words beginning with the definite article ה or the conjunction ו (including VC forms) will be found listed without those particles.

Try to give a possible meaning for each word you look up. Meaning will sometimes depend on context, but you should have a basic idea of the meaning from the information given in the lexicon.

WORD	FORM	ROOT	MEANING
דְּבָרֶיךָ	noun ms + suff 2ms	דָּבָר	*your words*
בְּדֶרֶךְ	prep בְּ + noun ms	דֶּרֶךְ	*in the way/path*
וְהַמֶּלֶךְ	Conj ו + def art + noun ms	מֶלֶךְ	*and the king*
פָּקַדְתִּי	Piel Perf 1s	פָּקַד	*I have mustered*
וַתִּשְׁלַח	Qal Impf 2ms	שָׁלַח	*and you sent/ stretched out*

a) נוֹדַע	Unit 6	_____	_____	_____
b) וְהַנּוֹרָא	Unit 9	_____	_____	_____
c) מְבֹרָךְ	Unit 10	_____	_____	_____
d) וּתְנַחֲמֵנִי	Unit 12	_____	_____	_____
e) אֲסַפְּרָה	Unit 13	_____	_____	_____
f) נִפְלְאוֹתֶיךָ	Unit 13	_____	_____	_____
g) אֲזַמְּרָה	Unit 13	_____	_____	_____
h) יִכָּשְׁלוּ	Unit 13	_____	_____	_____
i) אִבַּדְתָּ	Unit 13	_____	_____	_____
j) כּוֹנֵן	Unit 13	_____	_____	_____
k) וְנִפְקְחוּ	Unit 14	_____	_____	_____
l) דִּבֶּר	Unit 15	_____	_____	_____
m) הַגּוֹלָד	Unit 15	_____	_____	_____
n) צֻוָּה	Unit 15	_____	_____	_____
o) בְּהִוָּלֶד	Unit 15	_____	_____	_____
p) מָלַל	Unit 16	_____	_____	_____
q) גֵּרֵשׁ	Unit 16	_____	_____	_____

19.3 Commentaries

Sometimes looking up words in a dictionary is not quite enough to grasp the sense of the text. There are points where the grammar seems unusual or the words do not appear to fit together coherently. Some passages have puzzled readers for centuries; other passages are sometimes seen as ambiguous and readers have debated their true meaning.

Commentaries are books that discuss the meaning of the biblical text. They often confine themselves to one or two books of the Bible: for example a commentary on Genesis or a commentary on Ezra and Nehemiah. There are some commentaries on the whole Bible, but they tend to be less detailed than commentaries on single books.

Interpreting the text is an ancient phenomenon. We can see this in one of the most significant archaeological finds of the 20th century: the Dead Sea Scrolls. Some of the scrolls are biblical texts; some are other writings, including interpretive scrolls known as Pesherim (*pesher* means interpretation). It is widely believed that the scrolls were written about two thousand years ago, and the story of their discovery is legendary. They were found by shepherds in 1947 in a cave near the Dead Sea, just as Palestine was on the verge of being partitioned prior to the decision to create the state of Israel. One of the first three scrolls found in the caves was a *pesher*, or commentary, on the biblical book of Habakkuk. Here is an example of the kind of commentary practised centuries ago.

First, the text of Habakkuk 1:6 as we find it in the Hebrew Bible:

כִּי־הִנְנִי מֵקִים אֶת־הַכַּשְׂדִּים הַגּוֹי הַמַּר וְהַנִּמְהָר לְמֶרְחֲבֵי־אֶרֶץ לָרֶשֶׁת מִשְׁכָּנוֹת לֹא־לוֹ:

Translation:

For behold, I am raising up the Chaldeans, the bitter and impetuous nation, to expand across the earth and to seize dwellings that do not belong to them.

| כִּי־הִנְנִי | *For behold (me)* |
| מֵקִים | *raising up* (Hif Ptc קוּם) Hif: *to cause to rise* |

אֶת־הַכַּשְׂדִים	*the Chaldeans*. According to Genesis 22:22, Kesed (כֶּשֶׂד) is a son of Nahor, Abraham's brother. He is the ancestor of the Chaldeans. The Chaldeans were the people who lived in Babylon.
הַגּוֹי הַמַּר וְהַנִּמְהָר	*the nation the bitter and the impetuous*. The word מַר is an adjective from מָרַר, *to be bitter*. The word נִמְהָר is a Nif Ptc from מָהַר, *to be quick*.
לְמֶרְחֲבֵי־אֶרֶץ	*to expand (on) the earth*. The word לְמֶרְחֲבֵי is the preposition + Hif Inf Cstr from רָחַב, to be wide (Hif: *to enlarge oneself, to expand*)
לָרֶשֶׁת	to inherit Qal Inf Cstr יָרַשׁ, *to seize, to inherit*. Remember that infinitive constructs of *pe yod* verbs are often monosyllabic: they lose the initial י.
מִשְׁכָּנוֹת	*dwelling*: noun fp from שָׁכַן, *to lie down, rest, inhabit*. This noun often means the temple or the sacred dwelling place of God.
לֹא־לוֹ	*not to him*. The preposition ל is used here to indicate possession. The suffix is 3ms rather than 3mp because it agrees grammatically with הַגּוֹי, which is ms. However, in English we would probably say *to them*.

From this vantage point we can look at the Habakkuk *pesher*. In column 2 we find:

line 10   ....יא הנני מקים את

line 11   הכשדאים הגוי המ ...... הר

line 12   פשרו על הכתיאים א..... ה קלים וגבורים

line 13   במלחמה לאבד רכימ .... בממשלת

line 14   הכתיאים ירש.............ת ולוא יאמינו

line 15   .... בחוקי .. ל

It looks rather daunting at first. There are no vowels, there seem to be chunks of text missing (indicated by dots above), and even when we spot words we think we recognize they appear to be spelled differently. But if we place the text of the Hebrew Bible alongside the *pesher*, we should be able to spot a few similarities. Words in square brackets indicate material that is absent in the scroll. The scrolls are ancient and have been damaged, and there are many gaps in the text. However, there is also much that is thoroughly legible.

line 10   יא הנני מקים את

Hab   כִּי־הִנְנִי מֵקִים אֶת־

There seems to be a כ missing at the beginning of line 10, and an extra א in the word כִּי. Sometimes when words are spelled with an extra א it indicates that the text has been influenced by Aramaic spellings. Otherwise, the words of the *pesher* seem to correspond to the biblical text.

line 11   הכשדאים הגוי המ ...... הר

Hab   הַכַּשְׂדִּים הַגּוֹי הַמַּר וְהַנִּמְהָר

There are some missing letters where the scroll is torn, but nevertheless the phrase seems to be identical to the Hebrew Bible, although notice another extra א in הכשדאים.

line 12   פשרו על הכתיאים א..... ה קלים וגבורים

The quotation from Habakkuk has now finished, and the commentary begins. As there are no vowels, it is difficult for a beginner to read without help. But if you know the following words you may be able to make some sense of it:

interpretation	פֶּשֶׁר
Kittim (a nation)	כִּתִּיִּים
fast, light	קַל
strong, mighty	גִּבּוֹר

As in כשדאים, there is also an extra א in Kittim. So we get: *Its interpretation is concerning the Kittim* [.....] *fast and strong*

line 13   במלחמה לאבד רכים .... בממשלת

war, battle	מִלְחָמָה	from לָחַם *to fight*	
to destroy (Piel)	אִבֵּד		
dominion, reign	מֶמְשֶׁלֶת	from מָשַׁל *to rule*	

Thus: *in battle to destroy* [.....], *under the reign of*

line 14   הכתיאים ירש..............ת ולוא יאמינו

to trust, rely on (Hif)	אָמַן

Thus: *the Kittim* [.....] *and they will not trust*

line 15   בחוקי .. ל

ordinance, law	חֹק (cstr: חֻקֵי)

in the laws of [...]

There are quite a few gaps in our translation. So far our
translation of the column reads:

[*For*] *behold, I am raising up the Chaldeans, the* [*bitter and
impetuous*] *nation. Its interpretation is concerning the Kittim*
[.....] *fast and strong in battle to destroy* [.....]; *under the reign
of the Kittim* [.....] *and not trust in the laws of* [...]

Some scholars have attempted to fill in some of the blanks, based
on their knowledge of related texts and their ability to estimate
how much space the missing words would have taken up. Based
on their work, we can extrapolate that the text may have said
something like the following:

[*For*] *behold, I am raising up the Chaldeans, the* [*bitter and
impetuous*] *nation. Its interpretation is concerning the Kittim*
[*who are*] *fast and strong in battle to destroy* [*many people*].
Under the reign of the Kittim [*they will turn away from the way
of the covenant*] *and not trust in the laws of* [*God.*]

You will notice that the commentator interprets the prophecy
about the Chaldeans as a reference to the Kittim. The next
question, of course, is the identity of the Kittim. The name

is used in biblical Hebrew to refer to peoples of the northern Mediterranean. Many scholars consider that the Kittim mentioned in the Habakkuk *pesher* are the Romans, based on the details of the comments and the dating of the scrolls. The interesting thing is that the *pesher* takes an old prophecy and gives it a fresh twist. Unfortunately, there is no space here to discuss the *pesher* at length, but this example at least demonstrates how ancient the tradition of biblical commentary is.

Modern commentaries usually fall into three categories. There are commentaries that seek to comment on devotional issues, commentaries that aim to comment on scholarly issues, and commentaries that try to do both. Some commentaries are written from a particular theological perspective and can be located within a particular tradition. For example, there are Catholic commentaries, Presbyterian commentaries and Jewish commentaries. Many people feel that it is important to look at commentaries from their own tradition, and readers in that position might like to consult a trusted community leader for suggestions and advice.

One aspect of commentary that is particularly useful for learners of Hebrew is a discussion of the grammar and translation of the text. Some commentaries do not discuss the Hebrew text at all. While such commentaries may be useful in many ways, they will not usually be very helpful in understanding the Hebrew. If you can find a commentary that discusses the meaning and interpretation of the Hebrew text you will find it easier to grasp what is at stake in contested, difficult or ambiguous passages.

19.4 Exercise 2

Here are the first three verses of the text. Identify unknown forms and look them up in the lexicon. You will be able to compare your findings with the notes below to see if you are right.

וַיֹּאמֶר יִצְחָק אֶל־אַבְרָהָם אָבִיו וַיֹּאמֶר אָבִי וַיֹּאמֶר הִנֶּנִּי בְנִי וַיֹּאמֶר הִנֵּה הָאֵשׁ וְהָעֵצִים וְאַיֵּה הַשֶּׂה לְעֹלָה :

וַיֹּאמֶר אַבְרָהָם אֱלֹהִים יִרְאֶה־לּוֹ הַשֶּׂה לְעֹלָה בְּנִי וַיֵּלְכוּ שְׁנֵיהֶם יַחְדָּו :

וַיָּבֹאוּ אֶל־הַמָּקוֹם אֲשֶׁר אָמַר־לוֹ הָאֱלֹהִים וַיִּבֶן שָׁם אַבְרָהָם אֶת־הַמִּזְבֵּחַ וַיַּעֲרֹךְ אֶת־הָעֵצִים וַיַּעֲקֹד אֶת־יִצְחָק בְּנוֹ וַיָּשֶׂם אֹתוֹ עַל־הַמִּזְבֵּחַ מִמַּעַל לָעֵצִים :

19.5 Text: Genesis 22:7–12

Verses 10–12

verb: *to kill, to slaughter, to cut* שָׁחַט

pronoun: *anything* מְאוּמָה

adverb: *now* עַתָּה

verb: *to hold back, restrain* חָשַׂךְ

It is still important to read each verse aloud a few times to be sure of the pronunciation.

Verse 7

וַיֹּאמֶר יִצְחָק אֶל־אַבְרָהָם אָבִיו וַיֹּאמֶר אָבִי וַיֹּאמֶר הִנֶּנִּי בְנִי וַיֹּאמֶר הִנֵּה
הָאֵשׁ וְהָעֵצִים וְאַיֵּה הַשֶּׂה לְעֹלָה :

וַיֹּאמֶר יִצְחָק אֶל־אַבְרָהָם אָבִיו וַיֹּאמֶר אָבִי

Most of this phrase should be familiar territory. אָבִיו is אָב with a pronominal suffix 3ms; it looks a little like a plural form because of the י but in fact it is an irregular noun (see Unit 4, where the plurals of irregular nouns are given).

וַיֹּאמֶר הִנֶּנִּי בְנִי

The word הִנֶּנִּי is הִנֵּה with pronominal suffix 1s and could be translated *behold me* but as in verse 1 might be better translated *here I am* or even *yes*. בְנִי is בֵּן with pronominal suffix 3ms.

וַיֹּאמֶר הִנֵּה הָאֵשׁ וְהָעֵצִים וְאַיֵּה הַשֶּׂה לְעֹלָה

This phrase should be fairly straightforward. Remember that וְ can mean *but*.

Possible translation of Verse 7

And Isaac said to Abraham his father, 'Father,' and he said, 'Yes, my son?' And he said 'Behold the fire and the wood, but where is the lamb for the sacrifice?'

Verse 8

וַיֹּאמֶר אַבְרָהָם אֱלֹהִים יִרְאֶה־לּוֹ הַשֶּׂה לְעֹלָה בְּנִי וַיֵּלְכוּ שְׁנֵיהֶם יַחְדָּו :

אֱלֹהִים יִרְאֶה־לּוֹ הַשֶּׂה לְעֹלָה בְּנִי

The verb יִרְאֶה is Imperfect 3ms of רָאָה, which often means *to see* but can also mean *to provide*, as in this context. The use of the preposition לְ with a pronominal suffix is another construction like וַתֵּשֶׁב לָהּ in Genesis 21:16. Literally this means: *God will provide for himself the lamb for the burnt offering, my son.*

וַיֵּלְכוּ שְׁנֵיהֶם יַחְדָּו

This is the same as the last three words of verse 6.

Possible translation of Verse 8

And Abraham said, 'God himself will provide the lamb for an offering, my son.' And the two of them went on together.

Verse 9

וַיָּבֹאוּ אֶל־הַמָּקוֹם אֲשֶׁר אָמַר־לוֹ הָאֱלֹהִים וַיִּבֶן שָׁם אַבְרָהָם אֶת־הַמִּזְבֵּחַ וַיַּעֲרֹךְ אֶת־הָעֵצִים וַיַּעֲקֹד אֶת־יִצְחָק בְּנוֹ וַיָּשֶׂם אֹתוֹ עַל־הַמִּזְבֵּחַ מִמַּעַל לָעֵצִים :

וַיָּבֹאוּ אֶל־הַמָּקוֹם אֲשֶׁר אָמַר־לוֹ הָאֱלֹהִים

The first verb is the VC Impf 3mp of בּוֹא. Since it is a hollow verb, it is not constructed like קָטַל. We could translate אֲשֶׁר *about which* or *where*; the phrase is literally: *to the place which he said to him God.*

וַיִּבֶן שָׁם אַבְרָהָם אֶת־הַמִּזְבֵּחַ וַיַּעֲרֹךְ אֶת־הָעֵצִים

The verb וַיִּבֶן is VC Imperfect 3ms shortened (apocopated) from בָּנָה. Remember that many *lamed he* verbs lose the final ה in the VC 3ms form. We saw שָׁם in Unit 10. וַיַּעֲרֹךְ is VC Impf 3ms from עָרַךְ.

וַיַּעֲקֹד אֶת־יִצְחָק בְּנוֹ

This story is sometimes known as the Aqedah or Akedah: *the binding*. The name comes from the verb עָקַד, found here in VC Impf 3ms. בְּנוֹ is the noun בֵּן with pronominal suffix 3ms.

וַיָּשֶׂם אֹתוֹ עַל־הַמִּזְבֵּחַ מִמַּעַל לָעֵצִים

The verb וַיָּשֶׂם is VC Impf 3ms from שִׂים, which is a hollow verb and therefore not formed like קָטַל. The word אֹתוֹ is an object pronoun (see Unit 15). The phrase מִמַּעַל לָעֵצִים is literally: *above to the wood*.

Possible translation of Verse 9

And they came to the place where God had said, and Abraham built the altar there and he laid the wood and he bound Isaac his son and placed him on the altar above the wood.

Verse 10

וַיִּשְׁלַח אַבְרָהָם אֶת־יָדוֹ וַיִּקַּח אֶת־הַמַּאֲכֶלֶת לִשְׁחֹט אֶת־בְּנוֹ :

יִשְׁלַח אַבְרָהָם אֶת־יָדוֹ

The verb שָׁלַח can mean *to send* or to *stretch out*. The second meaning is probably more appropriate here. The verb is a fairly straightforward VC Impf 3ms. This is a classic example of Hebrew sentence structure: the verb comes first, followed by the subject and then the object. יָדוֹ is the noun יָד with pronominal suffix 3ms.

וַיִּקַּח אֶת־הַמַּאֲכֶלֶת לִשְׁחֹט אֶת־בְּנוֹ

The verb וַיִּקַּח is VC Impf 3ms from לָקַח; remember that לָקַח behaves like a *pe yod* verb in the Imperfect. The word לִשְׁחֹט is the Infinitive Construct of שָׁחַט and the Infinitive Construct is being used here in the sense of *to cut* or *to kill*.

Possible translation of Verse 10

Abraham stretched out his hand and took the knife to slaughter his son.

Verse 11

וַיִּקְרָא אֵלָיו מַלְאַךְ יְהוָה מִן־הַשָּׁמַיִם וַיֹּאמֶר אַבְרָהָם אַבְרָהָם וַיֹּאמֶר הִנֵּנִי :

וַיִּקְרָא אֵלָיו מַלְאַךְ יְהוָה מִן־הַשָּׁמַיִם

The verb וַיִּקְרָא is VC Impf 3ms from קָרָא. The ו here should probably be translated *but* rather than *and*. אֵלָיו is the preposition אֶל with pronominal suffix 3ms. It looks like a plural form because of the י but is in fact singular (see Unit 9). In Genesis

21 the calling was done by מַלְאַךְ אֱלֹהִים but here it is מַלְאַךְ יְהוָה. Again, we translate *the angel* rather than *an angel* because יְהוָה is definite, and that makes מַלְאַךְ definite (see Unit 7).

וַיֹּאמֶר אַבְרָהָם אַבְרָהָם וַיֹּאמֶר הִנֵּנִי

At first glance is may be difficult to know who is the subject of וַיֹּאמֶר. We are becoming used to seeing the verb וַיֹּאמֶר followed by the subject. However, it does not really make sense here for the subject of וַיֹּאמֶר to be אַבְרָהָם. The subject of the verb is more likely the angel, and the word וַיֹּאמֶר is followed by direct speech. Again, הִנֵּנִי can be translated *behold me* but in today's English might be better translated *here I am*.

Possible translation of Verse 11

But the angel of Yhwh spoke to him from heaven and he said, 'Abraham, Abraham.' And he said, 'Here I am.'

Verse 12

וַיֹּאמֶר אַל־תִּשְׁלַח יָדְךָ אֶל־הַנַּעַר וְאַל־תַּעַשׂ לוֹ מְאוּמָה כִּי עַתָּה יָדַעְתִּי
כִּי־יְרֵא אֱלֹהִים אַתָּה וְלֹא חָשַׂכְתָּ אֶת־בִּנְךָ אֶת־יְחִידְךָ מִמֶּנִּי :

וַיֹּאמֶר אַל־תִּשְׁלַח יָדְךָ אֶל־הַנַּעַר

The subject of the verb is the angel again. He issues a prohibition: אַל־תִּשְׁלַח. The verb תִּשְׁלַח is therefore a Jussive 2ms from שָׁלַח, though like so many Jussives it is spelled exactly the same as the Imperfect. יָדְךָ is the noun יָד with pronominal suffix 2ms. The preposition אֶל often means *to* but when used with שָׁלַח it means *against*. In biblical Hebrew, *to stretch out one's hand against* is an idiomatic way of saying *to injure* or *to harm*.

וְאַל־תַּעַשׂ לוֹ מְאוּמָה

This is another prohibition and therefore another Jussive: תַּעַשׂ is Jussive 2ms from עָשָׂה and just like the Imperfect of עָשָׂה it is often shortened: the final ה disappears.

כִּי עַתָּה יָדַעְתִּי כִּי־יְרֵא אֱלֹהִים אַתָּה

The first כִּי here is used in the sense of *because*; the second כִּי means *that*. עַתָּה is the word for *now* and should not be confused with אַתָּה meaning *you* (also found in this phrase). יָדַעְתִּי is a rather straightforward Perfect 3ms from יָדַע. The verb is a participle from יָרֵא. It is doubly weak because it is both *pe yod* and *lamed alef*, and so does not have the characteristic vowel pattern of the Participle (see Unit 14). Literally it could mean *you are fearing God* or *you are a fearer of God* but neither phrase is ideal in English. We might be better off translating simply *you fear God*.

וְלֹא חָשַׂכְתָּ אֶת־בִּנְךָ אֶת־יְחִידְךָ מִמֶּנִּי

The phrase וְלֹא חָשַׂכְתָּ might look like a Jussive after the Jussives earlier in this verse. However, the Jussive is formed like an Imperfect, and חָשַׂכְתָּ is a Perfect 2ms from חָשַׂךְ, so it cannot be Jussive. The phrase אֶת־בִּנְךָ אֶת־יְחִידְךָ was found in verse 2. The word מִמֶּנִּי is the preposition מִן with pronominal suffix 2ms (see Unit 9).

Possible translation of Verse 12

And he said, 'Do not injure the boy. And do not do anything to him, for now I know that you fear God and you did not hold back your only son from me.'

19.6 Suggestions

- Read commentaries on Genesis 22:7–12. This passage has received a great deal of theological, scholarly and artistic attention, and it should be interesting to read some of the things that have been written about it.

- Make sure you have learned the verb forms in the Qal for the verbs following the קָטַל model, and also the Qal Perfects and Imperfects of the weak verbs. If you are thoroughly familiar with the Qal forms, it will be easier to recognize other stems. There is a verb table on pages 293–6. Most people find it easiest to recite the Perfect by rote, followed by the Imperfect, and so on. Another method is to copy the list on to a series of flash cards with the name of the list on the back (e.g. Qal Perfect double *ayin* verbs). The verb table is not exhaustive, but provides most of the basic verbal forms.

- For extra practice with verb stems, look again at the verbs in Exercise 1. Make sure you understand exactly why the verb form is spelled that way. For example, look at נוֹדַע. You now know it is a Nifal Participle from יָדַע. Write the Nifal Participle of קָטַל next to it. Then look at the Nifal Participles of *pe yod* verbs and *lamed* guttural verbs, since יָדַע is doubly weak. You should be able to see how this form deviates from the קָטַל model and why. For example:

| Verb | יָדַע | קָטַל | שָׁלַח | יָשַׁב |
| Nif Ptc | נוֹדָע | נִקְטָל | נִשְׁלָח | נוֹשָׁב |

- The long-*a* vowel in the second syllable of נוֹדָע is clearly typical of Nifal Participles in most verbs, but the long-*o* vowel in the first syllable is a mark of Nifal Participles in *pe yod* verbs. However, there can be irregularities of spelling, so this exercise is not absolutely guaranteed to shed light on every form.

19.7 Summary

In this unit we have looked at

- using dictionaries and lexicons
- using commentaries
- the text of Genesis 22:7–12.

20.1 Sources and versions

It might come as a surprise to learn that the text you find in a Hebrew Bible is not replicated from manuscripts that are more than two thousand years old, or at least, not directly. One might imagine that manuscripts as important as the biblical texts would have been carefully preserved from antiquity and be available today in museums and libraries. However, the traditions of handling sacred texts did not permit them to be preserved after their useful life was over. If a scroll was damaged by accident or through wear and tear, it could become difficult to read accurately and could no longer be used. Unusable scrolls had to be buried. For this reason, and others, it is difficult to find very old manuscripts of the books of the Hebrew Bible.

Biblical texts were copied carefully by hand from earlier scrolls. The text we read today has been transmitted from ancient texts, even though we do not have the ancient manuscripts to look at. However, it was possible for some mistakes to be made during the copying, and the early manuscripts we have are not all precisely identical.

Today, most Hebrew Bibles that we can find in book stores and libraries are printed versions of the Masoretic Text (MT), which was compiled between the seventh and tenth centuries of the Common Era (CE). This was when the practice of writing vowels underneath the consonants became widespread; prior to the Masoretic Text, biblical Hebrew was written without vowels. The oldest manuscript we have of the Masoretic Text is about 1,100 years old. Some fragments of more ancient manuscripts have been preserved, but in general they are rather short.

The Masoretes, scholars who produced the Masoretic text, fixed not only the vowels, but also the divisions into books and chapters and verses. They standardized spelling and pronunciation, and they added cantillation marks: symbols that indicate how the texts should be read or sung. We have not looked at cantillation marks in this book because it is generally possible to understand the meaning of biblical Hebrew without knowing them. However, for reading aloud during public worship it would be important to learn them.

Interestingly enough, there are translations of the Hebrew texts that are much older than extant Hebrew manuscripts. One example is the Septuagint (an early Greek version, written LXX for short), which gets its name from the tradition that seventy translators arrived at identical versions. There are places where it differs from the Masoretic Text. We saw one example of this in Genesis 21:9 (unit 16). The earliest manuscripts we have of the Septuagint date from the fourth century CE, though the translation itself is usually dated about six centuries earlier.

Other early translations are the Targumim. Targum (Tg) means translation, and the Targumim are translations of the biblical texts into Aramaic, which was the language commonly spoken in the ancient Near East around two thousand years ago. It is closely related to Hebrew; however, not closely related enough, apparently, for speakers of Aramaic to understand biblical Hebrew perfectly, since the reason given for the existence of the Targumim is that worshippers no longer understood the Hebrew of the scrolls. Some of the Targumim follow the Hebrew very closely; others seem to provide additional commentary on the text.

A little later, around the fourth century CE, the LXX, Targumim and Hebrew manuscripts were sources for a translation of the biblical texts into Syriac, a dialect of Aramaic, and the language spoken in much of the Middle East from about the second to seventh centuries CE. This translation is known as the Peshitta (P), which means common or simple, and is still used in some Middle Eastern Christian communities today.

And of course, as we saw in Unit 19, since the discovery of the Dead Sea Scrolls we now have a further set of texts with which to work. The Dead Sea Scrolls are particularly interesting because the biblical texts sometimes agree with the LXX rather than the MT, as one might expect. They provide evidence of very early sources that differ somewhat from the tradition that led to the

MT. They are also some of the earliest manuscripts we have of the biblical texts.

All of these, the MT, the LXX, the Tg, the Peshitta and the Dead Sea Scrolls, are considered particularly valuable as sources that can be read alongside one another to help understand the meaning of the text. This is why in English translations some passages may follow the LXX rather than the MT.

It can be uncomfortable to deal with the idea of so many sources for the Bible. It might sound to some readers as if there are dozens of different Bibles going around; how can we know which is the correct one? It can, of course, feel a little threatening. Perhaps a more comfortable way to look at it is to acknowledge that there are numerous texts that can help us to understand better what the texts really mean.

Look at the following examples from manuscripts of 2 Samuel 1:5. They come from the Masoretic Text, Targum Jonathan, the Peshitta, a manuscript of Samuel from the Dead Sea Scrolls called 1QSam(a), and the Septuagint. It might be a good idea to read 2 Samuel 1 in English first, so that you have an idea of the context.

Syriac does not use the alphabet that we have learned for biblical Hebrew, but the Syriac of the Peshitta has been transliterated here into the familiar alphabet so that the similarities and differences can be seen. It was not possible to do the same with the Greek of the LXX, but it has been included for completeness, and for the sake of any readers who know some Greek.

The verses have been divided into columns to help you to compare the sections of the verse with the other versions.

MT:	מֵת שָׁאוּל וִיהוֹנָתָן בְּנוֹ:	אֵיךְ יָדַעְתָּ כִּי־	הַמַּגִּיד לוֹ	וַיֹּאמֶר דָּוִד אֶל־הַנַּעַר
TgJ:	מית שאול ויהונתן בריה:	איכדין ידעת ארי	דמחוי ליה	ואמר דויד לעולימא
P:	מיתו שאול ויונתן ברה:	איכנא	חוני	ואמר דויד לעלימא
1Q Sam (a):	מֵת שאול יהונתן בנו	אֵיךְ ידעת כּ־	המגיד לו	וַיאמר דוד אל־הנער

LXX και ειπεν δαυιδ τω παιδαριω τω απαγγελλοντι αυτω πως
οιδας οτι τεθνηκεν σαουλ και ιωναθαν ο υιος αυτου

Here are some possible translations of the above texts:

MT: *And David said to the young man* who told
        him, '*How do you know that Saul and his son
        Jonathan are dead?*'

TgJ: *And David said to the young man* who told
        him, '*How do you know that Saul and his son
        Jonathan are dead?*'

P: *And David said to the young man,* 'Tell me *how
        Saul and his son Jonathan* died.'

1QSam(a) *And David said to the young man* who told
        him, '*How do you know that Saul and his son
        Jonathan are dead?*'

LXX: *And David said to the boy* bringing the news,
        '*How* do you know that *Saul and his son
        Jonathan are dead?*'

The words in roman typeface indicate where the manuscripts
are at variance.

Here is some vocabulary so that you can compare the text with
the translations.

Pi Ptc	הַמַּגִּיד from נָגַד Pi: *to show, tell*. The initial is the definite article. Literal meaning of הַמַּגִּיד: *the one telling*	
adv:	אֵיךְ	*how?*
Qal Ptc:	מֵת	*dead*
noun ms:	עוּלֵים	*boy, young man*
relative:	ד	*who, which*
verb:	חוי	Pael (equiv of Heb Piel): *to show, tell*. The מ in דמחוי is a sign of the Ptc, as in Hebrew Piel.
adv:	אֵיכְדֵין	*how?*
conj:	אֲרֵי	*because, that*
noun ms:	בַר	*son* (equiv of Heb בֵּן)
adv:	אֵיכַן	*how?*

It can sometimes be helpful to look at other sources when the
MT is difficult to understand. For example, in 2 Samuel 1:8 the

Hebrew text of the MT may seem somewhat confused. The LXX is at variance with the MT, so we can see that (at least at one point in time) the text was understood slightly differently. (See below for a full discussion.) Many English translations of the Bible use the technique of comparing the MT with other versions such as the LXX when the text is difficult to understand.

20.2 Ketiv and Qere

Biblical manuscripts were copied by hand, and therefore it was possible for mistakes to be made in copying. When the Masoretes standardized the texts in about the ninth century, they did not want to edit the texts by replacing some words with other words. Instead, they made a note in the margin to indicate places where a different word might be appropriate. The word in the text remained in the written text, but when the text was read aloud the reader was supposed to use the word in the margin instead. They called the word in the text *Ketiv* (כְּתַב written) and the word in the margin *Qere* (קְרָא read).

To help with this process, the Masoretes wrote the vowel sounds of the Qere word underneath the consonants of the Ketiv word in the text. For example, in 2 Sam 1:8, The young man who brings news of Saul's death to David recounts his conversation with the deceased king:

וַיֹּאמֶר לִי מִי־אָתָּה וָיֹּאמַר אֵלָיו עֲמָלֵקִי אָנֹכִי

'He said to me, "Who are you?" and I said to him, "I am an Amalekite."'

The word וַיֹּאמֶר is the Ketiv. We might have expected to see it pointed וָיֹּאמַר, but in the margin (or in a footnote) there is a note: ואומר ק׳.

If the biblical text were written without vowels, a reader seeing the word ויאמר would probably be inclined to pronounce it *va-YŌ-mer*. With the vowels that have been added it looks as if one is expected to pronounce וָיֹּאמַר as *vā-YŌ-mar*. However, the note points us to the word ואומר which is pronounced *vā-ō-MAR*. And that is what the reader is expected to say out loud.

If we read the Ketiv instead of the Qere, the verse would read: 'He said to me, "Who are you?" and he said to him, "I am an Amalekite."' If we were to accept that reading, it would effectively indicate that the Amalekite was referring to himself as *he* rather than *I*, which would be unusual. And in fact, the LXX and the Peshitta both have a first-person verb here instead of the MT's third-person verb. So in this case, the MT appears to be preserving a variant reading that makes more sense than the received text.

The possibility of scribal errors is commonly given for the introduction of Qere readings, but in fact the situation may be more complicated that that. Some of the Qere words might testify to alternative manuscript traditions; others might indicate oral alternatives to the written text. Whatever the reason, the Qere words are now just as much a part of the received text as the Ketiv words; neither word is more correct, and neither word is incorrect. They simply co-exist peacefully.

In some cases, the vowels of the Qere reading are given without a footnote. For example, we have seen that the divine name יהוה is written with the vowels of אֲדֹנָי and it is always read *a-dōn-Ī* (see Unit 3). There is no need for a marginal note indicating the Qere of יהוה because it is always the same. Similarly, the pronoun הִיא (*she*) is often written הוא with a ו instead of a י. In a text without vowels, it is therefore identical to הוא meaning *he*. In order to distinguish between the two pronouns, the feminine is pointed with the *i* vowel of הִיא but the middle ו remains unchanged, thus: הִוא. The reader should not pronounce this word *heev* although it looks as if it should be pronounced that way. Instead, the reader is expected to know that הִוא is an alternate spelling of הִיא and say *hee*. Since this word is very common in the biblical text there is no marginal note. These examples are known as *Qere perpetuum*: they are always pronounced with a variation from the written text and do not require to be highlighted.

A great many occurrences of Qere readings do not significantly affect the meaning of the text. For example:

Job 42:2a   יָדַעְתָּ כִּי־כֹל תּוּכָל
Literally: *I know that all things you are able*; usually translated *I know that you can do all things*.

The Ketiv is יָדַעְתָּ. The Qere is יָדַעְתִּי and the only difference is the final י, which is how we would expect יָדַעְתִּי to be spelled.

20.3 Exercise 1

Here are some examples of Ketiv/Qere from the Bible. The words in bold are Ketiv. Work out how to read the verse using the vowels of the Ketiv and the consonants of the Qere. How would you fill in the blanks in the translations?

Qal Ptc	אֹרֵב	lying in wait
noun ms	אֲרִי	lion
adj cstr	גְּדָל־	great
adj	גְּרַל־	angry
noun ms	דֹּב	bear
Piel Perf 3ms	דִּבֶּר	he has spoken
noun fs	חֵמָה	heat, anger, poison, venom
Hif Impf 3ms	יָקֶם	Hif to raise, to confirm
pr noun	יְרוּשָׁלַיִם	Jerusalem
noun mp	מִסְתָּרִים	hiding places
Qal Ptc	נֹשֵׂא	lifting up, bearing
noun ms	עֹנֶשׁ	punishment

Ecclesiastes 4:17 שְׁמֹר **רַגְלֶיךָ** כַּאֲשֶׁר תֵּלֵךְ אֶל־בֵּית הָאֱלֹהִים

Guard _____ when you go to the house of God.

Qere רגלך ק׳

Daniel 9:12 וַיָּקֶם אֶת־**דְּבָרָיו** אֲשֶׁר־דִּבֶּר עָלֵינוּ

And he has confirmed _____ which he has spoken against us.

Qere דברו ק׳

Lamentations 3:10 דֹּב אֹרֵב הוּא לִי **אֲרִיה** בְּמִסְתָּרִים

To me he is a bear lying in wait; _____ in a hiding place.

Qere ארי ק׳

2 Chronicles 34:9   וַיָּשֻׁבִי יְרוּשָׁלָ͏ם

And _____ returned to Jerusalem.

Qere וישבו קי

Proverbs 19:19   גְּרָל־חֵמָה נֹשֵׂא עֹנֶשׁ

_____ anger will bear punishment

Qere גדל־ קי

(This last is very difficult to translate, so you are not expected to come up with a flawless translation. A suggestion will be sufficient.)

20.4 Accents and cantillation marks

Grammar: syllable and stress

A syllable is a sound that is part of a word. A word can have any number of syllables, and one of these syllables is stressed. For example:

one syllable	pal	PAL
two syllables	crystal	CRYS-tal
three syllables	denial	de-NI-al
four syllables	accidental	ac-ci-DEN-tal
five syllables	editorial	ed-i-TO-ri-al
six syllables	archaeological	ar-chae-o-LOG-i-cal

In some languages (e.g. Hungarian) the stress is always on the first syllable of a word, but in English, as you can see from the table above, the stress can occur in almost any syllable. In Hebrew the stress is usually on the last syllable of a word (e.g. סוּסָה *soo-SĀ*), but there are exceptions.

Some (though not all) Hebrew Bibles contain not only vowels but also accents and cantillation marks. These indicate how the text is to be read or sung. There are a great many of them, but for the purposes of private reading it is not necessary to understand or distinguish the cantillation marks. However, it may be useful to know that they can indicate where the stress comes in each word. For example:

without cantillation marks   בְּרֵאשִׁית בָּרָא אֱלֹהִים אֵת Genesis 1:1
הַשָּׁמַיִם וְאֵת הָאָרֶץ:

with cantillation marks   בְּרֵאשִׁית בָּרָא אֱלֹהִים אֵת Genesis 1:1
הַשָּׁמַיִם וְאֵת הָאָרֶץ:

As you can see, the marks indicate the places where the stress of each word can be found. In each of the first three words the stress is in the final syllable:

b^a-ray-SHEET   בְּרֵאשִׁית

bā-RĀ   בָּרָא

elō-HEEM   אֱלֹהִים

The word אֵת does not have a stress: it is read as if it were part of the next word. In this case the next word is הַשָּׁמַיִם, with the stress on the second-to-last syllable.

ayt ha-shā-MĪ-yim   אֵת הַשָּׁמַיִם

That is the usual pattern for nouns with dual endings: the same is the true of יָדַיִם hands, רַגְלַיִם feet, מַיִם water and so on. They are pronounced yā-DĪ-yim, rag-LĪ-yim and MĪ-yim respectively.

This time there is a stress in אֵת, because it has the conjunction ו in front of it. So the stress is on the second syllable of the word.

v^a-AYT   וְאֵת

The stress in הָאָרֶץ is on the second-to-last syllable because it is a segolate noun, like מֶלֶךְ (ME-lech) and נַעַר (NA-ar). These are outlined in Unit 16.

hā-ĀR-ets   הָאָרֶץ

Look again at the text of Genesis 1:1

בְּרֵאשִׁית בָּרָא אֱלֹהִים אֵת הַשָּׁמַיִם וְאֵת הָאָרֶץ:

Notice the wishbone-shaped mark under the ה of אֱלֹהִים. It is called *atnah* and it indicates that the reader should pause at this word, a little like the way a comma is used in English. You will usually see *atnah* underneath a word near the middle of a verse in the Bible.

The last word contains a small accent called *silluq*, which is the little line next to the second vowel in הָאָרֶץ. *Silluq* indicates that the reader should make a slightly longer pause than the pause at atnah. You will usually see silluq underneath the last word of a verse in the Bible. It functions a little like a full stop in English.

There is one other accent that is useful to know. It is called *meteg* and looks exactly like *silluq*. If you see it next to a ָ , it indicates that the vowel ָ is to be pronounced as a long-*a* vowel, rather than a short-*o* vowel. For example:

she has visited   פָּקְדָה   is pronounced *pāk-DĀH* and not *pok-DĀH*.

Of course, in some accents, these vowels are indistinguishable. Moreover, *meteg* is not found with every long-*a* vowel. It is only found where the structure of the word is such that an experienced reader might expect a short-*o* vowel instead of a long-*a* vowel. In general, it is best for beginners to assume that ָ is pronounced with a long-*a* vowel unless directed otherwise.

Knowing about these accents and about the cantillation marks can make it easier for us to read the biblical texts aloud, and can even help our understanding. If you incorrectly pronounce a word that you have seen before, you might have trouble recognizing it by its sound. If you pronounce it correctly, it should sound familiar.

If you are wondering why we did not learn about accents and cantillation marks from the beginning, the answer is this: a great many learners of biblical Hebrew find it complicated enough to learn a new alphabet which reads from right to left and whose vowels are found beneath the consonants. Learning cantillation marks and accents in the early stages can cause confusion and lead to discouragement.

20.5 Exercise 2

Here are some of the verses that we examined in previous units. Look through them carefully and mark each of the stressed syllables with a circle.

Psalm 25:8	טֽוֹב־וְיָשָׁ֥ר יְהוָ֑ה עַל־כֵּ֤ן יוֹרֶ֖ה חַטָּאִ֣ים בַּדָּֽרֶךְ׃
2 Samuel 12:7a	וַיֹּ֧אמֶר נָתָ֛ן אֶל־דָּוִ֖ד אַתָּ֥ה הָאִ֑ישׁ
Psalm 76:2	נוֹדָ֣ע בִּֽיהוּדָ֣ה אֱלֹהִ֑ים בְּיִשְׂרָאֵ֖ל גָּד֥וֹל שְׁמֽוֹ׃
Exodus 15:1a	אָ֣ז יָשִֽׁיר־מֹשֶׁה֩ וּבְנֵ֨י יִשְׂרָאֵ֜ל אֶת־הַשִּׁירָ֤ה הַזֹּאת֙ לַֽיהוָ֔ה
Ruth 1:1	וַיְהִ֗י בִּימֵי֙ שְׁפֹ֣ט הַשֹּׁפְטִ֔ים וַיְהִ֥י רָעָ֖ב בָּאָ֑רֶץ וַיֵּ֨לֶךְ אִ֜ישׁ מִבֵּ֧ית לֶ֣חֶם יְהוּדָ֗ה לָגוּר֙ בִּשְׂדֵ֣י מוֹאָ֔ב ה֥וּא וְאִשְׁתּ֖וֹ וּשְׁנֵ֥י בָנָֽיו׃
Deuteronomy 10:17	כִּ֚י יְהוָ֣ה אֱלֹֽהֵיכֶ֔ם ה֚וּא אֱלֹהֵ֣י הָֽאֱלֹהִ֔ים וַאֲדֹנֵ֖י הָאֲדֹנִ֑ים הָאֵ֨ל הַגָּדֹ֤ל הַגִּבֹּר֙ וְהַנּוֹרָ֔א אֲשֶׁר֙ לֹא־יִשָּׂ֣א פָנִ֔ים וְלֹ֥א יִקַּ֖ח שֹֽׁחַד׃
Job 1:21	וַיֹּאמֶר֩ עָרֹ֨ם יָצָ֜תִי מִבֶּ֣טֶן אִמִּ֗י וְעָרֹם֙ אָשׁ֣וּב שָׁ֔מָּה יְהוָ֣ה נָתַ֔ן וַֽיהוָ֖ה לָקָ֑ח יְהִ֛י שֵׁ֥ם יְהוָ֖ה מְבֹרָֽךְ׃
Isaiah 12:1–2	וְאָֽמַרְתָּ֙ בַּיּ֣וֹם הַה֔וּא אוֹדְךָ֣ יְהוָ֔ה כִּ֥י אָנַ֖פְתָּ בִּ֑י יָשֹׁ֤ב אַפְּךָ֙ וּֽתְנַחֲמֵֽנִי׃ ב הִנֵּ֨ה אֵ֣ל יְשׁוּעָתִ֔י אֶבְטַ֖ח וְלֹ֣א אֶפְחָ֑ד כִּֽי־עָזִּ֤י וְזִמְרָת֙ יָ֣הּ יְהוָ֔ה וַֽיְהִי־לִ֖י לִֽישׁוּעָֽה׃

20.6 Text: Genesis 22:13–20

Text

Read the text aloud a few times to be sure of the pronunciation. The cantillation marks should help you to stress the right syllables.

13 וַיִּשָּׂ֨א אַבְרָהָ֜ם אֶת־עֵינָ֗יו וַיַּרְא֙ וְהִנֵּה־אַ֔יִל אַחַ֕ר נֶאֱחַ֥ז בַּסְּבַ֖ךְ בְּקַרְנָ֑יו וַיֵּ֤לֶךְ אַבְרָהָם֙ וַיִּקַּ֣ח אֶת־הָאַ֔יִל וַיַּעֲלֵ֥הוּ לְעֹלָ֖ה תַּ֥חַת בְּנֽוֹ׃

14 וַיִּקְרָ֧א אַבְרָהָ֛ם שֵֽׁם־הַמָּק֥וֹם הַה֖וּא יְהוָ֣ה ׀ יִרְאֶ֑ה אֲשֶׁר֙ יֵאָמֵ֣ר הַיּ֔וֹם בְּהַ֥ר יְהוָ֖ה יֵרָאֶֽה׃

15וַיִּקְרָא מַלְאַךְ יְהוָה אֶל־אַבְרָהָם שֵׁנִית מִן־הַשָּׁמָיִם׃

16וַיֹּאמֶר בִּי נִשְׁבַּעְתִּי נְאֻם־יְהוָה כִּי יַעַן אֲשֶׁר עָשִׂיתָ אֶת־הַדָּבָר הַזֶּה וְלֹא חָשַׂכְתָּ אֶת־בִּנְךָ אֶת־יְחִידֶךָ׃

17כִּי־בָרֵךְ אֲבָרֶכְךָ וְהַרְבָּה אַרְבֶּה אֶת־זַרְעֲךָ כְּכוֹכְבֵי הַשָּׁמַיִם וְכַחוֹל אֲשֶׁר עַל־שְׂפַת הַיָּם וְיִרַשׁ זַרְעֲךָ אֵת שַׁעַר אֹיְבָיו׃

18וְהִתְבָּרְכוּ בְזַרְעֲךָ כֹּל גּוֹיֵי הָאָרֶץ עֵקֶב אֲשֶׁר שָׁמַעְתָּ בְּקֹלִי׃

19וַיָּשָׁב אַבְרָהָם אֶל־נְעָרָיו וַיָּקֻמוּ וַיֵּלְכוּ יַחְדָּו אֶל־בְּאֵר שָׁבַע וַיֵּשֶׁב אַבְרָהָם בִּבְאֵר שָׁבַע׃

20וַיְהִי אַחֲרֵי הַדְּבָרִים הָאֵלֶּה וַיֻּגַּד לְאַבְרָהָם לֵאמֹר הִנֵּה יָלְדָה מִלְכָּה גַם־הִוא בָּנִים לְנָחוֹר אָחִיךָ׃

Look up the words you do not recognize in the lexicon at the back of this book. It could be a great deal of work; you are advised to spend no more than half an hour at a time looking up words. Do one verse at a time (or even half a verse) if necessary.

Notes

There are a few textual issues that may be particularly difficult. Here are some helpful hints.

Verse 13

The meaning of the word אַחַר is not very clear in this context. We would normally expect it to have a 3ms suffix. LXX and P have *one* (אֶחָד) instead of *behind*.

Verse 14

The word רָאָה can mean *to see* or *to provide*, as we saw in verse 8. In the Nifal it can mean *to be provided* or *to appear*. The first time a form of it is used in this verse it is Qal Impf (יִרְאֶה), but the second time it is Nifal (יֵרָאֶה). Most translations use either the sense of *provide* or the sense of *appear* in both places.

Verse 16

The Nifal of שָׁבַע means *to swear*; there is no need to make it passive in translation. The phrase נְאֻם־יְהוָה is common in prophetic literature, along with כֹּה אָמַר יְהוָה (*thus says Yhwh*).

Verse 17

Notice the infinitive absolutes being used for emphasis. The phrase *to possess the gate of the enemy* is often understood as a way of saying *to conquer the enemy*.

Verse 18

The Hitpael here may have a reflexive sense, which is very common for Hitpael. However, many translations interpret this as a passive use of the Hitpael. The preposition בְּ is used in the sense of *by means of*. The phrase *to listen to someone's voice* is often a way of saying *to obey*.

Verse 19

This verse contains two forms that are easily confused:

VC Impf 3ms   וַיָּשָׁב   from   שׁוּב

VC Impf 3ms   וַיֵּשֶׁב   from   יָשַׁב

Verse 20

The phrase גַם־הוּא is probably best translated *also* rather than *also she*; it is idiomatic. Notice the Qere perpetuum.

Possible translation

You should now be in a position to make your own possible translation of the passage. It is often a good idea to make a rough, rather literal, translation first, and then to polish it up and make it sound more idiomatic. For example, some scholars say that it is not necessary to translate every VC Imperfect with an initial *and* because the ו is simply a feature of the construction of Hebrew narrative. It is widely considered acceptable to use words like *so* or *then* instead, or to leave out the *and* entirely.

Once you are happy with your translation, compare it with the possible translation below. Perfection is, sadly, out of our reach, but being able to make a good translation helps enormously with our understanding of the biblical texts.

13 *Abraham looked up and he noticed a ram behind him caught in a bush by its horns. So Abraham went and he took the ram and he sacrificed it instead of his son.*

14 *And Abraham called the name of that place 'Yhwh will provide' for it is said to this day 'On the mountain of Yhwh it will be provided.'*

15 *The angel of Yhwh called to Abraham a second time from the heavens*

16 *and he said, 'By myself I have sworn,' says Yhwh, 'Because you have done this thing and because you did not keep back your only son,*

17 *I will certainly bless you, and I will certainly multiply your offspring like the stars in the sky and the sand which is on the sea shore, and your offspring will possess the gate of his enemy.*

18 *And all the nations of the earth shall bless themselves through your offspring, because you have obeyed me.'*

19 *Then Abraham returned to his young men and they rose and they went together to Beersheba, and Abraham settled in Beersheba.*

20 *After these things Abraham was told, 'Behold, Milcah has also borne children to Nahor your brother.'*

20.7 Suggestions

- Look at a few English translations of the passages you examined in Exercise 1. Do they translate the Ketiv or the Qere?

- Look at commentaries on the text. This is a highly significant passage in several religious traditions and there are many possible perspectives on the text.

- Reviewing the biblical texts in earlier units should help to consolidate what you have learned throughout this book. If you have a Hebrew Bible you might like to look at a couple of verses either side, and expand your sense of the context. Context can be very helpful in translation.

- Consider what you might like to explore next in biblical Hebrew. Narrative is usually a little easier than poetry, so stories are particularly recommended at this point. You will need a Hebrew Bible if you wish to do this. Possibilities include:

- the story of Joseph (Genesis 37–40)
- the story of David and Goliath (1 Samuel 17)
- the book of Obadiah
- the book of Jonah
- the book of Ruth.

20.8 Summary

In this unit we have looked at

- the variety of manuscripts that represent sources or variants of the biblical texts

- the indications of ways in which the texts are to be read, using Qere and cantillation marks

- the text of Genesis 22:13–20.

afterword

There is much that it was not possible to explain in an introductory book, but working through this book should give a reader a good grasp of the basics. It is hoped that any reader who has reached the end of this book will have the confidence to begin to explore the biblical texts by him- or herself with the help of a dictionary or lexicon and perhaps a few commentaries. A good Hebrew grammar will explain the details of the vowel changes in weak verbs, the many ways in which the 'tenses' and stems can be used, and other advanced material.

Learning biblical Hebrew can be anything from a passing diversion to a lifetime's work. Whichever you wish to pursue, you should now have enough background to move forward. Your vocabulary extends to hundreds of words, and you will be able to work out many new forms in context. By now no doubt you have a very good grasp of the way biblical Hebrew works, and we hope that you have the confidence to learn new kinds of constructions as you encounter the text.

appendix 1: writing

alef		
bet		
gimel		
dalet		
he		
vav		
zayin		
chet		
tet		
yod		

kaf

lamed

mem

nun

samek

ayin

pe

tsade

qof

resh

sin/shin

tav

final kaf

final mem

final nun

final pe

final tsade

appendix 2: pronunciation

These pronunciations are approximate.

Consonants

b	בּ	book
ch	כ, ח	Always *ch* as in Scottish lo*ch*. Never *ch* as in *ch*eese.
d	ד	door
f	פ	fin
g	ג	Always hard, as in *g*old. Never soft, as in *g*in.
h	ה	help
k	כּ, ק	king
l	ל	land
m	מ	milk
n	נ	not
p	פּ	pin
r	ר	run
s	ס, שׂ	Always *s* as in *s*ock. Never *s* as in tree*s*, which sounds like *z*.
sh	שׁ	shock
t	ט, ת	time
ts	צ	tsar
v	בֿ, ו	van
y	י	young
z	ז	zone

Vowels

Short vowels

a	ֱ	pat
e	ֶ	set
i	ִ	hit
o	ָ	hot
u	ֻ	put

Long vowels

ā	ָ	blah
ay	ֵ	say
ee	ֵי	see
ō	ו	go
oo	וּ	zoo

Sheva

ᵃ	the first o in tomato

Vowel combinations

ī	ַי	as in fine
av	ו	as in *have*
av	יו	as in *have*
ay	ַי	as in *hay*

Capital letters represent stress. Thus: CAP-i-tal LET-ters re-pre-SENT stress.

Unit 3
Exercise 1

א ב ג ד ה ו ז ח ט י כ ל מ נ ס ע פ צ ק ר שׁ שׂ ת

Exercise 2

father and mother; garden and tree; horse and lamb; sea and mountain; sister and brother; hand and palm; sharp and light; woman and man; land and people; heart and voice

Each of these could also be translated *A father and a mother* etc.

Unit 4
Exercise 1

a) *the daughter* הַבַּת; *the garden* הַגַּן; *the sand* הַחוֹל; *the hand* הַיָּד; *the heart* הַלֵּבָב; *the path* הַדֶּרֶךְ; *the voice* הַקּוֹל; *the land* הָאָרֶץ; *the man* הָאִישׁ

b) *the man and the woman; the father and the mother; the sand and the sea; the horse and the cow; the brother and the sister*

Exercise 2

a) *horses* סוּסִים; *eyes* עֵינַיִם; *the princes* הַשָּׂרִים; *the princesses* הַשָּׂרוֹת; *the voices* הַקּוֹלִים; *cows* פָּרוֹת; *the hands* הַיָּדַיִם; *feet* רַגְלַיִם

b) *the hands and the feet; the horses and the mares; the mountains and the seas; the gardens and the paths*

Exercise 3

a man	אִישׁ	*the men*	הָאֲנָשִׁים
a daughter	בַּת	*the daughters*	הַבָּנוֹת
the mother	הָאֵם	*mothers*	אִמּוֹת
night	לַיְלָה	*nights*	לֵילוֹת
the days and the nights	הַיָּמִים וְהַלֵּילוֹת		
cities and princes	עָרִים וְשָׂרִים		

Unit 5

Exercise 1

The table should look like this:

he	הוּא	*they* (m)	הֵם or הֵמָּה
she	הִיא	*they* (f)	הֵנָּה
you (m)	אַתָּה	*you* (m)	אַתֶּם
you (f)	אַתְּ	*you* (f)	אַתֶּן
I	אֲנִי or אָנֹכִי	*we*	אֲנַחְנוּ

Exercise 2

He is the prince. הוּא הַשָּׂר; *She is the woman.* הִיא הָאִשָּׁה; *You are the brother.* אַתָּה הָאָח; *You are the princess.* אַתְּ הַשָּׂרָה; *I am the king.* אֲנִי הַמֶּלֶךְ or אָנֹכִי הַמֶּלֶךְ; *It is the mountain.* הוּא הָהָר; *It is the cow.* הִיא הַפָּרָה; *They are the sons.* הֵם הַבָּנִים or הֵמָּה הַבָּנִים; *They are the women.* הֵנָּה הַנָּשִׁים; *You are the fathers.* אַתֶּם הָאָבוֹת; *You are the daughters.* אַתֶּן הַבָּנוֹת; *We are the princes.* אֲנַחְנוּ הַשָּׂרִים; *They are the horses.* הֵם הַסּוּסִים or הֵמָּה הַסּוּסִים; *They are the cows.* הֵנָּה הַפָּרוֹת

Self-assessment

1) א ב ג ד ה ו ז ח ט י כ ל מ נ ס ע פ צ ק ר שׁ שׂ ת

2) a) ָ ַ ֻ ; b) וּ וֹ יְ ; c) ִ ֵ ; d) ֶ ֱ ֳ

3) a) א ה ח ע ר; b) ב ג ד כ פ ת;

4) a) הָאֵם; b) הַיָּד; c) הָאִישׁ; d) הַמֶּלֶךְ

5) a) סוּס וְסוּסָה; **e)** עִיר וָהָר; **d)** לַיְלָה וְיוֹם; **c)** שָׂרָה וְשָׂר; **b)** אִישׁ וְאִשָּׁה; **f)** אֶרֶץ וְיָם

6) a) *He is the man.* **b)** *They are the princes.* **c)** *We are the daughters.* **d)** *It is the city.* **e)** *You are the women.* **f)** *I am the sister.*

Unit 6
Exercise 1

3ms	קוֹלוֹ	*his voice*	3mp	קוֹלָם	*their voice*
3fs	קוֹלָהּ	*her voice*	3fp	קוֹלָן	*their voice*
2ms	קוֹלְךָ	*your voice*	2mp	קוֹלְכֶם	*your voice*
2fs	קוֹלֵךְ	*your voice*	2fp	קוֹלְכֶן	*your voice*
1cs	קוֹלִי	*my voice*	1cp	קוֹלֵנוּ	*our voice*
3ms	פָּרָתוֹ	*his cow*	3mp	פָּרָתָם	*their cow*
3fs	פָּרָתָהּ	*her cow*	3fp	פָּרָתָן	*their cow*
2ms	פָּרָתְךָ	*your cow*	2mp	פָּרַתְכֶם	*your cow*
2fs	פָּרָתֵךְ	*your cow*	2fp	פָּרַתְכֶן	*your cow*
1cs	פָּרָתִי	*my cow*	1cp	פָּרָתֵנוּ	*our cow*

my father; *your hands*; *our God* (or *our gods*, if referring to gods other than Yhwh); *their kings*; *his mother*

Exercise 2

The priest is small. קָטֹן הַכֹּהֵן; *The swords are sharp.* חַדּוֹת חֲרָבוֹת; *The places are holy.* קְדוֹשִׁים הַמְּקוֹמוֹת; *The prince is bad.* רַע הַשָּׂר; *The food is good.* טוֹבָה הָאֲכְלָה; *The house is empty.* רֵיק הַבַּיִת; *His love is beautiful.* יָפָה אַהֲבָתוֹ; *Our words are wise.* חֲכָמִים דְּבָרֵינוּ; *My knowledge is great.* גְּדוֹלָה דַּעְתִּי; *Your blessings are new.* חֲדָשׁוֹת בִּרְכוֹתֵיכֶם

Exercise 3

the sharp sword; *the great city* (or *the large city*); *the wise princesses*; *the holy words*; *the beautiful women*

Unit 7

Exercise 1

this name; this food; these words; these blessings; that house; that love; those places; those swords

זֶה *This is the priest.* הוּא *That is the heart.* זֹאת *This is the land.* אֵלֶּה *These are the nights.* הֵנָּה *Those are the heavens (or That is heaven).* אֵלֶּה *These are your mares.* הִיא *That is his cow.* הֵנָּה *Those are the women.*

Exercise 2

The man's wife. אֵשֶׁת הָאִישׁ; *The priest's word.* דְּבַר הַכֹּהֵן; *The kings of Israel.* מַלְכֵי יִשְׂרָאֵל; *David's son.* בֶּן דָּוִד; *The people's eyes.* עֵינֵי הָעָם; *The cities of Judah.* עָרֵי יְהוּדָה; *His horse's name.* שֵׁם סוּסוֹ; *My father's house.* בֵּית אָבִי

This is my father's wife. These are your king's words. That is his son's voice. Those are our princess's lips.

Unit 8

Exercise 1

as far as the city עַד הָעִיר; *on the skirt* עַל הַכָּנָף; *with my servant* עִם עַבְדִּי; *between the men* בֵּין הָאֲנָשִׁים; *with the young men* אֶת הַנְּעָרִים; *beneath the sun* תַּחַת הַשֶּׁמֶשׁ; *with an enemy* עִם אֹיֵב; *to his wife* אֶל אִשְׁתּוֹ

Exercise 3

1) *like an enemy;* 2) *with a loud voice;* 3) *from evening until morning;* 4) *before the king;* 5) *from this woman*

1) *Love (or kindness) is better than knowledge.* 2) *The people are bad and there is no knowledge in them.* 3) *You are in my hand.* 4) *She has a son.* 5) *We have these large (or great) horses.* OR: *These large horses are ours.*

Unit 9

Exercise 1

Prepositions אֶל עַל and עַד

3ms	*until him/it*	עָדָיו	3mp	*on them*	עֲלֵיהֶם
3fs	*on her/it*	עָלֶיהָ	3fp	*to them*	אֲלֵיהֶן
2ms	*as far as you*	עָדֶיךָ	2mp	*to you*	אֲלֵיכֶם
2fs	*on you*	עָלַיִךְ	2fp	*as far as you*	עֲדֵיכֶן
1s	*to me*	אֵלַי	1p	*to us*	אֵלֵינוּ

Prepositions תַּחַת and אַחֲרֵי לִפְנֵי

3ms	*under him/it*	תַּחְתָּיו	3mp	*before them*	לִפְנֵיהֶם
3fs	*after her/it*	אַחֲרֶיהָ	3fp	*under them*	תַּחְתֵּיהֶן
2ms	*under you*	תַּחְתֶּיךָ	2mp	*before you*	לִפְנֵיכֶם
2fs	*after you*	אַחֲרַיִךְ	2fp	*after you*	אַחֲרֵיכֶן
1s	*after me*	אַחֲרַי	1p	*under us*	תַּחְתֵּינוּ

Prepositions כְּ and מִן (remember, the suffixes on כְּ are not identical to those on מִן)

3ms	*from him/it*	מִמֶּנּוּ	3mp	*like them*	כָּהֶם
3fs	*like her/it*	כָּמוֹהָ	3fp	*from them*	מֵהֶן
2ms	*from you*	מִמְּךָ	2mp	*from you*	מִכֶּם
2fs	*like you*	כָּמוֹךְ	2fp	*like you*	כָּכֶן
1s	*from me*	מִמֶּנִּי	1p	*from us*	מִמֶּנּוּ

Exercise 2

Who is greater than Joseph? *David*. What does David have? *Horses and cows and wives*. What does Joseph lack? *A wife*. Who has the best horse? *David*. Which horse is white? *The smallest of Joseph's horses*.

Unit 10
Exercise 1

3ms	פָּקַד	כָּתַב	זָכַר
3fs	פָּקְדָה	כָּתְבָה	זָכְרָה
2ms	פָּקַדְתָּ	כָּתַבְתָּ	זָכַרְתָּ
2fs	פָּקַדְתְּ	כָּתַבְתְּ	זָכַרְתְּ

1s	פָּקַדְתִּי	כָּתַבְתִּי	זָכַרְתִּי
3p	פָּקְדוּ	כָּתְבוּ	זָכְרוּ
2mp	פְּקַדְתֶּם	כְּתַבְתֶּם	זְכַרְתֶּם
2fp	פְּקַדְתֶּן	כְּתַבְתֶּן	זְכַרְתֶּן
1p	פָּקַדְנוּ	כָּתַבְנוּ	זָכַרְנוּ

Exercise 2

The priest called to the people from his house. קָרָא הַכֹּהֵן אֶל־הָעָם מִבֵּתוֹ; *She remembered the name of my father's servant.* זָכְרָה שֵׁם עֶבֶד אָבִי; *This cow ate all my bread.* אָכְלָה הַפָּרָה הַזֹּאת אֶת־כָּל־לַחְמִי; *You created the trees of the field.* בָּרֵאתָ אֶת־עֲצֵי הַשָּׂדֶה; *You guarded the beautiful princess.* שָׁמַרְתְּ אֶת־הַשָּׂרָה הַיָּפָה; *I stood in the garden between the trees.* עָמַדְתִּי בַּגָּן בֵּין הָעֵצִים; *David and Solomon ruled in Judah.* מָשְׁלוּ דָוִד וּשְׁלֹמֹה בִּיהוּדָה; *You kept the law of Yhwh your God.* שְׁמַרְתֶּם אֶת־תּוֹרַת יְהוָה אֱלֹהֵכֶם; *You said to us there is no king in Israel.* אֲמַרְתֶּן אֵלֵינוּ אֵין מֶלֶךְ בְּיִשְׂרָאֵל; *We did not rest in the land of Egypt.* לֹא שָׁבַתְנוּ בְּאֶרֶץ מִצְרָיִם

Self-assessment

1) a) *our horse, their voice* (mp), *your horse* (ms), *his voice*
b) *your mares* (fp), *our cows, her mare, their voices*
c) קוֹלֵינוּ שֵׁרְתוֹ אָבִי **d)** טוֹבוֹת הַנָּשִׁים **e)** *Our oxen are good but our cows are bad.*

2) a) הַסּוּסוֹת הָאֵלֶּה **b)** זֶה (ms) and זֹאת (fs) **c)** הֵם (mp) and הֵנָּה (fp), הַסּוּסִים הָאֵלֶּה **d)** *This is my father's wife and that is his horse.*
e) *These are the words of the priests of the God of Israel.*

3) a) יֵשׁ לוֹ בֵּן **b)** בֵּין תַּחַת עַל אֶל **c)** *The king is greater* (or *larger*) *than the men.* **d)** בָּנוּ לָהֶם בָּהּ לִי **e)** *to a young man, in the city, like my servant*

4) a) אֵת and אֶת־. **b)** *like him, between them, from me, on you*
c) *vanity of vanities* **d)** *And David was* (or *is*) *the youngest.*
e) *The eldest of his sons is with my mother.*

(5) a) קָטַל קָטְלָה קָטַלְתָּ קָטַלְתְּ קָטַלְתִּי קָטְלוּ קְטַלְתֶּם קְטַלְתֶּן קָטַלְנוּ **b)** שָׁמְרוּ הָלַכְתִּי אָכְלָה מָשַׁל **c)** *She has walked* (or *gone*) *as far as the city.* **d)** *David and Daniel have eaten the bread.* **e)** *The king and his sons have ruled in all the land of Judah.* OR: *The king has ruled in all the land of Judah; he and his sons.*

Unit 11

Exercise 1

3ms	יִפְקֹד	יִכְתֹּב	יִזְכֹּר
3fs	תִּפְקֹד	תִּכְתֹּב	תִּזְכֹּר
2ms	תִּפְקֹד	תִּכְתֹּב	תִּזְכֹּר
2fs	תִּפְקְדִי	תִּזְכְּרִי	תִּזְכְּבִי
1s	אֶפְקֹד	אֶכְתֹּב	אֶזְכֹּר
3mp	יִפְקְדוּ	יִכְתְּבוּ	יִזְכְּרוּ
3fp	תִּפְקֹדְנָה	תִּכְתֹּבְנָה	תִּזְכֹּרְנָה
2mp	תִּפְקְדוּ	תִּכְתְּבוּ	תִּזְכְּרוּ
2fp	תִּפְקֹדְנָה	תִּכְתֹּבְנָה	תִּזְכֹּרְנָה
1p	נִפְקֹד	נִכְתֹּב	נִזְכֹּר

Exercise 2

You will rule over all the land of Israel. תִּמְשֹׁל בְּכָל־אֶרֶץ יִשְׂרָאֵל; *I will remember this day.* אֶזְכֹּר הַיּוֹם הַזֶּה; *We will judge those cities.* נִשְׁפֹּט אֶת־הֶעָרִים הָאֵלֶּה; *He/it will be blessed.* יְהִי מְבֹרָךְ; *They will keep the law.* יִשְׁמְרוּ אֶת־הַתּוֹרָה; *They will remember the name of Yhwh the God of gods.* תִּזְכֹּרְנָה שֵׁם יְהוָה אֱלֹהֵי אֱלֹהִים; *She will visit the women of Judah.* תִּפְקֹד אֶת־נָשֵׁי יְהוּדָה; *You will stand before the king and his servants.* תַּעַמְדוּ לִפְנֵי הַמֶּלֶךְ וְלִפְנֵי עֲבָדָיו; *You will rest under the tree which is in the field.* תִּשְׁבֹּתְנָה תַּחַת הָעֵץ אֲשֶׁר בַּשָּׂדֶה; *You will write in your books.* תִּזְכְּרִי בְּסִפְרֵיכֶן

Unit 12

Exercise 1

he has guarded	*and he will guard*
she has guarded	*and she will guard*
you have guarded	*and you will guard*
you have guarded	*and you will guard*

I have guarded	*and I will guard*
they have guarded	*and they will guard*
they have guarded	*and they will guard*
you have guarded	*and you will guard*
you have guarded	*and you will guard*
we have guarded	*and we will guard*

Exercise 2

וַיִּזְכֹּר אֶת־בְּרִיתְכֶם: *And he remembered your covenant.*

וַתִּכְתֹּב דִּבְרֵיכֶם בְּסֵפֶר: *And she wrote your words in a book.*

וָאֶמְשֹׁל בָּהֶם: *And I ruled over them.*

וַתֵּלַכְנָה בְּדַרְכֵי צְדָקָה: *And they (or you) (fp) walked in the paths of righteousness.*

וַתֹּאכְלוּ הַלֶּחֶם: *And you (mp) ate the bread.*

וַיִּשְׁמְרוּ אֶת־תּוֹרַת יְהוָה: *And they (mp) kept the law of Yhwh.*

וַתִּקְטֹל אִישׁ: *And you (ms) (or she) killed a man.*

וַיִּקְרָא שֵׁם בְּנוֹ שְׁלֹמֹה: *And he called the name of his son Solomon.*

וַיֹּאמֶר אֶשְׁפֹּט אֶת־כָּל־אֶרֶץ יְהוּדָה: *And he said, 'I will judge all the land of Judah.'*

וַיֹּאמְרוּ נִשְׁמֹר אֶת בֵּית הַמֶּלֶךְ: *And they said, 'We will guard the king's house.'*

Unit 13
Exercise 1

to send, stretch out שָׁלַח	*lamed* guttural	שָׁלְחָה	Perf 3fs *she has sent*
to put, place שִׂים	hollow	שָׂמָה	Perf 3fs *she has put*
to see רָאָה	doubly weak: *ayin* and *lamed* gutturals	רָאִינוּ	Perf 1p *we have seen*
to hear שָׁמַע	*lamed* guttural	שָׁמַעְתִּי	Perf 1s *I have heard*

to *drink* שָׁתָה	*lamed* guttural	שְׁתִיתֶם Perf 2mp *you have drunk*
to *go up* עָלָה	doubly weak: *pe* and *lamed* gutturals	עָלְתָה Perf 3fs *she has gone up*
to *come* בּוֹא	hollow	בָּא Perf 3ms *he has come*
to *give birth* יָלַד	*pe yod*	יָלַדְתְּ Perf 2fs *you have given birth*
to *go out* יָצָא	*pe yod*	יָצָאת Perf 2fs *you have gone out*
to *go down* יָרַד (e.g. to *Egypt*)	*pe yod*	יָרְדוּ Perf 3p *they have gone down*
to *die* מוּת	hollow	מַתֶּן Perf 2fp *you have died*
to *build* בָּנָה	*lamed* guttural	בָּנוּ Perf 3p *they have built*

Exercise 2

3ms	יֵלֵד	יֵרֵד
3fs	תֵּלֵד	תֵּרֵד
2ms	תֵּלֵד	תֵּרֵד
2fs	תֵּלְדִי	תֵּרְדִי
1s	אֵלֵד	אֵרֵד
3mp	יֵלְדוּ	יֵרְדוּ
3fp	תֵּלַדְנָה	תֵּרַדְנָה
2mp	תֵּלְדוּ	תֵּרְדוּ
2fp	תֵּלַדְנָה	תֵּרַדְנָה
1p	נֵלֵד	נֵרֵד

Unit 14
Exercise 1

VERB	*to eat*	*to reveal*	*to go down*
ROOT	אָכַל	גָּלָה	יָרַד
PARTICIPLE	אֹכֵל	גֹּלֶה	יֹרֵד
MEANING	*eating*	*revealing*	*going down*
IMPERATIVE	אֱכֹל	גְּלֵה	רֵד
MEANING	*eat!*	*reveal!*	*go down!*

VERB	*to sit*	*to die*	*to find*
ROOT	יָשַׁב	מוּת	מָצָא
PARTICIPLE	יֹשֵׁב	מֵת	מֹצֵא
MEANING	*sitting*	*dying*	*finding*
IMPERATIVE	שֵׁב	מוּת	מְצָא
MEANING	*sit!*	*die!*	*find!*

VERB	*to approach*	*to fall*	*to turn*
ROOT	נָגַשׁ	נָפַל	סָבַב
PARTICIPLE	נֹגֵשׁ	נֹפֵל	סוֹבֵב
MEANING	*approaching*	*falling*	*turning*
IMPERATIVE	גַּשׁ/גְּשָׁה	נְפֹל	סֹב
MEANING	*approach!*	*fall!*	*turn!*

VERB	*to stand*	*to visit*	*to arise*
ROOT	עָמַד	פָּקַד	קוּם
PARTICIPLE	עֹמֵד	פֹּקֵד	קָם
MEANING	*standing*	*visiting*	*arising*
IMPERATIVE	עֲמֹד	פְּקֹד	קוּם
MEANING	*stand!*	*visit!*	*arise!*

VERB	*to kill*	*to put*	*to send*
ROOT	קָטַל	שִׂים	שָׁלַח
PARTICIPLE	קֹטֵל	שָׂם	שֹׁלֵחַ
MEANING	*killing*	*putting*	*sending*
IMPERATIVE	קְטֹל	שִׂים	שְׁלַח
MEANING	*kill!*	*put!*	*send!*

VERB	*to hear*
ROOT	שָׁמַע
PARTICIPLE	שֹׁמֵעַ
MEANING	*hearing*
IMPERATIVE	שְׁמַע
MEANING	*hear!*

Exercise 2

a) Participle: עוֹמֵד **b)** Perfect: וְנָתַתִּי, Infinitive Construct: לָדַעַת
c) Imperative: שְׁמַע **d)** Infinitive Absolute: עָשֹׂה or יָכֹל , Imperfect
תּוּכַל or תַּעֲשֶׂה

Unit 15

Exercise 1

Yhwh will create them. יִבְרָא יהוה אֹתָם; *The king will
fear you.* יִירָא הַמֶּלֶךְ אֹתְךָ (the pronoun could be any of
אֹתָךְ אֹתָךְ אֶתְכֶם אֶתְכֶן); *David will not test me.* לֹא יִבְחַן דָּוִד אֹתִי; *My
mother will see them.* תִּרְאֶה אִמִּי אֹתָם (the pronoun could be אֹתָם
or אֹתָן); *The sword will cut you.* תִּכְרֹת הַחֶרֶב אֹתְךָ (the pronoun
could be any of אֹתָךְ אֹתְךָ אֶתְכֶם אֶתְכֶן); *We will swallow it.*
נִבְלַע אֹתָהּ (the pronoun could be אֹתוֹ or אֹתָהּ); *The women will
take you.* תִּקַּחְנָה הַנָּשִׁים אֶתְכֶם (the pronoun could be any of
אֹתָךְ אֹתְךָ אֶתְכֶם אֶתְכֶן); *I will send her.* אֶשְׁלַח אֹתָהּ (the pronoun
could be אֹתוֹ or אֹתָהּ); *Gideon will find us.* יִמְצָא גִדְעוֹן אֹתָנוּ;
He will answer you. יַעֲנֶה אֹתְךָ (the pronoun could be any of
אֹתָךְ אֹתְךָ אֶתְכֶם אֶתְכֶן)

Exercise 2

אֲשֶׁר אֲשֶׁר אֵי אֲשֶׁר מִי לָמָּה מָה

David came to the house which *is between the mountains. And he saw the servant* who *guards the house. And he said to him, 'Where is the woman* whose *father lives in this house?' And the servant said, 'Who are you?' And David answered, 'I am the king.' And the servant said, 'Why have you come?' And David said, 'I have come to visit Sarah. What is your name?'*

Self-assessment

1) a) Write out all the forms of the Imperfect of פָּקַד.

3ms	יִפְקֹד	3mp	יִפְקְדוּ
3fs	תִּפְקֹד	3fp	תִּפְקֹדְנָה
2ms	תִּפְקֹד	2mp	תִּפְקְדוּ
2fs	תִּפְקְדִי	2fp	תִּפְקֹדְנָה
1s	אֶפְקֹד	1p	נִפְקֹד

b) *My father has remembered the words of the priest which you wrote in a book.* **c)** *Yhwh will rule over you.* **d)** Usually future, but also past and present. **e)** Because it is a weak verb. It is *pe* guttural so the ע must take a complex *sheva* and it also attracts an *a* vowel under the י.

2) a) Past; **b)** *Sheva;* **c)** *And he went/walked as far as Judah.* **d)** *He was angry and he took his sword and I was afraid / I trembled.* **e)** Qal VC Imperfect 3ms of קוּם meaning *and he arose.*

3) a) *Lamed he* or ל״ה; **b)** *Infinitive Construct;* c) Qal Imperfect 3mp of יָדַע meaning *they will know.* **d)** They lose their initial נ. An example could be any one of

he will fall	יִפֹּל	*they will fall* (mp)	יִפְּלוּ
she will fall	תִּפֹּל	*they will fall* (fp)	תִּפֹּלְנָה
you will fall (ms)	תִּפֹּל	*you will fall* (mp)	תִּפְּלוּ
you will fall (fs)	תִּפְּלִי	*you will fall* (fp)	תִּפֹּלְנָה
I will fall	אֶפֹּל	*we will fall*	נִפֹּל

e) It is an extra ה, possibly to aid pronunciation.

4) a) Imperative. If you did not feel confident in your understanding of the verse, look it up in an English translation. b) *Write books.* c) The root שָׁלַח is *lamed* guttural and so its Participle form contains a *patach* furtive. d) *And Daniel answered me saying, 'Please sit and eat.'* e) It is used with a finite verb, e.g. מוֹת תָּמוּת literally *dying you will die* or *you will certainly die.*

5) a)

him	אֹתוֹ	*them*	אֹתָם
her	אֹתָהּ	*them*	אֹתָן
you (ms)	אֹתְךָ	*you* (mp)	אֶתְכֶם
you (fs)	אֹתָךְ	*you* (fp)	אֶתְכֶן
me	אֹתִי	*us*	אֹתָנוּ

b) *Why?* לָמָּה or לָמֶה *What?* מַה or מֶה *Who?* מִי c) *Whose* (*These are the men whose voices will sing songs.*) d) Participle שֹׁמֵעַ Infinitive Construct שְׁמֹעַ Infinitive Absolute שָׁמֹעַ; e) *Eight years old.*

Unit 16
Exercise 1

	NIFAL	MEANING
PERFECT		
3ms	נִפְקַד	*he has been visited*
3fs	נִפְקְדָה	*she has been visited*
2ms	נִפְקַדְתָּ	*you have been visited*
2fs	נִפְקַדְתְּ	*you have been visited*
1s	נִפְקַדְתִּי	*I have been visited*
3p	נִפְקְדוּ	*they have been visited*
2mp	נִפְקַדְתֶּם	*you have been visited*
2fp	נִפְקַדְתֶּן	*you have been visited*
1p	נִפְקַדְנוּ	*we have been visited*

IMPERFECT

3ms	יִפָּקֵד	he will be visited
3fs	תִּפָּקֵד	she will be visited
2ms	תִּפָּקֵד	you will be visited
2fs	תִּפָּקְדִי	you will be visited
1s	אֶפָּקֵד	I will be visited
3mp	יִפָּקְדוּ	they will be visited
3fp	תִּפָּקַדְנָה	they will be visited
2mp	תִּפָּקְדוּ	you will be visited
2fp	תִּפָּקַדְנָה	you will be visited
1p	נִפָּקֵד	we will be visited

Exercise 2

a) *Please live in my land.* מֶלֶךְ like דָּבָר like אֹיֵב אֶרֶץ like מֶלֶךְ

a) *Please live in my land.* אֶרֶץ like מֶלֶךְ

b) *Do not kill the guards.* שֹׁמֵר like אֹיֵב

c) *Let the heart of Moses be full.* לֵבָב like דָּבָר

d) *You must not touch my nose.* אַף like יָם

e) *Remember the righteousness of Solomon.* יְדָקָה like דָּבָר

f) *Let the judges of Israel rejoice.* שֹׁפֵט like אֹיֵב

g) *You must not destroy the sanctuaries of Judah.* קֹדֶשׁ like מֶלֶךְ

h) *Let my redeemer visit me.* גוֹאֵל like אֹיֵב

i) *Do not forget the mothers of the children (or sons) of Israel.* אֵם like יָם

j) *Do not fear my knowledge.* דַּעַת like מֶלֶךְ

Unit 17

Exercise 1

this great fire will consume us (Deuteronomy 5:25): תֹּאכְלֵנוּ הָאֵשׁ הַגְּדֹלָה צְדָקָה; *and he took them from the middle of the tent* (Joshua 7:3): וַיִּקָּחוּם מִתּוֹךְ הָאֹהֶל; *and Yhwh remembered* her (1 Samuel 1:19): וַיִּזְכְּרֶהָ יְהוָה; *and he loved him very much* (1 Samuel 16:21): וַיֶּאֱהָבֵהוּ מְאֹד; *and you did not know them* (Isaiah 48:6): וְלֹא יְדַעְתָּם; *we bless you from the house of Yhwh* (Psalm 118:26): בֵּרַכְנוּכֶם מִבֵּית יְהוָה; *Yhwh will guard you from all evil* (Psalm 121:7): יְהוָה יִשְׁמָרְךָ מִכָּל־רָע; *My God, my God, why have you abandoned me?* (Psalm 22:2; Engl. 22:1): אֵלִי הַזֹּאת לָמָה עֲזַבְתָּנִי

Exercise 2

	Perf. 3ms	Perf. 1s	Impf. 3mp
QAL	קָדֵשׁ	פָּקַדְתִּי	אֵלִי
MEANING	*he is holy*	*I have visited*	*they will gather*
PIEL	קִדֵּשׁ	פִּקַּדְתִּי	יַאַסְפוּ
MEANING	*he has consecrated*	*I have mustered*	*they will gather*
PUAL	קֻדַּשׁ	פֻּקַּדְתִּי	יֵאָסְפוּ
MEANING	*he has been consecrated*	*I have been mustered*	*they will be gathered*
HITPAEL	הִתְקַדֵּשׁ	הִתְפַּקַּדְתִּי	יִתְאַסְּפוּ
MEANING	*he has consecrated himself*	*I have mustered*	*they will be gathered together*

	Impv.	Perf. 3mp	Impf. 1p
QAL	קְדַשׁ	בָּקְעוּ	נִבְקַע
MEANING	*be holy*	*they have divided*	*we will divide*
PIEL	קַדֵּשׁ	בִּקְּעוּ	נְבַקַּע
MEANING	*consecrate*	*they have torn in pieces*	*we will tear in pieces*
PUAL	—	בֻּקְּעוּ	נְבֻקַּע
MEANING	—	*they have been torn in pieces*	*we will be torn in pieces*
HITPAEL	הִתְקַדֵּשׁ	הִתְבַּקְּעוּ	נִתְבַּקַּע
MEANING	*consecrate yourself*	*they have been torn*	*we will be torn*

	Impf. 3ms	Impv.	Part.
QAL	—	פְּקֹד	אֹסֵף
MEANING	—	*visit*	*gathering*
PIEL	יְוֶה	פַּקֵּד	מְאַסֵּף
MEANING	*he has commanded*	*muster*	*gathering*
PUAL	יְצֻוֶּה	—	מְאֻסָּף
MEANING	*he has been commanded*	*—*	*being gathered*
HITPAEL	—	הִתְפַּקֵּד	מִתְאַסֵּף
MEANING	—	*muster*	*being gathered together*

	Inf. Cstr.
QAL	בְּקֹעַ
MEANING	*to divide*
PIEL	בַּקַּע
MEANING	*to tear in pieces*
PUAL	בַּקַּע
MEANING	*to be torn in pieces*
HITPAEL	הִתְבַּקַּע
MEANING	*to be torn*

Unit 18

Exercise 1

a) הוֹשַׁעְתָּנוּ (Unit 11) Hifil Perf 2sm + suffix 1p יָשַׁע
He has saved us

b) אוֹדְךָ (Unit 12) Hifil Impf 1s + suff 2mp from ידה
I will praise you

c) אוֹדֶה (Unit 13) Hifil Impf 1s from ידה
I will praise

d) הֵינִיקָה (Unit 16) Hifil Perf 3fs from יָנַק
She will breastfeed

e) וְהַחֲזִיקִי (Unit 17) Hifil Impv 2fs from חָזַק
And hold

f) וַתַּשְׁקְ (Unit 17)   Hifil VC Imperfect 3fs from שָׁקָה
And she gave a drink [to ...]

Exercise 2

	Perfect		Imperfect
Qal	פָּקַד	Qal	יִפְקֹד
Nifal	נִפְקַד	Nifal	יִפָּקֵד
Piel	פִּקֵּד	Piel	יְפַקֵּד
Pual	פֻּקַּד	Pual	יְפֻקַּד
Hitpael	הִתְפַּקֵּד	Hitpael	יִתְפַּקֵּד
Hifil	הִפְקִיד	Hifil	יַפְקִיד
Hofal	הָפְקַד	Hofal	יָפְקַד

Unit 19
Exercise 1

a)	נוֹדָע	Nif ptc ms	יָדַע	*being known*
b)	וְהַנּוֹרָא	VC Nif ptc ms	יָרֵא	*being afraid*
c)	מְבֹרָךְ	Pual ptc ms	בָּרַךְ	*being blessed*
d)	וּתְנַחֲמֵנִי	VC Piel Impf 2ms + suff 1cs	נָחַם	*and you comforted me*
e)	אֲסַפְּרָה	Piel Impf 1s	סָפַר	*I will count, tell*
f)	נִפְלְאוֹתֶיךָ	Nif ptc pl + suff 2ms	פלא	*your great things*
g)	אֲזַמְּרָה	Piel Impf 1s + parag ה	זמר	*I will sing praises to*
h)	יִכָּשְׁלוּ	Nif Impf 3mp	כשל	*they will stumble*
i)	אִבַּדְתָּ	Piel Perf 2ms	אבד	*you have destroyed*
j)	כּוֹנֵן	Pilel Perf 3ms	כון	*he has established*
k)	וְנִפְקְחוּ	VC Nif Perf 3mp	פָּקַח	*and they will be opened*
l)	דִּבֶּר	Piel Perf 3ms	דָּבַר	*he has said, he has promised*

m) הַגּוֹלַד	Nif Perf 3ms	יָלַד	*being born*
n) צָוָּה	Piel Perf 3ms	צָוָה	*he has commanded*
o) בְּהִוָּלֶד	Prep בְּ + Nif Inf cstr	יָלַד	*in being born*
p) מִלֵּל	Piel Perf 3ms	מָלַל	*he said, he spoke*
q) גָּרֵשׁ	Piel Impv ms	גָּרַשׁ	*expel, drive away*

Unit 20

Exercise 1

Ecclesiastes 4:17

K: רַגְלֶיךָ

Q: רַגְלְךָ   *rag-l^a-CHĀ*

Meaning: either *your feet* (K) or *your foot* (Q)

Daniel 9:12

K: דְּבָרָיו

Q: דְּבָרוֹ   *d^a-vā-RŌ*

Meaning: either *his words* (K) or *his word* (Q)

Lamentations 3:10

K: אֲרִיה

Q: אֲרִי   *a-REE*

Meaning: *a lion* (Q). The Ketiv has no meaning.

2 Chronicles 34:9

K: וַיָּשֻׁבִי

Q: וַיָּשֻׁבוּ   *va-yā-SHOO-voo*

Meaning: *they returned* (Q); The Ketiv does not make sense.

The *dagesh* in the final י of וַיָּשֻׁבִי (K) represents the *dagesh* in the ו of וַיָּשֻׁבוּ (Q).

Proverbs 19:19

K: גְּרל־

Q: גִּדֹּל־ g^a-DŌL

Meaning: *angry* (K) or *great* (Q).

Neither meaning is easy to understand in the context. The LXX has *a malicious man will be severely punished* and most English translations follow this reading.

Exercise 2

Your circled syllables should correspond to the capitalized syllables in the transliteration.

Psalm 25:8	TŌV v^a-yā-SHĀR a-dō-NĪ al kayn yō-RE cha-tā-EEM ba-DĀR-ek
2 Samuel 12:7a	va-YO-mer nā-TĀN el dā-VID at-TĀ hā-EESH
Psalm 76:2	nō-DĀ bee-hoo-DĀ e-lo-HEEM b^a-yis-rā-AYL gā-DŌL sh^a-MŌ
Exodus 15:1a	āz yā-SHEER mō-SHE oov-NAY yis-rah-AYL et ha-shee-RĀ ha-ZŌT lā-dō-NĪ
Ruth 1:1	va-y^a-HEE bee-MAY sh^a-FŌT ha-shō-f^a-TEEM va-y^a-HEE rā-ĀV bā-ĀR-ets va-YAY-lech eesh mi-BAYT LE-chem y^a-HOO-dā lā-GOOR bis-DAY mō-ĀV hoo v^a-eesh-TŌ oosh-NAY vā-NAV
Deuteronomy 10:17	ki a-don-Ī e-lō-HAY-chem hoo e-lō-HAY hā-e-lō-HEEM va-a-dō-NAY hā-a-dō-NEEM, hā-AYL ha-gā-DŌL ha-gib-BŌR v^a-ha-nō-RĀ a-SHER lō yis-SĀ pā-NEEM v^a-lō yi-KACH SHŌ-chad
Job 1:21	va-YŌ-mer ā-RŌM yā-TSĀ-tee mi-BE-ten im-MEE v^a-ā-RŌM ā-SHOOV SHĀ-ma ā-dō-NĪ nā-TAN vā-dō-NĪ lā-KACH y^a-HEE shaym ā-dō-NĪ m^a-bō-RĀCH
Isaiah 12:1–2	v^a-ā-mar-TĀ bā-YŌM ha-HOO ōd-CHĀ ā-dō-NĪ kee ā-NAF-tā bee yā-SHŌV af-CHĀ oot-na-cha-MAY-nee. hin-NAY ayl y^a-shoo-ā-TEE ev-TACH v^a-LŌ ef-CHĀD; kee ā-ZEE v^a-zim-RĀ yāch ā-dō-NĪ va-y^a-hee-LEE lee-shoo-Ā

absolute In Hebrew, the form of a noun or adjective found in a dictionary.

Absolute: דָּבָר   Plural: דְּבָרִים   Construct: דְּבַר

Some nouns do not change in the construct (e.g. מֶלֶךְ).

accent A mark that indicates how a letter or word is supposed to be read. Accents are sometimes called diacritical marks. There are a number of types of accent in Hebrew, and the following have their own entries in this glossary: *atnah, dagesh, mappiq, maqqef, meteg, silluq.*

active voice A verb whose subject is doing something is said to be in the **active** voice. A verb whose subject is having something done to it/them is said to be in the **passive** voice.

Examples:

Active:	*Sarah has borne a son*	יָלְדָה שָׂרָה בֵּן
Passive:	*A son has been born to Sarah*	נוֹלַד לְשָׂרָה בֵּן

adjective A word that qualifies a noun: the *good* king, *big* horses. In Hebrew, an adjective used in this way comes **after** the noun it qualifies, and agrees with the noun in person, gender, number and definiteness.

Examples in Hebrew:

the good king הַמֶּלֶךְ הַטּוֹב   *big horses* סוּסִים גְּדוֹלִים

Adjectives can be used in Hebrew with the verb *to be* implied. In this case the adjective comes **before** the noun it qualifies, and agrees with the noun in person, gender and number but **not** definiteness.

Examples:

the king is good   טוֹב הַמֶּלֶךְ   horses are big   גְּדוֹלִים סוּסִים

An *adjectival construction* is a phrase containing at least one noun qualified by at least one adjective.

adverb   Adverbs can qualify several kinds of words. Qualifying a verb: I read *slowly*. Qualifying an adjective: Your work is *very* good. Qualifying another adverb: It all happened *quite* quickly.

Examples in Hebrew:

He lived there (qualifying a verb)   יָשַׁב שָׁם

The king is very good (qualifying an adjective)   טוֹב מְאֹד הַמֶּלֶךְ

My father walked very quickly   הָלַךְ אָבִי בִּמְהֵרָה מְאֹד

agreement   A change in a word's spelling so that it matches the words it is connected with. Examples:

The brothers are big and bad   גְּדוֹלִים רָעִים הָאַחִים

The mothers are good and wise   טוֹבוֹת וַחֲכָמוֹת הָאִמּוֹת

apocopation   Shortening of a word; very common in VC Imperfect forms of roots that end in ה. Example:

Root עָשָׂה *to make, to do*	VC Impf 3ms	VC Impf 3ms
(weak verb)	full form וַיַּעֲשֶׂה	apoc וַיַּעַשׂ

article   An article indicates definiteness. In English, there are two articles, the definite article: *the*, and the indefinite article: *a/an*. In Hebrew, the definite article is the letter ה vocalized with an *a* vowel or an *e* vowel and eliciting a *dagesh* in the first letter of the word (unless that letter is a guttural or ר). Example:

the man and the wise king   הָאִישׁ וְהַמֶּלֶךְ הֶחָכָם

Hebrew has no indefinite article. Examples:

a woman has judged Israel   שָׁפְטָה אִשָּׁה אֶת־יִשְׂרָאֵל

a king has eaten with a servant   אָכַל מֶלֶךְ עִם עֶבֶד

priests have kept the law   שָׁמְרוּ כֹהֲנִים אֶת־הַתּוֹרָה

assimilation   When a letter 'disappears' from a word and is represented in the next letter of the word by a *dagesh*. Example:

Root נָתַן *to give* (weak)   *I have given* נָתַתִּי (instead of נָתַנְתִּי)

atnah   An accent ֡, often found around the middle of a verse, and functioning a little like a comma.

***ayin* guttural verb**   A verb with a guttural as the middle letter of its root form. Example: שָׁחַט. See verb tables for conjugations.

***ayin yod* or *ayin vav* verb**   A verb with י or ו as the middle letter of its root form. Example: קוּם. See verb tables for conjugations.

clause   A sentence, or part of a sentence, that contains a verbal idea. English examples:

I saw that the sun had set in the west. In this example, *that the sun had set* is a clause but *in the west* is not, because it has no verb.

In Hebrew, a clause usually has a verb. However, certain verbless clauses have only an implied verb: the verb *to be*. Example: *the king is good* טוֹב הַמֶּלֶךְ

cohortative   A way of expressing commands to oneself, or expressing an intention. For example:

Let me remember your words   אֶזְכְּרָה דְּבָרֶיךָ

Let us make a covenant   נִכְרְתָה בְּרִית

comparative   A form that makes a comparison, in English often by adding the suffix *-er*: *The sun is bright*er than *the moon*. Comparatives can also be expressed by using *more ... than ...* : *I am* more *extrovert than* my sister.

In Hebrew, comparisons are made using the preposition מִן. For example:

A horse is bigger than a sheep   גָּדוֹל סוּס מִן שֶׂה

You are wiser than Daniel   חָכָם אַתָּה מִדָּנִיֵּאל

conjugation   All the forms of a verb. In English, for example, the verb *remember* is conjugated:

Present:	I, you, we, they	*remember*
	he, she, it	*remembers*

Present participle	*remembering*
Past	*remembered*
Past participle	*remembered*

English Infinitives and Imperatives are the same as the Present.

Hebrew conjugation tables list all the forms of the Perfect and Imperfect, and usually the Imperative, Infinitive and Participle for the Qal and for all the other stems (Nifal, Piel, Pual, Hifil, Hofal and Hitpael) of a verb.

conjunction   A word that connects two other words or phrases. Examples include *and, but, or*. In Hebrew, the sense of *and* and *but* is provided by the particle וֹ, usually vocalized with *sheva*.

Examples in Hebrew:

| *bad and good* | *daughter and son* | *Daniel and Deborah* |
| רַע וְטוֹב | בַּת וּבֵן | דָּנִאֵל וּדְבוֹרָה |

consonant   The alphabet we use to write English is made up of 5 vowels (AEIOU) and 21 consonants (all the rest of the letters). The Hebrew alphabet is composed entirely of consonants, although two of them are silent.

construct   One way of indicating possession in Hebrew (the other is the use of the preposition לְ). A word can be in *construct relationship* to another word, which involves placing it in front of the word it is in relationship to: *the man's horse* סוּס הָאִישׁ. Some words change their spelling when they are in construct relationship, and they are said to be in *construct state*:

a word דָּבָר   *God's word* דְּבַר אֱלֹהִים

Other words do not change spelling when they are in construct relationship:

a king מֶלֶךְ   *king of Israel* מֶלֶךְ יִשְׂרָאֵל

Words in construct relationship never take the definite article in Hebrew. However, when translating into English they must agree in definiteness with the word they are in relationship to:

a voice of a woman קוֹל אִשָּׁה   *the woman's voice* קוֹל הָאִשָּׁה

Any number of nouns can be placed in a *construct chain*:

dagesh   A dot in a letter that signifies any of the following:

doubling of the letter   example: סַבּוֹתִי   Qal Perf 1s of סָבַב

assimilation of a letter   example: יִפֹּל   Nif Impf 3ms of נָפַל

the definite article   example: הַמֶּלֶךְ

declension   A way of dividing nouns (and adjectives) into categories according to their spelling or the way they change in different contexts. The main declensions in Hebrew are:

Nouns with long-*a* type vowels	Example: דָּבָר *word*
Nouns with short-*e* type vowels	Example: מֶלֶךְ *king* (these are also known as segolate nouns)
Nouns with Participle-pattern vowels	Example: שֹׁמֵר *guard*
Consonant-doubling (*dagesh*) nouns	Example: יָם, *sea/seas* plural יַמִּים

definiteness   A way of expressing whether something can be identified. If we refer to *a blue house* the house cannot be identified: it could be any one of all the blue houses in the world. But if we refer to *the blue house* we are talking about a specific blue house and we can identify exactly which blue house we mean. In Hebrew, nouns are indefinite unless they take the definite article:

Indefinite: *a house*   בַּיִת   Definite: *the house*   הַבַּיִת

However, proper nouns are definite:

Israel   יִשְׂרָאֵל   *David*   דָּוִד

demonstrative   A word that singles out a particular thing (or things) for attention. In English, demonstratives are *this*, *these*, *that*, *those*. Demonstratives can be used as adjectives or as pronouns.

Without demonstrative	*the house*	הַבַּיִת
With demonstrative	*this house*	הַבַּיִת הַזֶּה
Demonstrative adjective	*this house is big*	גָּדוֹל הַבַּיִת הַזֶּה
Demonstrative pronoun	*this is the big house*	זֶה הַבַּיִת הַגָּדוֹל

direct speech Speech that is quoted directly, as opposed to indirect speech, which is reported indirectly. Examples:

Direct	*And he said, 'I have eaten the fruit.'*	וַיֹּאמֶר אָכְלִי אֶת־הַפְּרִי
Indirect	*And he said that he had eaten the fruit.*	וַיֹּאמֶר כִּי־אָכַל אֶת־הַפְּרִי

Direct speech is often introduced with the Infinitive Construct of the verb אָמַר, which is לֵאמֹר:

And he answered saying, 'I have eaten the fruit.'
וַיַּעַן לֵאמֹר אָכְלִי אֶת־הַפְּרִי

double *ayin* verb A verb in which the second and third root letters are identical. Example: סָבַב. See verb tables for conjugations.

geminate verb See double *ayin* verb

gender A division of nouns, and words that qualify nouns, into different kinds. The different kinds of nouns in Hebrew are known as *masculine* and *feminine*. Sometimes this reflects gender that is considered inherent:

man אִישׁ masculine *woman* אִשָּׁה feminine

However, nouns that might not be considered inherently gendered nevertheless are described as masculine or feminine:

day יוֹם masculine *hand* יָד feminine

Some languages have a neuter gender, but Hebrew does not. However, some words in Hebrew are of *common* gender, which means that they can be either masculine or feminine. Example: שֶׁמֶשׁ *sun*.

gentilic adjective A word describing a person or people by their place of origin, such as Glaswegian, Scottish, European. Hebrew examples are:

guttural Any of the letters ה, ע, א or ח. The term *guttural* refers to how they are, or were, pronounced. They have certain properties that separate them from other consonants, except the letter ר, which behaves like a *guttural*: they cannot take *dagesh*; they take a complex *sheva* instead of a simple *sheva*; they attract *a* vowels; they cause changes in the vowel patterns of weak verbs.

Hifil One of the Hebrew verb stems. It represents a change to the form of a verb to indicate a causative effect:

Root בּוֹא Qal *to come*, Hif *to bring* (i.e. *to cause to come*) (weak verb)

| Qal Perf 3ms | בָּא | *he came* |
| Hifil Perf 3ms | הֵבִיא | *he brought* |

Hitpael One of the Hebrew verb stems. It is an intensive form related to the Piel, and it represents a change to the form of the verb to indicate a reflexive effect:

Root קָדַשׁ Qal *to be holy*, Hit *to consecrate oneself*

| Qal | קָדַשׁ | *he is holy* |
| Hitpael | הִתְקַדֵּשׁ | *he has consecrated himself* |

Hofal One of the Hebrew verb stems. A passive form of the Hifil.

Root בּוֹא Qal *to come*, Hif *to bring* (i.e. *to cause to come*) (weak verb)

Qal Perf 3ms	בָּא	*he came*
Hifil Perf 3ms	הֵבִיא	*he brought* (e.g. a present)
Hofal Perf 3ms	הוּבָא	*he was brought* (e.g. by guards)

hollow verb See *ayin vav* or *ayin yod* verb

idiom A form of expression that is characteristic of a language and that does not make literal sense. Examples:

English *He has two left feet* (he finds dancing a challenge)

Hebrew גָּדוֹל יהוה מִכָּל־הָאֱלֹהִים *Yhwh is great from all the gods*, meaning *Yhwh is greater than all the gods*.

However, some Hebrew idioms have made their way into English via translations of the Bible. Examples:

to pour out one's heart   שִׁפְכוּ־לְפָנָיו לְבַבְכֶם (Ps 62:9 [Engl. 62:8]) *Pour out your heart before him.*

the skin of one's teeth   וָאֶתְמַלְּטָה בְּעוֹר שִׁנָּי (Job 19:20) *I have escaped by the skin of my teeth.*

imperative   A verbal form that indicates the giving of orders or instructions.

Root הָלַךְ *to go* (weak verb)

Imperfect	תֵּלֵךְ	*you will go*
Imperative	לֵךְ	*go!*

imperfect   A verbal form that expresses an idea of incomplete action. Often translated with an English future tense, but can be translated with English past or present tenses. Forms include all persons, genders and numbers. Example

Root זָכַר *to remember* (strong verb)

3ms	יִזְכֹּר	3mp	יִזְכְּרוּ
3fs	תִּזְכֹּר	3fp	תִּזְכֹּרְנָה
2ms	תִּזְכֹּר	2mp	תִּזְכְּרוּ
2fs	תִּזְכְּרִי	2fp	תִּזְכֹּרְנָה
1s	אֶזְכֹּר	1p	נִזְכֹּר

infinitive   A verb form that has no finite parts. In English, infinitives are usually expressed with the preposition *to*: *to go, to sleep, to think*. There are two kinds of infinitive in Hebrew.

The Infinitive Construct is frequently used in the same way as the English infinitive, with the preposition לְ:

to remember   לִזְכֹּר   *to visit*   לִפְקֹד

The Infinitive Absolute is frequently used with a finite form of the same verb to indicate emphasis:

I will certainly bless you   בָּרֵךְ אֲבָרֶכְךָ

you certainly will not die   לֹא־מוֹת תְּמֻתוּן

interjection   A word that conveys emotion without having much grammatical function in the sentence. Examples in English are words like *hurray* and *ouch*. A common example in Hebrew is הִנֵּה *behold*.

interrogative   A word that asks a question. In Hebrew the commonest are:

Who ... ?	מִי	*Where ... ?*	אֵי or אִי
What ... ?	מֶה or מַה	*When ... ?*	מָתַי
Why ... ?	לָמֶה or לָמָּה	*How ... ?*	אֵיךְ

jussive   A means of giving commands or instructions in the 2nd or 3rd person. Usually, but not always, identical in form to the Imperfect. Also used for prohibitions in the 3rd person. Examples:

he will kill them	יִקְטֹל אוֹתָם	Imperfect 3ms
let him kill them	יִקְטֹל אוֹתָם	Jussive 3ms
kill them	קְטֹל אוֹתָם	Imperative 2ms
do not kill them	אַל תִּקְטֹל אוֹתָם	Jussive 2ms + negative particle אַל
you absolutely must not kill them	לֹא תִּקְטֹל אוֹתָם	Jussive 2ms + negative particle לֹא

lamed alef **verb**   A verb with א as the final letter of its root form. Example: מָצָא. See verb tables for conjugations.

lamed **guttural verb**   A verb with a guttural as the final letter of its root form. Example: שָׁלַח. See verb tables for conjugations.

Ketiv   A word in the written text of the Hebrew Bible that is substituted when the text is read aloud. The word read instead is called the Qere.

mappiq   A dot in the letter ה to indicate that it is to be pronounced as a consonant (roughly similar to the pronunciation of ח). Frequently found in 3fs pronominal suffixes:

to her לָהּ   *her horse* סוּסָהּ

maqqef   A line like a hyphen that joins two words so that they are pronounced as if they were one word. For example: *all the land of Israel* כָּל־אֶרֶץ יִשְׂרָאֵל

meteg   An accent that is used to mark occasions where ָ is to be pronounced *ā* rather than *o*. In fact ָ is almost always pronounced *ā*, but in closed unstressed syllables it is generally pronounced as a short-*o* vowel. Therefore, in closed unstressed syllables where it needs to be pronounced as an *a* vowel, the meteg reminds the reader of the pronunciation. For example:

she has remembered זָכְרָה   *and he lived* וַיִּשֶׁב

Nifal   One of the Hebrew verb stems. Often translated as a passive form of the Qal.

Root פָּקַד Qal *to visit*, Nif *to be visited*

| Qal Perf 3ms | פָּקַד | *he has visited* |
| Nifal Perf 3ms | נִפְקַד | *he has been visited* |

noun   The name of a thing, a person or a place. Examples:

house בַּיִת   *Abraham* אַבְרָהָם   *Egypt* מִצְרַיִם

number   Forms of a word that indicate how many of something there are. In English we have two possibilities: singular and plural. In Hebrew, there is a third option: dual. Example:

Singular יָד *hand*   Plural יָדוֹת *hands*   Dual יָדַיִם *hands*
                       (non-human, e.g. the   (human)
                       arms of a chair)

Hebrew verbs also come in singular and plural:

Singular שָׁמַרְתִּי *I have guarded*   Plural שָׁמַרְנוּ *We have guarded*

object   Put simply, the thing that something happens to. The subject of a sentence does something, the verb indicates what is being done, and the object indicates what it is being done to. Example:

Sentence: אָהֲבָה מִיכַל דָּוִד   *Michal loved David*

Subject: מִיכַל *Michal*   Verb: אָהֲבָה *loved*   Object: דָּוִד *David*

object marker   A Hebrew particle (אֵת) that identifies the object(s) of a verb. There is no English word that translates it. If a verb has multiple objects, they can each take an object marker. Example:

Joseph commanded Moses to eat the bread
צִוָּה יוֹסֵף אֶת־מֹשֶׁה לֶאֱכוֹל אֶת־הַלֶּחֶם

paragogic   An extra letter usually added to make a word easier to pronounce. In Hebrew we commonly find paragogic ה and paragogic ן. Examples:

Usual form	תְּמוּתוּ	*you will die*	(Qal Impf 2mp from מוּת)
With paragogic ן	תְּמֻתוּן	*you will die*	
Usual form	נֵלֵךְ	*we will go*	(Qal Impf 1p from הָלַךְ)
With paragogic ה	נֵלְכָה	*we will go*	

participle   A form of the verb that works like an adjective. Example:

He was judging *the people of the land*   הוּא שֹׁפֵט אֶת־עַם הָאָרֶץ

However, in Hebrew the Participle can also function like a noun. Example:

He is the judge   הוּא הַשֹּׁפֵט

particle   A word that has a grammatical function but does not change form. An example in English is the word *to* used as part of the infinitive, e.g. *to sing* or *to dance*. Hebrew has numerous particles. Some words that are described as particles may also be described in other ways: for example, the particle גַּם is sometimes known as the conjunction גַּם.

passive   A verb whose subject is having something done to it/ them is said to be in the **passive** voice. See **active** for examples.

patach furtive An *a* vowel (called *patach*) that looks as if it is creeping into a word. Common under the last letter of *lamed* guttural verbs in certain forms. Examples:

Ptc שֹׁמֵעַ *hearing*　　　　Inf cstr שְׂמֹחַ *to rejoice*

pause There are usually two places in a verse of biblical Hebrew where the reader is required to pause: at the points indicated by *atnah* and *silluq*. Some words take a longer vowel when they are in pause. However, the meaning does not change. Example:

Usual form	בַּדֶּרֶךְ	*in the path*
Pausal form	בַּדָּרֶךְ	*in the path*

pe alef verb A verb with an א as the first letter of its root form. Example: אָכַל. See verb tables for conjugations.

pe guttural verb A verb with a guttural as the first letter of its root form. Example: עָמַד. See verb tables for conjugations.

pe nun verb A verb with an נ as the first letter of its root form. Example: נָגַשׁ. See verb tables for conjugations.

pe vav or pe yod verbs A verb with a ו or י as the first letter of its root form. Example: יָשַׁב. See verb tables for conjugations.

perfect A verbal form that expresses an idea of incomplete action. Often translated with an English past tense, but can be translated with English future or present tenses. Forms include all persons, genders and numbers. Example:

Root כָּתַב *to write* (strong verb)

3ms	כָּתַב	3p	כָּתְבוּ
3fs	כָּתְבָה		
2ms	כָּתַבְתָּ	2mp	כְּתַבְתֶּם
2fs	כָּתַבְתְּ	2fp	כְּתַבְתֶּן
1s	כָּתַבְתִּי	1p	כָּתַבְנוּ

Piel One of the Hebrew verb stems. It represents a change to the form of a verb to indicate an intensive effect:

Root שָׁבַר Qal *to break*, Pi *to shatter*

Qal Perf 3ms	שָׁבַר	*it broke*
Pi Perf 3ms	שִׁבֵּר	*it shattered*

pointing Another word for the vowels added to the consonantal Hebrew text. Also known as vocalization.

pronoun A word that stands in place of a noun. In English, for example, we could say: *My sister has visited me*; *Deborah has visited me*; *A woman has visited me*. Or we could simply say *She has visited me*, with *she* (pronoun) standing in place of *my sister*, *Deborah* or *the woman*.

prefix A letter or letters that are added to the beginning of a word to indicate its meaning. Examples:

Imperfect forms	יִקְטֹל	*he has killed*	prefix יְ
Inseparable prepositions	לַיהוָה	*to Yhwh*	prefix לְ

preposition A word that indicates a relationship between a noun or pronoun and other words in the sentence. Example:

The angel stood under the tree   עָמַד הַמַּלְאָךְ תַּחַת הָעֵץ

The word *under* describes where the angel is in relation to the tree.

pronominal suffixes A letter or letters that are added to the end of a word to indicate which person is involved. Each suffix represents a pronoun. A pronominal suffix can be added to a noun to indicate possession, to a verb to indicate its object, or to prepositions to indicate the relationship between the subject and the object, expressed by a pronoun. Even interjections in Hebrew can take pronominal suffixes. Examples:

noun	סוּסוֹ	his *horse*
verb	אֲהַבְתִּךָ	*I love* you
preposition	לָהֶם	*to* them
interjection	הִנְנִי	(Literally, *Behold* me), *here I am*

proper noun The name of a person or place. Examples:

Gideon   גִּדְעוֹן   *Bethlehem*   בֵּיתלֶחֶם

Pual One of the Hebrew verb stems. A passive form of the Piel.

Root שָׁבַר Qal *to break*, Pi *to shatter*

Qal Perf 3ms	שָׁבַר	*it broke*
Piel Perf 3ms	שִׁבֵּר	*it shattered*
Pual Perf 3ms	שֻׁבַּר	*it was shattered*

Qal One of the Hebrew verb stems. This stem is known as the 'light' form because it is the basic form of the verb, without the additions of the other stems (such as the נ prefix of the Nifal, the *dagesh* in the middle root letter of the Piel, or the ה prefix of the Hifil).

Qere A word in the margins beside the text of the Hebrew Bible. It is intended to be read aloud as a substitute for one of the written words, and its pointing is given within the word it replaces. See also **Ketiv**. A few Ketiv words are not given marginal Qere readings; instead the vowels of the Qere are simply written into the Ketiv without an accompanying note. These words are always read as Qere and are called Qere perpetuum. Example: the name of God is always read *a-dō-NĪ* and is written with the vowels of אֲדֹנָי, thus: יְהוָה.

reduplicated verbs See double *ayin* verbs.

reflexive A means of referring to oneself. In English, reflexive ideas are frequently expressed with words like *myself* or *yourselves*. Example: *He opened the oven and burned himself.* In Hebrew, the reflexive is generally expressed by the Hitpael stem.

relative pronoun A word that expresses a relationship between a clause and its context in the sentence. In English we distinguish between *who, which* and *that*. In Hebrew they are all represented by אֲשֶׁר. Example:

The place which you are standing on is holy ground.
הַמָּקוֹם אֲשֶׁר אַתָּה עוֹמֵד עָלָיו אַדְמַת־קֹדֶשׁ הוּא

root The word that forms the basis of a Hebrew verb. Most roots have three letters, though roots such as קוּם are sometimes described as biliteral (having two letters). In this case, and others like it, the letter ו is considered to be a vowel rather than a consonant.

silluq   An accent that is identical in form to *meteg* but has an entirely different function. It marks the pause at the end of a verse, functioning a little like a full stop.

stem   One of the seven categories of Hebrew verbs. Each stem has distinctive features and each stem has a distinctive range of meanings. The seven stems are: **Qal, Nifal, Piel, Pual, Hitpael, Hifil** and **Hofal**. Verbs can be conjugated within each of the stems. However, not all verbs are actually found in all stems in biblical Hebrew.

stress   The point where a word is emphasized. Examples:

English	the *hap* in *happy*
Hebrew	the בָר in דָּבָר

strong verb   A verb that follows the קָטַל pattern and has no vowels (י or ו), no gutturals, and no ר in its root. Neither should it begin with נ or be reduplicated.

subject   The part of a sentence that indicates who or what is doing something. In the following sentence, *the king* (הַמֶּלֶךְ) is the subject: *The king gave his horse to me* נָתַן הַמֶּלֶךְ לִי סוּסוֹ.

suffix   A letter or letters that are added to the end of a word to indicate its meaning. Examples:

Perfect forms	קָטַלְתִּי	I *have killed*	suffix תִּי
Pronominal suffixes	יְהַלְלָהּ	*he will praise* her	suffix הָּ

superlative   A word used to indicate that something transcends others of its type. In English, this is done by adding the ending -*est*; example: *tall*est, *fast*est. It can also be done by using the term *the most*: *She is* the most *talkative child in her class*. In Hebrew, superlatives can be expressed in a number of ways. One of the most common is by means of the **construct** relationship. Examples:

the youngest of his sons	קְטֹן בָּנָיו
the holiest place (literally *the holy of holies*)	קֹדֶשׁ הַקֳּדָשִׁים

syllable One of the sounds in a word. In the word מַאֲכֶלֶת there are four syllables: מַ and אֲ and כֶ and לֶת.

Vav Consecutive The means by which Hebrew verbs use the conjunction ו to link a series of verbs. In English, this often requires changing the translating tense from future to past (for VC Imperfect) or from past to future (for VC Perfect). Example:

He will guard   יִשְׁמֹר   *And he guarded*   וַיִּשְׁמֹר

verb A word that denotes some kind of activity.

vocalization See **pointing**.

vowel In English, the letters AEIO and U (and sometimes Y) represent vowel sounds. However, the Hebrew alphabet is made up entirely of consonants. Vowel sounds are represented by dots and dashes underneath the consonants, although the long-*o* vowel is written above the consonant.

weak verb A verb that contains a letter that cannot take *dagesh* (the gutturals and ר), or is prone to disappear at the beginning of a word (נ), or otherwise causes the verb to depart from the קָטַל strong-verb pattern, is known as a weak verb.

Table 1 Qal: strong verbs

QAL					
Strong verbs	קָטַל	שָׁמַר	פָּקַד	כָּתַב	זָכַר
Perfect					
3ms	קָטַל	שָׁמַר	פָּקַד	כָּתַב	זָכַר
3fs	קָטְלָה	שָׁמְרָה	פָּקְדָה	כָּתְבָה	זָכְרָה
2ms	קָטַלְתָּ	שָׁמַרְתָּ	פָּקַדְתָּ	כָּתַבְתָּ	זָכַרְתָּ
2fs	קָטַלְתְּ	שָׁמַרְתְּ	פָּקַדְתְּ	כָּתַבְתְּ	זָכַרְתְּ
1s	קָטַלְתִּי	שָׁמַרְתִּי	פָּקַדְתִּי	כָּתַבְתִּי	זָכַרְתִּי
3p	קָטְלוּ	שָׁמְרוּ	פָּקְדוּ	כָּתְבוּ	זָכְרוּ
2mp	קְטַלְתֶּם	שְׁמַרְתֶּם	פְּקַדְתֶּם	כְּתַבְתֶּם	זְכַרְתֶּם
2fp	קְטַלְתֶּן	שְׁמַרְתֶּן	פְּקַדְתֶּן	כְּתַבְתֶּן	זְכַרְתֶּן
1p	קָטַלְנוּ	שָׁמַרְנוּ	פָּקַדְנוּ	כָּתַבְנוּ	זָכַרְנוּ
Imperfect					
3ms	יִקְטֹל	יִשְׁמֹר	יִפְקֹד	יִכְתֹּב	יִזְכֹּר
3fs	תִּקְטֹל	תִּשְׁמֹר	תִּפְקֹד	תִּכְתֹּב	תִּזְכֹּר
2ms	תִּקְטֹל	תִּשְׁמֹר	תִּפְקֹד	תִּכְתֹּב	תִּזְכֹּר
2fs	תִּקְטְלִי	תִּשְׁמְרִי	תִּפְקְדִי	תִּכְתְּבִי	תִּזְכְּרִי
1s	אֶקְטֹל	אֶשְׁמֹר	אֶפְקֹד	אֶכְתֹּב	אֶזְכֹּר
3mp	יִקְטְלוּ	יִשְׁמְרוּ	יִפְקְדוּ	יִכְתְּבוּ	יִזְכְּרוּ
3fp	תִּקְטֹלְנָה	תִּשְׁמֹרְנָה	תִּפְקֹדְנָה	תִּכְתֹּבְנָה	תִּזְכֹּרְנָה
2mp	תִּקְטְלוּ	תִּשְׁמְרוּ	תִּפְקְדוּ	תִּכְתְּבוּ	תִּזְכְּרוּ
2fp	תִּקְטֹלְנָה	תִּשְׁמֹרְנָה	תִּפְקֹדְנָה	תִּכְתֹּבְנָה	תִּזְכֹּרְנָה
1p	נִקְטֹל	נִשְׁמֹר	נִפְקֹד	נִכְתֹּב	נִזְכֹּר
Imperative ms	קְטֹל	שְׁמֹר	פְּקֹד	כְּתֹב	זְכֹר
Infinitive Cstr	קְטֹל	שְׁמֹר	פְּקֹד	כְּתֹב	זְכֹר
Infinitive Abs	קָטוֹל	שָׁמוֹר	פָּקוֹד	כָּתוֹב	זָכוֹר
Participle	קֹטֵל	שֹׁמֵר	פֹּקֵד	כֹּתֵב	זֹכֵר
Jussive 3ms	יִקְטֹל	יִשְׁמֹר	יִפְקֹד	יִכְתֹּב	יִזְכֹּר

Verb Table 2 Qal: weak verbs

QAL

Weak verbs	*Pe guttural*	*Ayin guttural*	*Lamed guttural*	*Pe yod/ Pe vav*	*Ayin yod/ Ayin vav*
Perfect					
3ms	עָמַד	שָׁחַט	שָׁלַח	יָשַׁב	קָם
3fs	עָמְדָה	שָׁהֲטָה	שָׁלְחָה	יָשְׁבָה	קָמָה
2ms	עָמַדְתָּ	שָׁחַטְתָּ	שָׁלַחְתָּ	יָשַׁבְתָּ	קַמְתָּ
2fs	עָמַדְתְּ	שָׁחַטְתְּ	שָׁלַחְתְּ	יָשַׁבְתְּ	קַמְתְּ
1s	עָמַדְתִּי	שָׁחַטְתִּי	שָׁלַחְתִּי	יָשַׁבְתִּי	קַמְתִּי
3p	עָמְדוּ	שָׁהֲטוּ	שָׁלְחוּ	יָשְׁבוּ	קָמוּ
2mp	עֲמַדְתֶּם	שְׁחַטְתֶּם	שְׁלַחְתֶּם	יְשַׁבְתֶּם	קַמְתֶּם
2fp	עֲמַדְתֶּן	שְׁחַטְתֶּן	שְׁלַחְתֶּן	יְשַׁבְתֶּן	קַמְתֶּן
1p	עָמַדְנוּ	שָׁחַטְנוּ	שָׁלַחְנוּ	יָשַׁבְנוּ	קַמְנוּ
Imperfect					
3ms	יַעֲמֹד	יִשְׁחַט	יִשְׁלַח	יֵשֵׁב	יָקוּם
3fs	תַּעֲמֹד	תִּשְׁחַט	תִּשְׁלַח	תֵּשֵׁב	תָּקוּם
2ms	תַּעֲמֹד	תִּשְׁחַט	תִּשְׁלַח	תֵּשֵׁב	תָּקוּם
2fs	תַּעַמְדִי	תִּשְׁחֲטִי	תִּשְׁלְחִי	תֵּשְׁבִי	תָּקוּמִי
1s	אֶעֱמֹד	אֶשְׁחַט	אֶשְׁלַח	אֵשֵׁב	אָקוּם
3mp	יַעַמְדוּ	יִשְׁחֲטוּ	יִשְׁלְחוּ	יֵשְׁבוּ	יָקוּמוּ
3fp	תַּעֲמֹדְנָה	תִּשְׁחַטְנָה	תִּשְׁלַחְנָה	תֵּשַׁבְנָה	תְּקוּמֶינָה
2mp	תַּעַמְדוּ	תִּשְׁחֲטוּ	תִּשְׁלְחוּ	תֵּשְׁבוּ	תָּקוּמוּ
2fp	תַּעֲמֹדְנָה	תִּשְׁחַטְנָה	תִּשְׁלַחְנָה	תֵּשַׁבְנָה	תְּקוּמֶינָה
1p	נַעֲמֹד	נִשְׁחַט	נִשְׁלַח	נֵשֵׁב	נָקוּם
Imperative ms	עֲמֹד	שְׁחַט	שְׁלַח	שֵׁב	קוּם
Infinitive Cstr	עֲמֹד	שְׁחַט	שְׁלֹחַ	שֶׁבֶת	קוּם
Infinitive Abs	עָמוֹד	שָׁחוֹט	שָׁלוֹחַ	יָשׁוֹב	קוֹם
Participle	עֹמֵד	שֹׁחֵט	שֹׁלֵחַ	יֹשֵׁב	קָם
Jussive 3ms	יַעֲמֹד	יִשְׁחַט	יִשְׁלַח	יֵשֵׁב	יָקֹם

Weak verbs	Pe nun	Double Ayin	Pe alef	Lamed alef	Lamed he
Perfect					
3ms	נָגַשׁ	סָבַב	אָכַל	מָצָא	גָּלָה
3fs	נָגְשָׁה	סָבְבָה	אָכְלָה	מָצְאָה	גָּלְתָה
2ms	נָגַשְׁתָּ	סַבּוֹתָ	אָכַלְתָּ	מָצָאתָ	גָּלִיתָ
2fs	נָגַשְׁתְּ	סַבּוֹת	אָכַלְתְּ	מָצָאת	גָּלִית
1s	נָגַשְׁתִּי	סַבּוֹתִי	אָכַלְתִּי	מָצָאתִי	גָּלִיתִי
3p	נָגְשׁוּ	סָבְבוּ	אָכְלוּ	מָצְאוּ	גָּלוּ
2mp	נְגַשְׁתֶּם	סַבּוֹתֶם	אֲכַלְתֶּם	מְצָאתֶם	גְּלִיתֶם
2fp	נְגַשְׁתֶּן	סַבּוֹתֶן	אֲכַלְתֶּן	מְצָאתֶן	גְּלִיתֶן
1p	נָגַשְׁנוּ	סַבּוֹנוּ	אָכַלְנוּ	מָצָאנוּ	גָּלִינוּ
Imperfect					
3ms	יִגַּשׁ	יָסֹב	יֹאכַל	יִמְצָא	יִגְלֶה
3fs	תִּגַּשׁ	תָּסֹב	תֹּאכַל	תִּמְצָא	תִּגְלֶה
2ms	תִּגַּשׁ	תָּסֹב	תֹּאכַל	תִּמְצָא	תִּגְלֶה
2fs	תִּגְּשִׁי	תָּסֹבִּי	תֹּאכְלִי	תִּמְצְאִי	תִּגְלִי
1s	אֶגַּשׁ	אָסֹב	אֹכַל	אֶמְצָא	אֶגְלֶה
3mp	יִגְּשׁוּ	יָסֹבּוּ	יֹאכְלוּ	יִמְצְאוּ	יִגְלוּ
3fp	תִּגַּשְׁנָה	תְּסֻבֶּינָה	תֹּאכַלְנָה	תִּמְצֶאנָה	תִּגְלֶינָה
2mp	תִּגְּשׁוּ	תָּסֹבּוּ	תֹּאכְלוּ	תִּמְצְאוּ	תִּגְלוּ
2fp	תִּגַּשְׁנָה	תְּסֻבֶּינָה	תֹּאכַלְנָה	תִּמְצֶאנָה	תִּגְלֶינָה
1p	נִגַּשׁ	נָסֹב	נֹאכַל	נִמְצָא	נִגְלֶה
Imperative ms	גַּשׁ/גְּשָׁה	סֹב	אֱכֹל	מְצָא	גְּלֵה
Infinitive Cstr	גֶּשֶׁת	סֹב	אֱכֹל	מְצֹא	גְּלוֹת
Infinitive Abs	נָגוֹשׁ	סָבוֹב	אָכוֹל	מָצוֹא	גָּלֹה
Participle	נֹגֵשׁ	סוֹבֵב	אֹכֵל	מֹצֵא	גֹּלֶה
Jussive 3ms	יִגַּשׁ	יָסֹב	יֹאכַל	יִמְצָא	יִגֶל

Table 3 All stems: strong verbs (קָטַל)

N.B. Tables for the other stems of the weak verbs are outside the scope of this book. However, they can be found in Hebrew grammars.

	QAL	NIFAL	PIEL	PUAL	HITP.	HIFIL	HOFAL
Perfect							
3ms	קָטַל	נִקְטַל	קִטֵּל	קֻטַּל	הִתְקַטֵּל	הִקְטִיל	הָקְטַל
3fs	קָטְלָה	נִקְטְלָה	קִטְּלָה	קֻטְּלָה	הִתְקַטְּלָה	הִקְטִילָה	הָקְטְלָה
2ms	קָטַלְתָּ	נִקְטַלְתָּ	קִטַּלְתָּ	קֻטַּלְתָּ	הִתְקַטַּלְתָּ	הִקְטַלְתָּ	הָקְטַלְתָּ
2fs	קָטַלְתְּ	נִקְטַלְתְּ	קִטַּלְתְּ	קֻטַּלְתְּ	הִתְקַטַּלְתְּ	הִקְטַלְתְּ	הָקְטַלְתְּ
1s	קָטַלְתִּי	נִקְטַלְתִּי	קִטַּלְתִּי	קֻטַּלְתִּי	הִתְקַטַּלְתִּי	הִקְטַלְתִּי	הָקְטַלְתִּי
3p	קָטְלוּ	נִקְטְלוּ	קִטְּלוּ	קֻטְּלוּ	הִתְקַטְּלוּ	הִקְטִילוּ	הָקְטְלוּ
2mp	קְטַלְתֶּם	נִקְטַלְתֶּם	קִטַּלְתֶּם	קֻטַּלְתֶּם	הִתְקַטַּלְתֶּם	הִקְטַלְתֶּם	הָקְטַלְתֶּם
2fp	קְטַלְתֶּן	נִקְטַלְתֶּן	קִטַּלְתֶּן	קֻטַּלְתֶּן	הִתְקַטַּלְתֶּן	הִקְטַלְתֶּן	הָקְטַלְתֶּן
1p	קָטַלְנוּ	נִקְטַלְנוּ	קִטַּלְנוּ	קֻטַּלְנוּ	הִתְקַטַּלְנוּ	הִקְטַלְנוּ	הָקְטַלְנוּ
Imperfect							
3ms	יִקְטֹל	יִקָּטֵל	יְקַטֵּל	יְקֻטַּל	יִתְקַטֵּל	יַקְטִיל	יָקְטַל
3fs	תִּקְטֹל	תִּקָּטֵל	תְּקַטֵּל	תְּקֻטַּל	תִּתְקַטֵּל	תַּקְטִיל	תָּקְטַל
2ms	תִּקְטֹל	תִּקָּטֵל	תְּקַטֵּל	תְּקֻטַּל	תִּתְקַטֵּל	תַּקְטִיל	תָּקְטַל
2fs	תִּקְטְלִי	תִּקָּטְלִי	תְּקַטְּלִי	תְּקֻטְּלִי	תִּתְקַטְּלִי	תַּקְטִילִי	תָּקְטְלִי
1s	אֶקְטֹל	אֶקָּטֵל	אֲקַטֵּל	אֲקֻטַּל	אֶתְקַטֵּל	אַקְטִיל	אָקְטַל
3mp	יִקְטְלוּ	יִקָּטְלוּ	יְקַטְּלוּ	יְקֻטְּלוּ	יִתְקַטְּלוּ	יַקְטִילוּ	יָקְטְלוּ
3fp	תִּקְטֹלְנָה	תִּקָּטַלְנָה	תְּקַטֵּלְנָה	תְּקֻטַּלְנָה	תִּתְקַטֵּלְנָה	תַּקְטֵלְנָה	תָּקְטַלְנָה
2mp	תִּקְטְלוּ	תִּקָּטְלוּ	תְּקַטְּלוּ	תְּקֻטְּלוּ	תִּתְקַטְּלוּ	תַּקְטִילוּ	תָּקְטְלוּ
2fp	תִּקְטֹלְנָה	תִּקָּטַלְנָה	תְּקַטֵּלְנָה	תְּקֻטַּלְנָה	תִּתְקַטֵּלְנָה	תַּקְטֵלְנָה	תָּקְטַלְנָה
1p	נִקְטֹל	נִקָּטֵל	נְקַטֵּל	נְקֻטַּל	נִתְקַטֵּל	נַקְטִיל	נָקְטַל
Impv ms	קְטֹל	הִקָּטֵל	קַטֵּל	—	הִתְקַטֵּל	הַקְטֵל	—
Inf Cstr	קְטֹל	הִקָּטֵל	קַטֵּל	קֻטַּל	הִתְקַטֵּל	הַקְטִיל	הָקְטַל
Inf Abs	קָטוֹל	הִקָּטֵל	קַטֵּל	קֻטַּל	הִתְקַטֵּל	הַקְטֵל	הָקְטֵל
Ptc	קֹטֵל	נִקְטָל	מְקַטֵּל	מְקֻטָּל	מִתְקַטֵּל	מַקְטִיל	מָקְטָל
Juss 3ms	יִקְטֹל	יִקָּטֵל	יְקַטֵּל	יְקֻטַּל	יִתְקַטֵּל	יַקְטֵל	יָקְטַל

Abbreviations

1	first person	Impv	Imperative
2	second person	Inf	Infinitive
3	third person	m	masculine
abs	absolute	Nif	Nifal
adj	adjective	p	plural
adv	adverb	parag	paragogic (extra)
Cohort	Cohortative	pass	passive
conj	conjunction	Perf	Perfect
cstr	construct	Pi	Piel
f	feminine	pr noun	proper noun
gent	gentilic	prep	preposition
Hif	Hifil	Ptc	Participle
Hit	Hitpael	s	singular
Hof	Hofal	suff	suffix
Impf	Imperfect	VC	Vav Consecutive

Entry	Related words	Form	Meaning/Look up Hebrew entry
אָב		noun ms	*father*
	אָבוֹת	noun mp	*fathers*
	אֲבוֹת	noun mp cstr	*fathers of*
	אָבִיו	noun ms + suff 3ms	*his father*
	אַבְרָהָם	pr noun ms	*Abraham*
אָבַד		verb	*to be lost, to wander, to perish*; Pi *to destroy*
אִבַּדְתָּ		Pi Perf 2ms	אָבַד
אֲבוֹת		noun mp cstr	אָב
אָבוֹת		noun mp	אָב
אֶבְטַח		Qal Impf 1s	בָּטַח
אָבִי		noun ms + suff 1s	אָב
אָבִיו		noun ms + suff 3ms	אָב
אַבְרָהָם		pr noun ms	אָב
אֲבָרֶכְךָ		Pi Impf 1s + suff 2ms	בָּרַךְ
אֲדֹנָי		noun ms	דוּן
אֲדֹנִים		noun mp	דוּן
אֵדַע		Qal Impf 1s	יָדַע
אָהַב		verb	*to love*
	אַהֲבָה	noun fs	*love*
אַהֲבָה		noun fs	אָהַב
אָהַבְתָּ		Qal Perf 2ms	אָהַב
אוֹדֶה		Hif Impf 1s	יָדָה
אוֹדְךָ		Hif Impf 1s + suff 2mp	יָדָה
אוֹיְבַי		noun mp + suff 1s	אָיַב
אָז		adv	*then, therefore*
אֶזְכֹּר		Qal Impf 1s	זָכַר
אֶזְכְּרָה		Cohort 1s	זָכַר
אֲזַמְּרָה		Pi Impf 1s + parag ה	זָמַר
אֹזֶן		noun fs	*ear*
	אָזְנַיִם	noun f dual	
אָח		noun ms	*brother*

Entry	Related words	Form	Meaning/Look up Hebrew entry
	אֲחִי	noun ms cstr	*brother of*
	אֲחֵי	noun mp cstr	*brothers of*
	אַחִים	noun mp	*brothers*
	אָחוֹת	noun fs	*sister*
	אֲחָיוֹת	noun fp	*sisters*
אֶחָד		numeral	*one*
	אַחַד	numeral cstr	*one of*
אָחַז		verb	*to seize, catch;* Nif *to be caught*
אֲחִי		noun ms cstr	אָח
אֲחֵי		noun mp cstr	אָח
אֲחָיוֹת		noun fp	אָח
אָחִיךְ		noun ms + suff 2ms	אָח
אַחִים		noun mp	אָח
אַחַר		prep	אַחַר
אָחַר		verb	*to stay;* Pi *to linger*
	אָחוֹר	noun ms (also adv)	*back part, west* (adv: *back*)
	אַחַר	prep	*after*
	אַחֲרֵי	prep	*after*
	אַחֲרָיו	prep + suff 3ms	*after him* (or *it*)
אַחֲרֵי		prep	אַחַר
אַחֲרַי		prep + suff 1s	אַחַר
אַחֲרֶיהָ		prep + suff 3fs	אַחַר
אַחֲרֵיהֶם		prep + suff 3mp	אַחַר
אַחֲרֵיהֶן		prep + suff 3fp	אַחַר
אַחֲרָיו		prep + suff 3ms	אַחַר
אַחֲרֶיךָ		prep + suff 2ms	אַחַר
אַחֲרַיִךְ		prep + suff 2fs	אַחַר
אַחֲרֵיכֶם		prep + suff 2mp	אַחַר
אַחֲרֵיכֶן		prep + suff 2fp	אַחַר
אַחֲרֵינוּ		prep + suff 1p	אַחַר
אָחֹת		noun fs	אָח

Entry	Related words	Form	Meaning/Look up Hebrew entry
אֵי		pronoun cstr	*Where ... ?*
	אֵי	pronoun	*Where ... ?*
	אֵיךְ	pronoun	*How ... ?*
אָיַב		verb	*to hate, to be an enemy*
	אֹיֵב	noun ms	*enemy*
	אֹיְבִים	noun mp	*enemies*
אֹיֵב		noun ms	אָיַב
אֹיְבִי		noun ms + suff 1s	אָיַב
אֹיְבֵי		noun mp cstr	אָיַב
אֹיְבָיו		noun ms + suff 3ms	אָיַב
אֹיְבִים		noun mp	אָיַב
אֵיךְ		pronoun	אֵי
אַיִל		noun ms	*ram*
אֵין		adv cstr	*there is not, there are not*; abs is אַיִן
אִישׁ		noun ms	*man*
אַךְ		adv	*only, but*
אָכוֹל		Qal Inf abs	אָכַל
אֱכֹל		Qal Inf cstr	אָכַל
אֱכֹל		Qal Impv 2ms	אָכַל
אָכַל		verb	*to eat*
	אָכְלָה	noun fs	*food*
	מַאֲכֶלֶת	noun fs	*knife*
אֹכֵל		Qal Ptc	אָכַל
אָכְלָה		Qal Perf 3fs	אָכַל
אָכְלָה		noun fs	אָכַל
אָכְלוּ		Qal Perf 3p	אָכַל
אֲכַלְכֶם		Qal Perf 2mp	אָכַל
אֲכַלְנוּ		Qal Perf 1p	אָכַל
אָכַלְתְּ		Qal Perf 2fs	אָכַל
אָכַלְתָּ		Qal Perf 2ms	אָכַל
אָכַלְתִּי		Qal Perf 1s	אָכַל

Entry	Related words	Form	Meaning/Look up Hebrew entry
אֲכַלְתֶּם		Qal Perf 2mp	אָכַל
אֲכַלְתֶּן		Qal Perf 2fp	אָכַל
אֶכְתֹּב		Qal Impf 1s	כָּתַב
אֶכְתְּבָה		Cohort 1s	כָּתַב
אֵל		noun ms	God, god
	אֱלֹהִים	noun ms, mp	God, gods
	אֱלֹהֵי	pr noun cstr	God of
	כֵּאלֹהִים	prep כְּ + אֱלֹהִים	like God
אֶל		prep	to
	אֵלָיו	prep + suff 3ms	to him (or it)
אַל		negative particle	not
אֵלֶּה		pronoun mp and fp	these
אֱלֹהֵי		pr noun cstr	אֵל
אֱלֹהִים		noun ms	אֵל
אֱלֹהִים		pr noun mp	אֵל
אֵלַי		prep + suff 1s	אֶל
אֵלֶיהָ		prep + suff 3fs	אֶל
אֲלֵיהֶם		prep + suff 3mp	אֶל
אֲלֵיהֶן		prep + suff 3fp	אֶל
אֵלָיו		prep + suff 3ms	אֶל
אֵלֶיךָ		prep + suff 2ms	אֶל
אֵלַיִךְ		prep + suff 2fs	אֶל
אֲלֵיכֶם		prep + suff 2mp	אֶל
אֲלֵיכֶן		prep + suff 2fp	אֶל
אֵלֵינוּ		prep + suff 1p	אֶל
אֵלֵךְ		Qal Impf 1s	הָלַךְ
אֵם		noun fs	mother
	אִמּוֹת	noun fp	mothers
	אִמּוֹ	noun fs + suff 3ms	his mother
אָמָה		noun fs	handmaid
אִמּוֹ		noun fs + suff 3ms	אֵם
אִמּוֹת		noun fp	אֵם
אִמִּי		noun fs + suff 1s	אֵם

Entry	Related words	Form	Meaning/Look up Hebrew entry
אָמַר		verb	*to say*
	וַיֹּאמֶר	Qal VC Impf 3ms	*and he said*
	וַיֹּאמְרוּ	Qal VC Impf 3mp	*and they said*
אֹמַר		Qal Impf 1s	אָמַר
אָמְרָה		Qal Perf 3fs	אָמַר
אָמַרְתְּ		Qal Perf 3fs	אָמַר
אֶמְשֹׁל		Qal Impf 1s	מָשַׁל
אֲנַחְנוּ		pronoun 1p	*we*
אֲנִי		pronoun 1s	*I*
אָנֹכִי		pronoun 1s	*I*
אָנַף		verb	*to be angry*
	אַף	noun ms	*nose, anger*
אָנַפְתָּ		Qal Perf 2ms	אָנַף
אָנַשׁ		verb	*to be mortal*
	אֲנָשִׁים	noun mp	*men*
	אַנְשֵׁי	noun mp cstr	*men of*
	אִשָּׁה	noun fs	*woman*
	אֵשֶׁת	noun fs cstr	*woman of, wife of*
	נָשִׁים	noun fp	*women*
	נְשֵׁי	noun fp cstr	*women of*
	אִשְׁתּוֹ	noun fs + suff 3ms	*his wife*
אַנְשֵׁי		noun mp cstr	אָנַשׁ
אֲנָשִׁים		noun mp	אָנַשׁ
אָסֹב		Qal Impf 1s	סָבַב
אֲסַפְּרָה		Pi Impf 1s	סָפַר
אֶעֶלְצָה		Qal Impf 1s + parag ה	עָלַץ
אֶעֱמֹד		Qal Impf 1s	עָמַד
אַף		conj	*also, moreover, indeed*; אַף כִּי *is it so that ... ?*
אַף		noun ms	אָנַף
אֶפְחַד		Qal Impf 1s	פָּחַד
אַפְּךָ		noun ms + suff 2ms	אָנַף

Entry	Related words	Form	Meaning/Look up Hebrew entry
אֶפֹּל		Qal Impf 1s	נָפַל
אֲפַקֵּד		Pi Impf 1s	פָּקַד
אֶפְקֹד		Qal Impf 1s	פָּקַד
אֶפְקְדָה		Cohort 1s	פָּקַד
אַפְקִיד		Hif Impf 1s	פָּקַד
אֶקְטֹל		Qal Impf 1s	קָטַל
אֶקָּטֵל		Nif Impf 1s	קָטַל
אֶרְאֶה		Qal Impf 1s	רָאָה
אֶרֶץ		noun fs	*land*
	אֲרָצוֹת	noun fp	*lands*
	אַרְצוֹת	noun fp cstr	*lands of*
אֲרָצוֹת		noun fp	אֶרֶץ
אַרְצוֹת		noun fp cstr	אֶרֶץ
אֵשׁ		noun ms and fs	*fire*
אֵשֵׁב		Qal Impf 1s	יָשַׁב
אִשָּׁה		noun fs	אָנַשׁ
אָשׁוּב		Qal Impf 1s	שׁוּב
אֲשִׂימֶנּוּ		Qal Impf 1s	שִׂים
אֶשְׂמְחָה		Qal Impf 1s + parag ה	שָׂמַח
אֲשֶׁר		pronoun m and f	*that, which, who*
	כַּאֲשֶׁר	prep כְּ + pronoun	*as, when*
אֵשֶׁת		noun fs cstr	אָנַשׁ
אִשְׁתּוֹ		noun fs + suff 3ms	אָנַשׁ
אַתְּ		pronoun 2fs	*you*
אֵת (1)		particle	object marker (no English word translates it)
	אֹתוֹ	pronoun 3ms	*him*
	אֹתָם	pronoun 3mp	*them*
אֵת (2)		prep	*with*
	אִתּוֹ	prep + suff 3ms	*with him* (or *it*)
	אִתָּם	prep + suff 3mp	*with them*
אִתָּהּ		prep + suff 3fs	אֵת (2)

Entry	Related words	Form	Meaning/Look up Hebrew entry
אַתָּה		pronoun 2ms	*you*
אֹתָה		pronoun 3fs	אֵת (1)
אִתּוֹ		prep + suff 3ms	אֵת (2)
אֹתוֹ		pronoun 3ms	אֵת (1)
אִתִּי		prep + suff 1s	אֵת (2)
אֹתִי		pronoun 1s	אֵת (1)
אִתְּךָ		prep + suff 2ms	אֵת (2)
אִתָּךְ		prep + suff 2fs	אֵת (2)
אֹתְךָ		pronoun 2ms	אֵת (1)
אֹתָךְ		pronoun 2fs	אֵת (1)
אִתְּכֶם		prep + suff 2mp	אֵת (2)
אֶתְכֶם		pronoun 2mp	אֵת (1)
אִתְּכֶן		prep + suff 2fp	אֵת (2)
אֶתְכֶן		pronoun 2fp	אֵת (1)
אִתָּם		prep + suff 3mp	אֵת (2)
אַתֶּם		pronoun 2mp	*you*
אֹתָם		pronoun 3mp	אֵת (1)
אִתָּן		prep + suff 3fp	אֵת (2)
אַתֶּן		pronoun 2fp	*you*
אֹתָן		pronoun 3fp	אֵת (1)
אִתָּנוּ		prep + suff 1p	אֵת (2)
אֹתָנוּ		pronoun 1p	אֵת (1)
אֶתְקַדֵּשׁ		Hit Impf 1s	קָדֵשׁ
בְּ		prep	*in, with*
	בּוֹ	prep + suff 3ms	*in/with him* (or *it*)
בָּאַר		verb	Pi *to engrave*
	בְּאֵר	noun fs	*well*
	בְּאֵר שֶׁבַע	pr noun	*Beersheba*
בָּאָרֶץ		prep בְּ + noun fs cstr	אֶרֶץ
בַּבֹּקֶר		prep בְּ + noun ms	בֹּקֶר
בַּדֶּרֶךְ		prep בְּ + noun ms	דֶּרֶךְ
בָּהּ		prep + suff 3fs	בְּ

Entry	Related words	Form	Meaning/Look up Hebrew entry
בְּהִוָּלֵד		prep בְּ + Nif Inf cstr	יָלַד
בָּהֶם		prep + suff 3mp	בְּ
בָּהֶן		prep + suff 3fp	בְּ
בָּהָר		prep בְּ + noun ms	הַר
בּוֹ		prep + suff 3ms	בְּ
בּוֹא		verb	Qal *to come*; Hif *to bring*; Hof *to be brought*
בְּזַרְעֶךָ		prep בְּ + noun ms + suff 2ms	זֶרַע
בָּחַן		verb	*to try, test*
בָּטַח		verb	*to cling to, trust, rely on*
בֶּטֶן		noun fs	*belly, womb*
בִּי		prep + suff 1s	בְּ
בְּיָדוֹ		prep בְּ + noun fs + suff 3ms	יָד
בִּיהוּדָה		prep בְּ + pr noun ms	יְהוּדָה
בַּיּוֹם		prep בְּ + noun ms	יוֹם
בִּימֵי		prep בְּ + noun mp cstr	יוֹם
בִּין		verb	*to discern, distinguish*
	בֵּין	prep	*between*
	בֵּינוֹ	prep + suff 3ms	*between him* (or *it*)
בֵּין		prep	בֵּין
בֵּינָהּ		prep + suff 3fs	בֵּין
בֵּינוֹ		prep + suff 3ms	בֵּין
בֵּינִי		prep + suff 1s	בֵּין
בֵּינֵיהֶם		prep + suff 3mp	בֵּין
בֵּינֵיהֶן		prep + suff 3fp	בֵּין
בֵּינֵיכֶם		prep + suff 2mp	בֵּין
בֵּינֵיכֶן		prep + suff 2fp	בֵּין
בֵּינֵינוּ		prep + suff 1p	בֵּין
בֵּינְךָ		prep + suff 2ms	בֵּין

Entry	Related words	Form	Meaning/Look up Hebrew entry
בֵּינֵךְ		prep + suff 2fs	בֵּין
בְּיִצְחָק		prep בְּ + pr noun ms	צָחַק
בְּיִשְׂרָאֵל		prep בְּ + pr noun ms	שָׂרָה
בֵּית		noun ms cstr	בָּנָה
בַּיִת		noun ms	בָּנָה
בֵּית לֶחֶם		pr noun	בָּנָה
בְּךָ		prep + suff 2ms	בְּ
בָּךְ		prep + suff 2fs	בְּ
בָּכָה		verb	to weep, lament
בָּכֶם		prep + suff 2mp	בְּ
בָּכֶן		prep + suff 2fp	בְּ
בָּלַה		verb	to swallow
בְּמִדְבַּר		prep בְּ + noun ms	דָּבַר
בְּמוֹת		prep בְּ + noun ms cstr	מוּת
בְּמֵישָׁרִים		prep בְּ + noun mp (also an adverb)	יָשַׁר
בֵּן		noun ms	בָּנָה
בֶּן		noun ms cstr	בָּנָה
בָּנָה		verb	to build
	בַּיִת	noun ms	house
	בֵּן	noun ms	son
	בֵּית	noun ms cstr	house of
	בֶּן	noun ms cstr	son of
	בָּנִים	noun mp	sons
	בָּתִּים	noun mp	houses
	בַּת	noun fs	daughter
	בֵּית לֶחֶם	pr noun	Bethlehem
	בְּנוֹ	noun ms + suff 3ms	his son
בְּנוֹ		noun ms + suff 3ms	בָּנָה
בָּנוּ		prep + suff 1p	בְּ
בָּנוֹת		noun fp	בָּנָה
בְּנוֹת		noun fp cstr	בָּנָה
בְּנִי		noun ms + suff 1s	בָּנָה

Entry	Related words	Form	Meaning/Look up Hebrew entry
בְּנֵי		noun mp cstr	בָּנָה
בָּנָיו		noun mp + suff 3ms	בָּנָה
בָּנִים		noun mp	בָּנָה
בִּנְךָ		noun ms + suff 2ms (in pause for בִּנְךָ)	בָּנָה
בִּנְךָ		noun ms + suff 2ms	בָּנָה
בְּסֻכָּךְ		prep בְּ + noun ms	סָכַךְ
בְּעֵינֶיךָ		prep בְּ + noun mp + suff 2ms	עַיִן
בְּקֹלָהּ		prep בְּ + noun ms + suff 3fs	קוֹל
בְּקֹלִי		prep בְּ + noun ms + suff 1s	קוֹל
בָּקַע		verb	Pi *to divide, split*
בָּקַר		verb	Pi *to search, observe*
	בֹּקֶר	noun ms	*morning*
	בְּקָרִים	noun mp	*mornings*
	בָּקְרֵי	noun mp cstr	*mornings of*
	בָּקְרִי	noun ms + suff 1s	*my morning*
בֹּקֶר		noun ms	בָּקָר
בָּקְרִי		noun ms + suff 1s	בָּקָר
בָּקְרֵי		noun mp cstr	בָּקָר
בְּקָרִים		noun mp	בָּקָר
בְּקַרְנָיו		prep בְּ + noun fs + suff 3ms	קֶרֶן
בָּרָא		verb	*to create, to form, to make*
בְּרֵאשִׁית		prep בְּ + noun fs	רֹאשׁ
בָּרָה		verb	*to cut*
	בְּרִית	noun fs	*covenant*
בְּרִית		noun fs	בָּרָה
בָּרַךְ		verb	*to kneel*; Pi *to bless, give thanks*
	בֶּרֶךְ	noun fs	*knee*

Entry	Related words	Form	Meaning/Look up Hebrew entry
בְּרָכָה		noun fs	*blessing*
בָּרֵךְ		Pi Inf abs	בָּרַךְ
בֶּרֶךְ		noun ms	בָּרַךְ
בְּרָכָה		noun fs	בָּרַךְ
בְּרָכוֹת		noun fp	בָּרַךְ
בִּרְכַּיִם		noun f dual	בָּרַךְ
בִּשְׂדֵי		prep בְּ + noun mp cstr	שָׂדֶה
בְּשׁוּב		prep בְּ + Qal Inf cstr	שׁוּב
בַּת		noun fs	בָּנָה
בְּתוֹךְ		prep בְּ + noun ms	*in the middle*
בָּתֵּי		noun mp cstr	בָּנָה
בָּתִּים		noun mp	בָּנָה
גְּאוּלִים		Qal Ptc mp	גָּאַל
גָּאַל		verb	*to redeem*
	גּוֹאֵל	noun ms	*redeemer*
גָּבַר		verb	*to be strong*
	גִּבֹּר	adj ms	*strong*
גָּדוֹל		adj ms	גָּדַל
גָּדַל		verb	*to be great, to grow*
	גָּדוֹל	adj ms	*great, large*
גָּדַע		verb	*to cut off*
	גִּדְעוֹן	pr noun ms	*Gideon*
גּוֹאֵל		noun ms	גָּאַל
גּוֹי		noun ms	*nation*
	גּוֹיִם	noun mp	*nations*
גּוֹיֵי		noun mp cstr	גּוֹי
גּוּר		verb	*to live* (temporarily)
גָּלָה		verb	*to uncover, reveal;* Pi *to uncover, reveal*
גְּלֵה		Qal Impv 2ms	גָּלָה
גָּלֹה		Qal Inf abs	גָּלָה
גֹּלֶה		Qal Ptc	גָּלָה

Entry	Related words	Form	Meaning/Look up Hebrew entry
גָּלוּ		Qal Perf 3mp	גָּלָה
גְּלוֹת		Qal Inf cstr	גָּלָה
גָּלִינוּ		Qal Perf 1p	גָּלָה
גָּלִית		Qal Perf 2fs	גָּלָה
גָּלִיתָ		Qal Perf 2ms	גָּלָה
גָּלִיתִי		Qal Perf 1s	גָּלָה
גְּלִיתֶם		Qal Perf 2mp	גָּלָה
גְּלִיתֶן		Qal Perf 2fp	גָּלָה
גָּלְתָה		Qal Perf 3fs	גָּלָה
גַּם		conj	*also*
גָּמַל		verb	*to wean*
גַּן		noun ms and fs	גָּנַן
גָּנַן		verb	*to protect*
	גַּן	noun ms and fs	*garden*
גָּעַר		verb	*to rebuke*
גָּעַרְתָּ		Qal Perf 2ms	גָּעַר
גָּרַשׁ		verb	*to drive away, expel*
גָּרֵשׁ		Pi Impv 2ms	גָּרַשׁ
גַּשׁ		Qal Impv 2ms	נָגַשׁ
גְּשָׁה		Qal Impv 2ms	נָגַשׁ
גֶּשֶׁת		Qal Inf cstr	נָגַשׁ
דָּבַר		verb	*to speak, promise*
	דָּבָר	noun ms	*word, thing*
	דְּבַר	noun ms cstr	*word of*
	מִדְבָּר	noun ms	*desert*
	דְּבָרִים	noun mp	*words*
דָּבָר		noun ms	דָּבַר
דְּבַר		noun ms cstr	דָּבַר
דִּבֶּר		Pi Perf 3ms	דָּבַר
דְּבָרִי		noun ms + suff 1s	דָּבַר
דִּבְרֵי		noun mp cstr	דָּבַר
דְּבָרֶיךָ		noun mp + suff 2ms	דָּבַר

Entry	Related words	Form	Meaning/Look up Hebrew entry
דְּבָרִים		noun mp	דָּבָר
דּוֹד		noun ms	*beloved*
	דָּוִד	pr noun ms	*David*
דּוּן		verb	*to govern, judge*
	דִּין	noun ms	*judgement, cause*
	דָּנִאֵל	pr noun ms	*Daniel*
	מִדְיָן	pr noun ms	*Midian*
דִּין		noun ms	דּוּן
דִּינִי		noun ms + suff 1s	דּוּן
דָּנִאֵל		pr noun ms	דּוּן
דַּעַת		Qal Inf cstr	יָדַע
דַּעַת		noun fs	יָדַע
דָּרַךְ		verb	*to tread*
	דֶּרֶךְ	noun ms	*way, path*
הִגָּמֵל		Nif Inf cstr	גָּמַל
הוּא		pronoun 3ms	*he, that*
	הוּא	pronoun 3fs	*she, that*
	הִיא	pronoun 3fs	*she, that*
הוֹשַׁעְתָּנוּ		Hif Perf 2ms + suffix 1p	יָשַׁע
הַחֲזִיקִי		Hif Impv fs	חָזַק
הִיא		pronoun 3fs	הוּא
הָיָה		verb	*to be*
הֱיִיתֶם		Qal Perf 2mp	הָיָה
הֵינִיקָה		Hif Perf 3fs	יָנַק
הָלַךְ		verb	Qal *to go, walk;* Pi *to go, walk*
	יֵלֵךְ	Qal Impf 3ms	
	לֵךְ	Qal Impv ms	
הָלְכָה		Qal Perf 3fs	הָלַךְ
הָלְכוּ		Qal Perf 3p	הָלַךְ
הָלַכְנוּ		Qal Perf 1p	הָלַךְ

Entry	Related words	Form	Meaning/Look up Hebrew entry
הָלַכְתְּ		Qal Perf 2fs	הָלַךְ
הָלַכְתָּ		Qal Perf 2ms	הָלַךְ
הָלַכְתִּי		Qal Perf 1s	הָלַךְ
הֲלַכְתֶּם		Qal Perf 2mp	הָלַךְ
הֲלַכְתֶּן		Qal Perf 2fp	הָלַךְ
הָלַל		verb	Pi *to praise*
הֵם		pronoun 3mp	*they, those*
	הֵמָּה	pronoun 3mp	*they*
	הֵנָּה	pronoun 3fs	*they*
הֵן	הִנֵּה	interjection	*behold*
	הִנְנִי	interj הִנֵּה + suff 1s	
הֵנָּה		pronoun 3fs	הֵם
הִנְנִי		interj הִנֵּה + suff 1s	הֵן
הַעֲלֵהוּ		Hif Impv ms + suff 3ms	עָלָה
הַפְקֵד		Hif Impv ms	פָּקַד
הַפְקֵד		Hif Inf abs	פָּקַד
הִפְקַדְנוּ		Hif Perf 1p	פָּקַד
הִפְקַדְתָּ		Hif Perf 2ms	פָּקַד
הִפְקַדְתִּי		Hif Perf 1s	פָּקַד
הִפְקַדְתֶּם		Hif Perf 2mp	פָּקַד
הִפְקַדְתֶּן		Hif Perf 2fp	פָּקַד
הִפְקִיד		Hif Perf 3ms	פָּקַד
הַפְקִיד		Hif Inf cstr	פָּקַד
הִפְקִידָה		Hif Perf 3fs	פָּקַד
הִפְקִידוּ		Hif Perf 3fp	פָּקַד
הִפְקַדְתְּ		Hif Perf 2fs	פָּקַד
הִקְטִיל		Hif Perf 3ms	קָטַל
הַקְטִיל		Hif Inf cstr	קָטַל
הַקְטֵל		Hif Impv 2ms	קָטַל
הָקְטֵל		Hof Inf cstr	קָטַל
הָקְטַל		Hof Perf 3ms	קָטַל
הַר		noun ms	*mountain*

Entry	Related words	Form	Meaning/Look up Hebrew entry
	הָרִים	noun mp	*mountains*
הָרָה		verb	*to conceive, to be pregnant*
הַרְחֵק		Hif Inf abs	רָחַק
הָרִים		noun mp	הַר
הִתְבָּרֲכוּ		Hit Perf 3p	בָּרַךְ
הִתְפַּקֵּד		Hit Perf 3ms	פָּקַד
הִתְקַדֵּשׁ		Hit Perf 3ms	קָדַשׁ
הִתְקַטֵּל		Hit Impv 2ms	קָטַל
הִתְקַטֵּל		Hit Inf cstr	קָטַל
הִתְקַטֵּל		Hit Perf 3ms	קָטַל
ו		particle	*and, but*
זֹאת		pronoun fs	זֶה
זָבַח		verb	*to slaughter for sacrifice*
	מִזְבֵּחַ	noun ms	*altar*
זֶה		pronoun ms	*this*
	זֹאת	pronoun fs	*this*
זָקֵן		verb	*to be old*
	זְקֻנִים	noun mp	*old age*
זָכַר		verb	*to remember*
	זֵכֶר	noun ms	*remembrance, memory*
זִכְרָם		noun ms + suff 3mp	זֵכֶר
זָמַר		verb	*to sing praises*
	זִמְרָה	noun fs	*song, praise, music*
זִמְרָת		noun fs cstr	זָמַר
זְקֻנִים		noun mp	זָקֵן
זָרַע		verb	*to scatter*
	זֶרַע	noun ms	*seed, progeny, family*
זַרְעֲךָ		noun ms + suff 2ms	זֶרַע

Entry	Related words	Form	Meaning/Look up Hebrew entry
חָבַשׁ		verb	to bind, saddle (an animal)
חַד		adj ms	חָדַד
חָדַד		verb	to be sharp
חָדַשׁ		verb	Pi to make new
	חָדָשׁ	adj ms	new
חוּל		verb	to dance; Hif to shake
	חוֹל	noun ms	sand
חוּר		verb	to be white
חָזַק		verb	to be strong; Hif with בְּ to hold
	חָזָק	adj ms	strong, powerful
חָטָא		verb	to miss, to sin
	חַטָּא	noun ms	sinner
	חַטָּאת	noun fs	sin
חַטָּאִים		noun mp	חָטָא
חַטָּאת		noun fs	חָטָא
חָי		noun ms	חָיַי
חַיָּה		noun fs	חָיַי
חָיָה		verb	to live
חָיַי		verb	to live
	חָי	noun ms	living thing
	חַיָּה	noun fs	living thing
חַיַּת		noun fp cstr	חָיַי
חָכַם		verb	to be wise
	חָכְמָה	noun fs	wisdom
	חָכָם	adj ms	wise
חָכְמָה		noun fs	חָכַם
חֲלוֹם		noun ms	חָלַם
חָלַם		verb	to dream
	חֲלוֹם	noun ms	dream

Entry	Related words	Form	Meaning/Look up Hebrew entry
חֲמוֹר		noun ms and fs	חָמַר
חָמַר		verb	*to be red*
	חֲמוֹר	noun ms and fs	*donkey*
חֲמֹרוֹ		noun m and s + suff 3ms	
חֵמֶת		noun ms	*container*
חֵמַת		noun fs cstr	חֵמֶת
חָסַד		verb	Hit *to show oneself kind*
	חֶסֶד	noun ms	love, kindness
חָר		noun ms	חוּר
חָרַב		verb	*to destroy*
	חֶרֶב	noun fs	*sword*
	חָרְבָּה	noun fs	*desolation, ruin*
חֶרֶב		noun fs	חָרַב
חָרְבָּה		noun fs	חָרַב
חֲרָבוֹת		noun fp	חָרַב
חָשַׂךְ		verb	*to hold back, restrain*
חָשַׂכְתָּ		Qal Perf 2ms	חָשַׂךְ
טוֹב		adj ms	*good*
טוֹבָה		adj fs	טוֹב
טוֹבוֹת		adj fp	טוֹב
טוֹבִים		adj mp	טוֹב
סָחָה		verb	*to shoot*
יֹאבְדוּ		Qal Impf 3mp	אָבַד
יֵאָמֵר		Nif Impf 3ms	אָמַר
יָבֹאוּ		Qal Impf 3mp	בּוֹא
יָבֵל		noun fs	*world, earth*
יִבֶן		Qal Impf 3ms apoc	בָּנָה
יְבַקַּע		Pi Impf 3ms	בָּקַע
יֻגַּד		Hof Impf 3ms	נָגַד

Entry	Related words	Form	Meaning/Look up Hebrew entry
יִגְדַּל		Qal Impf 3ms	גָּדַל
יִגְלוּ		Qal Impf 3mp	גָּלָה
יִגָּמֵל		Nif Impf 3ms	גָּמַל
יָד		noun fs	*hand*
	יָדוֹ	noun fs + suff 3ms	*his hand*
	יָדַיִם	noun f dual	*hands*
יָדָה		verb	*to throw*; Hif *to thank, praise*
	יְהוּדָה	pr noun ms	*Judah*
יָדוֹ		noun fs + suff 3ms	יָד
יָדוֹעַ		Qal Inf abs	יָדַע
יָדַיִם		noun f dual	יָד
יָדִין		Qal Impf 3ms	דוּן
יָדְךָ		noun fs + suff 2ms	יָד
יָדֵךְ		noun fs + suff 2fs	יָד
יֵדַע		Qal Impf 3ms	יָדַע
יָדַע		verb	*to know*
	דַּעַת	noun fs	*knowledge*
יֹדֵעַ		Qal Ptc ms	יָדַע
יֵדְעוּ		Qal Impf 3mp	יָדַע
יֹדְעֵי		Qal Ptc mp cstr	יָדַע
יָדַעְתִּי		Qal Perf 1s	יָדַע
יָהּ		pr noun ms	יְהוָה
יְהוּדָה		pr noun ms	יָדָה
יְהוָה		pr noun ms	*name of God*
	יָהּ	pr noun ms	abbreviation of יְהוָה
יְהוֹשֻׁעַ		pr noun ms	יָשַׁע
יְהִי		Qal Impf 3ms	הָיָה
יוֹדֵעַ		Qal Ptc	יָדַע
יוֹם		noun ms	*day*
	יְמֵי	noun mp cstr	*days of*
	יָמִים	noun mp	*days*
יוֹסֵף		pr noun ms	יָסַף

Entry	Related words	Form	Meaning/Look up Hebrew entry
יוֹרֶה		Qal Ptc	יָרָה
יַחְבֹּשׁ		Qal Impf 3ms	חָבַשׁ
יָחַד		verb	*to be united, to be one*
	יַחְדָּו	adv	*together*
	יָחִיד	adj ms	*only*
יַחְדָּו		adv	יָחַד
יָחִיד		adj ms	יָחַד
יְחִידְךָ		adj ms + suff 2ms	יָחַד
יִירַשׁ		Qal Impf 3ms	יָרַשׁ
יִכְלוּ		Qal Impf 3mp apoc	כָּלָה
יִכָּשְׁלוּ		Nif Impf 3mp	כָּשַׁל
יָלַד		verb	Qal *to give birth*; Hif *to beget*; Hof *to be born*
	יֶלֶד	noun ms	*child*
יֶלֶד		noun ms	יָלַד
יָלְדָה		Qal Perf 3fs	יָלַד
יֵלֶךְ		Qal Impf 3ms	הָלַךְ
יֵלְכוּ		Qal Impf 3mp	הָלַךְ
יַם		noun ms cstr	יָם
יָם		noun ms	*sea*
	יַם	noun ms cstr	*sea of*
	יַמִּים	noun mp	*seas*
יְמֵי		noun mp cstr	יוֹם
יַמִּי		noun ms + suff 1s	יָם
יַמֵּי		noun mp cstr	יָם
יַמִּים		noun mp	יָם
יָמִים		noun mp	יוֹם
יִמְשֹׁל		Qal Impf 3ms	מָשַׁל
יִמְשְׁלוּ		Qal Impf 3mp	מָשַׁל
יָנַק		verb	*to suck*; Hif *to breastfeed*
יָסֹב		Qal Impf 3ms	סָבַב

Entry	Related words	Form	Meaning/Look up Hebrew entry
יָסֹבּוּ		Qal Impf 3mp	סָבַב
יָסַף		verb	to add, increase
	יוֹסֵף	pr noun ms	Joseph
יָעַד		verb	to appoint
	מוֹעֵד	noun ms	time
יַעֲלֵהוּ		Impf 3ms + suff 3ms	עָלָה
יַעֲמֹד		Qal Impf 3ms	עָמַד
יַעַמְדוּ		Qal Impf 3mp	עָמַד
יַעֲקֹד		Qal Impf 3ms	עָקַד
יַעֲרֹךְ		Qal Impf 3ms	עָרַךְ
יַעַשׂ		Qal Impf 3ms apoc	עָשָׂה
יָפֶה		adj ms	יָפֶה
יָפָה		verb	to be beautiful
	יָפֶה	adj ms	beautiful
	יָפָה	adj fs	יָפֶה
יִפֹּל		Qal Impf 3ms	נָפַל
יִפְּלוּ		Qal Impf 3mp	נָפַל
יְפַקֵּד		Pi Impf 3ms	פָּקַד
יְפַקְּדוּ		Pi Impf 3mp	פָּקַד
יִפְקְדוּ		Qal Impf 3mp	פָּקַד
יִפְקְדוּהוּ		Qal Impf 3mp + suff 3ms	פָּקַד
יִפְקְדֵנִי		Qal Impf 3ms + suff 1s	פָּקַד
יִפְקוֹד		Qal Impf 3ms	פָּקַד
יִפְקַח		Qal Impf 3ms	פָּקַח
יַפְקִיד		Hif Impf 3ms	פָּקַד
יַפְקִידוּ		Hif Impf 3mp	פָּקַד
יָצָא		verb	to go out, to be born
יִצְחָק		pr noun ms	צָחַק
יִצְחֲקוּ		Qal Impf 3mp	צָחַק
יָצָאתִי		Qal Perf 1s	יָצָא
יִקַּח		Qal Impf 3ms	לָקַח
יָקְטַל		Hof Impf 3ms	קָטַל

Entry	Related words	Form	Meaning/Look up Hebrew entry
יַקְטִיל		Hif Impf 3ms	קָטַל
יְקֻטַּל		Pual Impf 3ms	קָטַל
יִקָּטֵל		Nif Impf 3ms	קָטַל
יִקְטֹל		Qal Impf 3ms	קָטַל
יִקְטְלוּ		Qal Impf 3mp	קָטַל
יִקָּטְלוּ		Nif Impf 3mp	קָטַל
יָּקָם		with prefix וַ : VC Qal Impf 3ms	קוּם
יָקֻמוּ		Qal Impf 3mp	קוּם
יִקָּרֵא		Nif Impf 3ms	קָרָא
יִקְרָא		Qal Impf 3ms	קָרָא
יָרֵא		verb	*to be afraid, to fear*
יִרְא		Qal Impf 3ms apoc	רָאָה
יָרֵא		Qal Ptc	יָרֵא
יֵרָאֶה		Nif Impf 3ms	רָאָה
יִרְאֶה		Qal Impf 3ms	רָאָה
יָרַד		verb	*to go down (e.g. to Egypt)*
יָרָה		verb	*to show, teach, instruct, shoot*
	תּוֹרָה	noun fs	*law, instruction*
יָרַע		Qal Impf 3ms	רָעַע
יָרַשׁ		verb	*to inherit, to possess*
יִירַשׁ		Qal Impf 3ms	יָרַשׁ
יֵשׁ		adv	*there is, there are*
יִשָּׂא		Qal Impf 3ms	נָשָׂא
יָשַׁב		verb	*to sit, to live*
יָּשָׁב		with prefix וַ : VC Qal Impf 3ms	שׁוּב
יָשֹׁב		Qal Impf 3ms apoc	שׁוּב
יֵשֵׁב		Qal Impf 3ms	יָשַׁב
יֵשֵׁב		Qal Impf 3ms	יָשַׁב
יֹשֵׁב		Qal Ptc	יָשַׁב
יֵשְׁבוּ		Qal Impf 3mp	יָשַׁב

Entry	Related words	Form	Meaning/Look up Hebrew entry
יָשַׁבְתָּ		Qal Perf 2ms	יָשַׁב
יָשׁוֹב		Qal Inf abs	יָשַׁב
יְשׁוּעָה		noun fs	יָשַׁע
יְשׁוּעָתִי		noun fs + suff 1s	יָשַׁע
יַשְׁכֵּם		Hif Impf 3ms	שָׁכַם
יִשְׁלַח		Qal Impf 3ms	שָׁלַח
יִשְׁלָחֶהָ		Qal Impf 3ms + suff 3fs	שָׁלַח
יָשֶׂם		with prefix וַ : VC Impf 3ms	שִׂים
יִשְׁמַע		Qal Impf 3ms	שָׁמַע
יִשְׁמֹר		Qal Impf 3ms	שָׁמַר
יִשְׁמְרוּ		Qal Impf 3mp	שָׁמַר
יָשַׁע		verb	Hif *to save, deliver*
	יְהוֹשֻׁעַ	pr noun ms	*Joshua*
	יְשׁוּעָה	noun fs	*help, salvation*
יִשְׁפֹּט		Qal Impf 3ms	שָׁפַט
יָשַׁר		verb	*to be right, straight, upright*
	יָשָׁר	adj ms	*right, upright, honest*
	מֵישָׁר	noun ms	*righteousness, justice, equity*
יָשָׁר		adj ms	יָשַׁר
יִשְׂרָאֵל		pr noun ms	שָׂרָה
יִתֵּן		Qal Impf 3ms	נָתַן
יִתְקַדֵּשׁ		Hit Impf 3ms	קָדַשׁ
יִתְקַדְּשׁוּ		Hit Impf 3mp	קָדַשׁ
יִתְקַטֵּל		Hit Impf 3ms	קָטַל
כְּ		prep	*as, like*
	כָּמוֹהוּ	prep + suff 3ms	*like him* (or *it*)
כַּאֲשֶׁר		prep כְּ + pronoun	אֲשֶׁר
כָּבֵד		verb	*to be heavy, difficult*
	כָּבֵד	adj ms	*heavy, difficult*

Entry	Related words	Form	Meaning/Look up Hebrew entry
כָּהֶם		prep + suff 3mp	כְּ
כָּהֵן		prep + suff 3fp	כְּ
כָּהֵן		verb	Pi *to prepare, to act as a priest*
	כֹּהֵן	noun ms	*priest*
	כֹּהֲנִים	noun mp	*priests*
כֹּהֲנֵי		noun mp cstr	כָּהֵן
כֹּהֲנִי		noun ms + suff 1s	כָּהֵן
כֹּהֲנִים		noun mp	כָּהֵן
כּוֹכָב		noun ms	*star*
כּוּן		verb	*to establish*
	כֵּן	adv	*therefore*
כּוֹנֵן		Pi Perf 3ms	כּוּן
כָּחוֹל		prep כְּ + noun ms	חוֹל
כִּי		adv	*because, that*
כְּכוֹכְבֵי		prep כְּ + noun mp cstr	כּוֹכָב
כָּכֶם		prep + suff 2mp	כְּ
כָּכֶן		prep + suff 2fp	כְּ
כֹּל		noun ms	כָּלַל
כָּל־		noun ms	כָּלַל
כָּלָה		verb	*to be finished*
כָּלַל		verb	*to complete*
	כֹּל	noun ms	*all, entirety, the whole*
	כָּל־	noun ms	*all, entirety, the whole*
כָּמוֹהָ		prep + suff 3fs	כְּ
כָּמוֹהוּ		prep + suff 3ms	כְּ
כָּמוֹךְ		prep + suff 2fs	כְּ
כָּמוֹךָ		prep + suff 2ms	כְּ
כָּמוֹנוּ		prep + suff 1p	כְּ
כָּמוֹנִי		prep + suff 1s	כְּ
כְּמִשְׁתַּחֲוֵי		prep כְּ + Pi Ptc	שָׁחָה

Entry	Related words	Form	Meaning/Look up Hebrew entry
כֵּן		adv	כון
כָּנָף		noun fs	*wing, skirt* (of a robe)
כִּסֵּא		noun ms	*seat, throne*
כִּסְאוֹ		noun ms + suff 3ms	כִּסֵּא
כַּף		noun fs	כָּפַף
כָּפַף		verb	*to bend, bow down*
	כַּף	noun fs	*palm* (of hand)
כָּרַת		verb	*to cut*
כָּשַׁל		verb	*to stumble*
כָּתַב		verb	*to write*
כְּתֹב		Qal Impv 2ms	כָּתַב
כִּתְבוּ		Qal Impv 2fs	כָּתַב
כִּתְבִי		Qal Impv 2mp	כָּתַב
כְּתֹבְנָה		Qal Impv 2fp	כָּתַב
לְ		prep	*to, at, for*
	לוֹ	prep + suff 3ms	*to/at/for him* (or *it*)
לֹא		adv	*not*
לְאַבְרָהָם		prep לְ + pr noun ms	אָב
לְאֹם		noun ms	*people, nation*
לְאֻמִּים		prep לְ + noun mp	לְאֹם
לֵבָב		noun ms	*heart*
	לֵב	noun ms	*heart*
לִבִּי		noun ms + suff 1s	לֵבָב
לְגוֹי		prep לְ + noun ms	גּוֹי
לָגוּר		prep לְ + Inf cstr	גּור
לָהּ		prep + suff 3fs	לְ
לָהֶם		prep + suff 3mp	לְ
לָהֶן		prep + suff 3fp	לְ
לוֹ		prep + suff 3ms	לְ
לִזְקֵנָיו		prep לְ + noun ms + suff ms	זָקֵן

Entry	Related words	Form	Meaning/Look up Hebrew entry
לִי		prep + suff 1s	לְ
לַיהוה		prep + לְ + pr noun	יהוה
לַיְלָה		noun ms	*night*
	לֵילוֹת	noun mp	*nights*
לִישׁוּעָה		prep לְ + noun fs	יֶשַׁע
לְךָ		prep + suff 2ms	לְ
לֵךְ		Qal Impv ms	הָלַךְ
לָךְ		prep + suff 2fs	לְ
לָכֶם		prep + suff 2mp	לְ
לֶחֶם		noun ms	*bread*
לָכֶן		prep + suff 2fp	לְ
לְכִסֵּא		pref לְ + noun ms	כִּסֵּא
לָמָה		pronoun	מָה
לָמֶה		pronoun	מָה
לַמּוֹעֵד		prep לְ + noun ms	יָעַד
לִמְשֹׁל		Qal Inf cstr	מָשַׁל
לַמִּשְׁפָּט		prep לְ + noun ms	שָׁפַט
לָנוּ		prep + suff 1p	לְ
לְנָחוֹר		prep לְ + pr noun ms	נָחוֹר
לָנֶצַח		adv	נָצַח
לְעוֹלָם		prefix לְ noun ms	עָלַם
לְעָלָה		prep לְ + noun fs	עָלָה
לַעֲמֹד		Qal Inf cstr	עָמַד
לָעֵצִים		prep לְ + noun mp	עֵצָה
לִפְנֵי		prep	פָּנָה
לָקַח		verb	*to take*
	יִקַּח	Qal Impf 3ms	
	קַח	Qal Impv 2ms	
לָקֹחַ		Qal Inf abs	לָקַח
לֹקֵחַ		Qal Ptc	לָקַח
לָקְחָה		Qal Perf 3fs	לָקַח
לָקְחוּ		Qal Perf 3p	לָקַח
לָקַחְנוּ		Qal Perf 1p	לָקַח

Entry	Related words	Form	Meaning/Look up Hebrew entry
לְקַחְתָּ		Qal Perf 2ms	לָקַח
לָקַחַתְּ		Qal Perf 2fs	לָקַח
לָקַחְתִּי		Qal Perf 1s	לָקַח
לְקַחְתֶּם		Qal Perf 2mp	לָקַח
לְקַחְתֶּן		Qal Perf 2fp	לָקַח
לִקְטֹל		Qal Inf cstr	קָטַל
לִשְׁחֹט		prep לְ + Qal Inf cstr	שָׁחַט
לִשְׁמֹר		Qal Inf cstr	שָׁמַר
לְשָׂרָה		prep לְ + pr noun fs	שָׂרָה
מְאֹד		adv	*very*
מֵאָה		numeral	*one hundred*
	מְאַת	numeral cstr	
מְאוּמָה		pronoun	מָה
מַאֲכֶלֶת		noun fs	אָכַל
מֵאֶרֶץ		prep מִן + noun fs cstr	אֶרֶץ
מְאַת		numeral cstr	מֵאָה
מִבֶּטֶן		prep מִן + noun ms	בֶּטֶן
מִבֵּית		prep מִן + noun ms cstr	בָּנָה
מְבֹרָךְ		Pual Ptc ms	בָּרַךְ
מִדְבָּר		noun ms	דָּבַר
מִדְיָן		pr noun ms	דּוּן
מַה		pronoun ms	*what ... ?*
	מְאוּמָה	pronoun	*anything*
	מָה	pronoun	*what ... ?*
מֵהֶם		prep + suff 3mp	מִן
מֵהֶן		prep + suff 3fp	מִן
מוֹאָב		pr noun ms	*Moab*
	מוֹאָבִי	gent noun ms	*Moabite*
	מוֹאָבִית	gent noun fs	*Moabite*
מוֹאָבִיּוֹת		gent noun fp	מוֹאָב
מוֹאָבִים		gent noun mp	מוֹאָב
מוֹאָבִית		gent noun fs	מוֹאָב

Entry	Related words	Form	Meaning/Look up Hebrew entry
מוּל		verb	*to cut off, to circumcise*
מוֹעֵד		noun ms	יָעַד
מוּת		verb	*to die*
	מָוֶת	noun ms	*death*
מוֹת		Qal Inf cstr	מוּת
מָוֶת		noun ms	מוּת
מִזְבֵּחַ		noun ms	זָבַח
מָחָה		verb	*to destroy*
מָחִיתָ		Qal Perf 2ms	מָחָה
מִי		pronoun	*who ... ?*
מִיַּד		prep מִן + noun fs cstr	יָד
מִיהוּדָה		prep מִן + pr noun ms	יְהוּדָה
מִיכַל		pr noun fs	*Michal*
מַיִם		noun f dual	*water*
מֵישָׁר		noun ms	יָשַׁר
מִכֶּם		prep + suff 2mp	מִן
מִכֶּן		prep + suff 2fp	מִן
מָלֵא		verb	*to be full*; Pi *to fill*
מַלְאָךְ		noun ms	*angel, messenger*
מָלַךְ		verb	*to reign, to be king*
	מֶלֶךְ	noun ms	*king*
	מִלְכָּה	pr noun fs	*Milcah*
	מְלָכִים	noun mp	*kings*
מִלְכָּה		pr noun fs	מֶלֶךְ
מַלְכֵי		noun mp cstr	מֶלֶךְ
מַלְכִּי		noun ms + suff 1s	מֶלֶךְ
מְלָכִים		noun mp	מֶלֶךְ
מָלַל		verb	*to say, speak*
מִלֵּל		Pi Perf 3ms	מָלַל
מִמְּךָ		prep + suff 2ms	מִן
מִמֵּךְ		prep + suff 2fs	מִן
מִמֶּלֶךְ		prep מִן + noun ms	מֶלֶךְ

Entry	Related words	Form	Meaning/Look up Hebrew entry
מִמֶּנָּה		prep + suff 3fs	מִן
מִמֶּנּוּ		prep + suff 1p or prep + suff 3ms	מִן
מִמֶּנִּי		prep + suff 1s	מִן
מִמַּעַל		adv	עָלָה
מִן		prep	*from*
	מִמֶּנּוּ	prep + suff 3ms	*from him* (or *it*)
מֵעִירְךָ		prep מִן + noun mf + suff 2ms	עוּר
מִפָּנֶיךָ		noun mp + suff 2ms	פָּנֶה
מְפַקֵּד		Pi Ptc	פָּקַד
מַפְקִיד		Hif Ptc	פָּקַד
מִפְּרִי		prep מִן + noun ms	פָּרָה
מָצָא		verb	*to find*
מְצָא		Qal Impv 2ms	מָצָא
מֹצֵא		Qal Ptc	מָצָא
מָצוֹא		Qal Inf abs	מָצָא
מְצַחֵק		Pi Ptc	צָחַק
מִצְרִי		gent noun ms	מִצְרַיִם
מִצְרִיּוֹת		gent noun fp	מִצְרַיִם
מִצְרַיִם		pr noun mp	*Egypt*
	מִצְרִי	gent noun ms	*Egyptian*
	מִצְרִית	gent noun fs	*Egyptian*
מִצְרִים		gent noun mp	מִצְרַיִם
מִקֶּדֶם		noun ms	קֶדֶם
מָקוֹם		noun ms	קוּם
מְקוֹמוֹת		noun mp	קוּם
מַקְטִיל		Hif Ptc	קָטַל
מָקְטָל		Hof Ptc	קָטַל
מְקֻטָּל		Pual Ptc	קָטַל
מֵרָחֹק		adv	רָחַק
מֹרִיָּה		pr noun	*Moriah*
מֹשֶׁה		pr noun ms	*Moses*

Entry	Related words	Form	Meaning/Look up Hebrew entry
מָשַׁל		verb	*to rule*
מְשֹׁל		Qal Inf cstr or Impv ms	מָשַׁל
מָשְׁלָה		Qal Perf 3fs	מָשַׁל
מָשְׁלוּ		Qal Perf 3p	מָשַׁל
מָשַׁלְנוּ		Qal Perf 1p	מָשַׁל
מָשַׁלְתְּ		Qal Perf 2fs	מָשַׁל
מָשַׁלְתָּ		Qal Perf 2ms	מָשַׁל
מָשַׁלְתִּי		Qal Perf 1s	מָשַׁל
מְשַׁלְתֶּם		Qal Perf 2mp	מָשַׁל
מְשַׁלְתֶּן		Qal Perf 2fp	מָשַׁל
אֶשְׁמֹר		Qal Impf 1s	שָׁמַר
מִשְׁמָר		noun ms	שָׁמַר
מִשְׁמֶרֶת		noun fs	שָׁמַר
מִשְׁפָּט		noun ms	שָׁפַט
מִשְׁפָּטִי		noun ms + suff 1s	שָׁפַט
מִשְׁתֶּה		noun ms	שָׁתָה
מָתַי		adv	*when ... ?*
מִתְקַטֵּל		Hit Ptc	קָטַל
נָא		particle	*please*
נֶאֱחָז		Nif Ptc	אָחַז
נֹאכַל		Qal Impf 1p	אָכַל
נָאַם		verb	*to speak, declare*
	נְאֻם	noun (Qal Ptc pass) m cstr	*oracle, declaration*
נָבָא		verb	Nif *to prophesy*
	נָבִיא	noun ms	*prophet*
נְבִיא		noun ms cstr	נָבָא
נָבִיא		noun ms	נָבָא
נְבִיאִי		noun ms + suff 1s	נָבָא
נְבִיאֵי		noun mp cstr	נָבָא
נְבִיאִים		noun mp	נָבָא

Entry	Related words	Form	Meaning/Look up Hebrew entry
נָגַד		verb	Hif *to tell, declare; to praise*
נֶגֶד		prep	*in front of, opposite*
נָגוֹעַ		Qal Inf abs	נָגַע
נָגוֹשׁ		Qal Inf abs	נָגַשׁ
נָגַע		verb	*to touch*
נְגֹעַ		Qal Inf cstr	נָגַע
נָגַשׁ		verb	*to approach*
נֹגֵשׁ		Qal Ptc ms	נָגַשׁ
נֵדַע		Qal Impf 1p	יָדַע
נוֹגֵעַ		Qal Ptc ms	נָגַע
נוֹדָע		Nif Ptc ms	יָדַע
נוֹלַד		Nif Perf 3ms	יָלַד
נוֹרָא		Nif Ptc ms	יָרֵא
נִזְכֹּר		Qal Impf 1p	זָכַר
נִזְכְּרָה		Cohort 1p	זָכַר
נָחוֹר		pr noun ms	*Nahor*
נָחַם		verb	Pi *to comfort, console*
נָחָשׁ		noun ms	*serpent*
נִכְתֹּב		Qal Impf 1p	כָּתַב
נִכְתְּבָה		Cohort 1p	כָּתַב
נֵלֵךְ		Qal Impf 1p	הָלַךְ
נֵלְכָה		Qal Impf 1p	הָלַךְ
נִמְשֹׁל		Qal Impf 1c	מָשַׁל
נָסֹב		Qal Impf 1p	סָבַב
נָסָה		verb	Pi *to test, try*
נִסָּה		Pi Perf 3ms	נָסָה
נַעֲמֹד		Qal Impf 1p	עָמַד
נַעַר		noun ms	*young man, servant*
נַעֲרִי		noun ms + suff 1s	נַעַר
נַעֲרֵי		noun mp cstr	נַעַר
נְעָרָיו		noun mp + suff 3ms	נַעַר

Entry	Related words	Form	Meaning/Look up Hebrew entry
נְעָרִים		noun mp	נַעַר
נָפוֹל		Qal Inf abs	נָפַל
נָפַל		verb	*to fall*
נְפֹל		Qal Inf cstr or Impv ms	נָפַל
נִפֹּל		Qal Impf 1p	נָפַל
נֹפֵל		Qal Ptc	נָפַל
נִפְלָאוֹת		noun (Nif Ptc) fp	פָּלָא
נִפְלְאוֹתֶיךָ		Nif Ptc p + suff 2ms	פָּלָא
נְפַקֵּד		Pi Impf 1p	פָּקַד
נִפְקֹד		Qal Impf 1p	פָּקַד
נִפְקְדָה		Cohort 1p	פָּקַד
נִפְקְחוּ		Nif Perf 3p	פָּקַח
נַפְקִיל		Hif Impf 1p	פָּקַד
נָצַח		verb	Pi *to excel*; Nif *to be perfect, complete*
	לָנֶצַח	adv	*forever*
נִקְטַל		Nif Perf 3ms	קָטַל
נִקְטֹל		Qal Impf 1p	קָטַל
נִקָּטֵל		Nif Impf 1p	קָטַל
נִקְטְלָה		Nif Perf 3fs	קָטַל
נִקְטְלוּ		Nif Perf 3p	קָטַל
נִקְטַלְנוּ		Nif Perf 1p	קָטַל
נִקְטַלְתָּ		Nif Perf 2ms	קָטַל
נִקְטַלְתְּ		Nif Perf 2fs	קָטַל
נִקְטַלְתִּי		Nif Perf 1s	קָטַל
נִקְטַלְתֶּם		Nif Perf 2mp	קָטַל
נִקְטַלְתֶּן		Nif Perf 2fp	קָטַל
נָשָׂא		verb	*to lift, carry*
נֵשֵׁב		Qal Impf 1p	יָשַׁב
נִשְׁבַּעְתִּי		Nif Perf 1s	שׁבע
נָשׁוּבָה		Qal Impf 1p + paragogic ה	שׁוּב
נְשֵׁי		noun fp cstr	אֱנָשׁ

Entry	Related words	Form	Meaning/Look up Hebrew entry
נָשִׁים		noun fp	אָנַשׁ
נִשְׁמֹר		Qal Impf 1p	שָׁמַר
נִשְׁתַּחֲוֶה		Hit Impf 1p	שָׁחָה
נָתַן		verb	*to give*
	יִתֵּן	Qal Impf 3ms	*he gave*
	נָתָן	pr noun ms	*Nathan*
	נָתַתִּי	Qal Perf 1s	*I have given*
נָתְנָה		Qal Perf 3fs	נָתַן
נָתְנוּ		Qal Perf 3p	נָתַן
נָתַנּוּ		Qal Perf 1p	נָתַן
נָתַק		verb	*to pull off, tear away*; Pi *to tear apart, tear to pieces*
נִתְקַדֵּשׁ		Hit Impf 1p	קָדַשׁ
נָתַשׁ		verb	*to tear, destroy*
נָתַשְׁתָּ		Qal Perf 2ms	נָתַשׁ
נָתַתְּ		Qal Perf 2fs	נָתַן
נָתַתָּ		Qal Perf 2ms	נָתַן
נָתַתִּי		Qal Perf 1s	נָתַן
נְתַתֶּם		Qal Perf 2mp	נָתַן
נְתַתֶּן		Qal Perf 2fp	נָתַן
סֹב		Qal Inf cstr or Impv ms	סָבַב
סָבַב		verb	*to turn*
סָבְבָה		Qal Perf 3fs	סָבַב
סָבְבוּ		Qal Perf 3p	סָבַב
סָבוֹב		Qal Inf abs	סָבַב
סַבּוֹנוּ		Qal Perf 1p	סָבַב
סַבּוֹת		Qal Perf 2fs	סָבַב
סַבּוֹתָ		Qal Perf 2ms	סָבַב
סַבּוֹתִי		Qal Perf 1s	סָבַב
סַבּוֹתֶם		Qal Perf 2mp	סָבַב
סַבּוֹתֶן		Qal Perf 2fp	סָבַב

Entry	Related words	Form	Meaning/Look up Hebrew entry
סָבַךְ		verb	*to entwine*
	סְבָךְ	noun ms	*thicket*
סוֹבֵב		Qal Ptc	סָבַב
סוּס		noun ms	*horse*
	סוּסָה	noun fs	*mare*
	סוּסוֹ	noun ms + suff 3ms	*his horse*
סוּסָה		noun fs	סוּס
סוּסָהּ		noun ms + suff 3fs	סוּס
סוּסוֹ		noun ms + suff 3ms	סוּס
סוּסוֹת		noun fp	סוּס
סוּסוֹתַי		noun fp + suff 1s	סוּס
סוּסוֹתֶיהָ		noun fp + suff 3fs	סוּס
סוּסוֹתֵיהֶם		noun fp + suff 3mp	סוּס
סוּסוֹתֵיהֶן		noun fp + suff 3fp	סוּס
סוּסוֹתָיו		noun fp + suff 3ms	סוּס
סוּסוֹתֶיךָ		noun fp + suff 2ms	סוּס
סוּסוֹתַיִךְ		noun fp + suff 2fs	סוּס
סוּסוֹתֵיכֶם		noun fp + suff 2mp	סוּס
סוּסוֹתֵיכֶן		noun fp + suff 2fp	סוּס
סוּסוֹתֵינוּ		noun fp + suff 1p	סוּס
סוּסִי		noun ms + suff 1s	סוּס
סוּסַי		noun mp + suff 1s	סוּס
סוּסֶיהָ		noun mp + suff 3fs	סוּס
סוּסֵיהֶם		noun mp + suff 3mp	סוּס
סוּסֵיהֶן		noun mp + suff 3fp	סוּס
סוּסָיו		noun mp + suff 3ms	סוּס
סוּסֶיךָ		noun mp + suff 2ms	סוּס
סוּסַיִךְ		noun mp + suff 2fs	סוּס
סוּסֵיכֶם		noun mp + suff 2mp	סוּס
סוּסֵיכֶן		noun mp + suff 2fp	סוּס
סוּסִים		noun mp	סוּס
סוּסֵינוּ		noun mp + suff 1p	סוּס
סוּסְךָ		noun ms + suff 2ms	סוּס

Entry	Related words	Form	Meaning/Look up Hebrew entry
סוּסֵךְ		noun ms + suff 2fs	סוּס
סוּסְכֶם		noun ms + suff 2mp	סוּס
סוּסְכֶן		noun ms + suff 2fp	סוּס
סוּסָם		noun ms + suff 3mp	סוּס
סוּסָן		noun ms + suff 3fp	סוּס
סוּסֵנוּ		noun ms + suff 1p	סוּס
סוּסָתָהּ		noun fs + suff 3fs	סוּס
סוּסָתוֹ		noun fs + suff 3ms	סוּס
סוּסָתִי		noun fs + suff 1s	סוּס
סוּסָתְךָ		noun fs + suff 2ms	סוּס
סוּסָתֵךְ		noun fs + suff 2fs	סוּס
סוּסַתְכֶם		noun fs + suff 2mp	סוּס
סוּסַתְכֶן		noun fs + suff 2fp	סוּס
סוּסָתָם		noun fs + suff 3mp	סוּס
סוּסָתָן		noun fs + suff 3fp	סוּס
סוּסָתֵנוּ		noun fs + suff 1p	סוּס
סוּר		verb	*to turn, depart*
סַךְ		noun ms	סָכַךְ
סָכַךְ		verb	*to cover*
	סַךְ	noun ms	*crowd*
סָפַד		verb	*to mourn*
סָפַר		verb	*to count*; Pi *to tell*
	סֵפֶר	noun ms	*book*
	סְפָרִים	noun mp	*books*
סִפְרִי		noun ms + suff 1s	סָפַר
סִפְרֵי		noun mp cstr	סָפַר
סְפָרִים		noun mp	סָפַר
עָבַד		verb	*to work*
	עֶבֶד	noun ms	*servant*
עָבַר		verb	*to pass over, to go* (used with בְּ)
עַד		prep	עֵדָה

Entry	Related words	Form	Meaning/Look up Hebrew entry
עֵד		noun ms	עֵדָה
עַד־כֹּה		adv	עֵדָה
עָדָה		verb	to pass by
	עַד	prep	until, as far as
	עַד	noun ms	eternity
	עָדָיו	prep + suff 3ms	as far as him (or it)
	עֵת	noun fs	time
	עַתָּה	adv	now
עָדַי		prep + suff 1s	עֵדָה
עָדֶיהָ		prep + suff 3fs	עֵדָה
עֲדֵיהֶם		prep + suff 3mp	עֵדָה
עֲדֵיהֶן		prep + suff 3fp	עֵדָה
עָדָיו		prep + suff 3ms	עֵדָה
עָדֶיךָ		prep + suff 2ms	עֵדָה
עָדַיִךְ		prep + suff 2fs	עֵדָה
עֲדֵיכֶם		prep + suff 2mp	עֵדָה
עֲדֵיכֶן		prep + suff 2fp	עֵדָה
עָדֵינוּ		prep + suff 1p	עֵדָה
עוֹלָה		noun fs	עָלָה
עוֹלָם		noun ms	עָלַם
עוּר		verb	to wake up, watch
	עִיר	noun fs	city
	עָרִים	noun fp	cities
עַז		adj ms	עָזַז
עֹז		noun ms	עָזַז
עָזַב		verb	to abandon, forsake
עַזָּה		adj fs	עָזַז
עָזַז		verb	to be strong, to make strong
	עַז	adj ms	strong
	עַזָּה	adj fs	strong
עֻזִּי		noun ms + suff 1s	עָזַז
עַיִן		noun fs	eye

Entry	Related words	Form	Meaning/Look up Hebrew entry
	עֵין	noun fs cstr	*eye of*
	עֵינַיִם	noun f dual	*eyes*
עֵינֵי		noun fp cstr	עַיִן
עֵינֶיהָ		noun f dual + suff 3fs	עַיִן
עֵינָיו		noun f dual + suff 3ms	עַיִן
עֵינֵיכֶם		noun f dual + suff 2mp	עַיִן
עֵינַיִם		noun f dual	עַיִן
עִיר		noun fs	עוּר
עַל		prep	עָלָה
עַל אֹדֹת		adv	עָלָה
עַל־כֵּן		adv	עָלָה
עָלָה		verb	Qal *to go up*; Hif *to offer*
	עַל אֹדֹת	adv	*on account of, because of*
	עֹלָה	noun fs	*burnt offering*
	עוֹלָה	noun fs	*burnt offering*
	עַל	prep	*on, upon, against*
	מִמַּעַל	adv	*above*
	עַל־כֵּן	adv	*therefore*
	עָלָיו	prep + suff 3ms	*on him* (or *it*)
עֹלָה		noun fs	עָלָה
עָלַי		prep + suff 1s	עָלָה
עָלֶיהָ		prep + suff 3fs	עָלָה
עֲלֵיהֶם		prep + suff 3mp	עָלָה
עֲלֵיהֶן		prep + suff 3fp	עָלָה
עָלָיו		prep + suff 3ms	עָלָה
עֶלְיוֹן		adj ms	עָלָה
עָלֶיךָ		prep + suff 2ms	עָלָה
עָלַיִךְ		prep + suff 2fs	עָלָה
עֲלֵיכֶם		prep + suff 2mp	עָלָה
עֲלֵיכֶן		prep + suff 2fp	עָלָה
עָלֵינוּ		prep + suff 1p	עָלָה

Entry	Related words	Form	Meaning/Look up Hebrew entry
עָלַם		verb	*to hide, conceal*
	עוֹלָם	noun ms	*hidden time, unlimited time, ancient times*
עָלַץ		verb	*to rejoice*; + בְּ = *rejoice in*
עַם		noun ms	עָמַם
עִם		prep	עָמַם
עָמַד		verb	*to stand*
עֲמֹד		Qal Inf cstr or Impv ms	עָמַד
עֹמֵד		Qal Ptc	עָמַד
עִמָּהּ		prep + suff 3fs	עָמַם
עִמּוֹ		prep + suff 3ms	עָמַם
עָמוֹד		Qal Inf abs	עָמַד
עַמִּי		noun ms + suff 1s	עָמַם
עַמֵּי		noun mp cstr	עָמַם
עִמִּי		prep + suff 1s	עָמַם
עַמִּים		noun mp	עָמַם
עִמְּךָ		prep + suff 2ms	עָמַם
עִמָּךְ		prep + suff 2fs	עָמַם
עִמָּכֶם		prep + suff 2mp	עָמַם
עִמָּכֶן		prep + suff 2fp	עָמַם
עִמָּם		prep + suff 3mp	עָמַם
עָמַם		verb	*to hide, conceal*
	עַם	noun ms	*people*
	עִם	prep	*with*
	עִמּוֹ	prep + suff 3ms	*with him* (or *it*)
	עַמִּים	noun mp	*peoples*
עִמָּן		prep + suff 3fp	עָמַם
עִמָּנוּ		prep + suff 1p	עָמַם
עָנָה		verb	*to answer*
עֵץ		noun ms	עָצָה
עָצָה		verb	*to close* (the eyes); Arabic *to be hard*

Entry	Related words	Form	Meaning/Look up Hebrew entry
	עֵץ	noun ms	*tree*
עֲצֵי		noun mp cstr	עֵצָה
עָקַב		verb	*to take by the heel*
	עֵקֶב	adv	*because*
	עֵקֶב אֲשֶׁר	adv	*because*
עָקַד		verb	*to bind*
עָרַג		verb	*to long for* (used with אֶל)
עָרוּם		adj m	עָרֹם
עָרֵי		noun fp cstr	עוּר
עָרִים		noun fp	עוּר
עָרַךְ		verb	*to lay in rows*
עָרַם		verb	*to be cunning*
	עָרֹם	adj ms	*naked*
	עָרוּם	adj m	*clever, cunning, prudent*
עָשָׂה		verb	*to do, make, accomplish*
	יַעַשׂ	Qal Impf 3ms apoc	*he made*
עָשִׂיתָ		Qal Perf 2ms	עָשָׂה
עֵת		noun fs	עָדָה
עַתָּה		adv	עָדָה
פָּאָה		verb	Hif *to blow*
	פֶּה	noun ms	*mouth*
	פָּארָן	pr noun ms	*Paran*
פֶּה		noun ms	פָּאָה
פֹּה		adv	*here*
פַּח		noun ms	פָּחַח
פָּחַד		verb	*to tremble, be afraid*
פָּחַח		verb	Hif *to ensnare*
	פַּח	noun ms	*snare*
פָּלָא		verb	Nif *to be extraordinary*

Entry	Related words	Form	Meaning/Look up Hebrew entry
	נִפְלָאוֹת	noun (Nif Ptc) fp	*great deeds, greatness*
פֶּן		conj	פָּנָה
פָּנֶה		noun ms	פָּנָה
פָּנָה		verb	*to turn, turn oneself*
	לִפְנֵי	prep	*in front of*
	פֶּן	conj	*lest*
	פָּנֶה	noun ms	*face*
	פָּנִים	noun mp	*face(s)*
פָּנִים		noun mp	פָּנָה
פָּקַד		verb	*to visit*; Pi *to muster*; Hif *to appoint*; Hof *to be appointed*
פִּקֵּד		Pi Perf 3ms	פָּקַד
פַּקֵּד		Pi Impv ms	פָּקַד
פַּקֵּד		Pi Inf cstr	פָּקַד
פָּקֹד		Pi Inf abs	פָּקַד
פֻּקַּד		Pual Perf 3ms	פָּקַד
פִּקְּדָה		Pi Perf 3fs	פָּקַד
פִּקְּדוּ		Pi Perf 3p	פָּקַד
פָּקְדוּ		Qal Perf 3p	פָּקַד
פְּקָדוּהוּ		Qal Impf 3mp + suff 3ms	פָּקַד
פִּקַּדְנוּ		Pi Perf 2fp	פָּקַד
פְּקָדֵנִי		Qal Impf 3ms + suff 1s	פָּקַד
פִּקַּדְתְּ		Pi Perf 2fs	פָּקַד
פִּקַּדְתָּ		Pi Perf 2ms	פָּקַד
פִּקַּדְתִּי		Pi Perf 1s	פָּקַד
פִּקַּדְתֶּם		Pi Perf 3p	פָּקַד
פִּקַּדְתֶּן		Pi Perf 2mp	פָּקַד
פָּקַח		verb	*to open* (eyes)
פַּר		noun ms	פָּרַר
פָּרָה		verb	*to be fertile, fruitful*
	פְּרִי	noun ms	*fruit*

Entry	Related words	Form	Meaning/Look up Hebrew entry
פָּרָה		noun fs	פָּרַר
פָּרוֹת		noun fp	פָּרָה
פְּרִי		noun ms	פָּרָה
פָּרִים		noun mp	פָּרַר
פָּרַר		verb	*to break in pieces*
	פַּר	noun ms	*ox, bull*
	פָּרָה	noun fs	*cow*
פָּתַח		verb	*to open*
צָדַק		verb	*to be righteous, just*
	צֶדֶק	noun ms	*justice*
	צְדָקָה	noun fs	*righteousness*
צְדָקָה		noun fs	צָדַק
צָוָה		verb	Pi *to appoint, to command*
	צִיּוֹן	pr noun	*Zion*
צִוָּה		Piel Perf 3ms	צָוָה
צָחַק		verb	*to laugh, mock*
	צְחֹק	noun ms	*laughter, ridicule*
	יִצְחָק	pr noun ms	*Isaac*
צִיּוֹן		pr noun	צָוָה
קָדוֹשׁ		adj ms	קָדַשׁ
קָדַם		verb	*to precede*
	מִקֶּדֶם	noun ms	*olden time, of old; east; formerly*
קָדַשׁ		verb	Qal *to be holy*; Pi *to sanctify, consecrate*
	קָדוֹשׁ	adj ms	*holy*
קִדַּשׁ		Pi Perf 3ms	קָדַשׁ
קֹדֶשׁ		noun ms	קָדַשׁ
קַדֵּשׁ		Pi Impf 3ms	קָדַשׁ
קוֹל		noun ms	*voice*

Entry	Related words	Form	Meaning/Look up Hebrew entry
קוֹם		Qal Inf abs	קוּם
קוּם		verb	*to arise*
	יָקָם	with prefix וַ : VC Impf 3ms	*and he arose*
	מָקוֹם	noun ms	*place*
	קָם	Qal Perf 3ms	*he has arisen*
קוּם		Qal Inf cstr or Impv ms	קוּם
קוּמִי		Qal Impv 2fs	קוּם
קוֹשׁ		verb	*to lay snares*
	קֶשֶׁת	noun fs	*bow* (weapon)
קַח		Qal Impv 2ms	לָקַח
קַחַת		Qal Inf cstr	לָקַח
קָטוֹל		Qal Inf abs	קָטַל
קָטַל		verb	*to kill*
קְטֹל		Qal Inf cstr or Impv ms	קָטַל
קֹטֵל		Qal Ptc	קָטַל
קֻטַּל		Pual Impv 2ms	קָטַל
קֻטַּל		Pual Perf 3ms	קָטַל
קָטְלָה		Qal Perf 3fs	קָטַל
קָטְלוּ		Qal Perf 3p	קָטַל
קָטַלְנוּ		Qal Perf 1p	קָטַל
קָטַלְתְּ		Qal Perf 2fs	קָטַל
קָטַלְתָּ		Qal Perf 2ms	קָטַל
קָטַלְתִּי		Qal Perf 1s	קָטַל
קְטַלְתֶּם		Qal Perf 2mp	קָטַל
קְטַלְתֶּן		Qal Perf 2fp	קָטַל
קָטֹן		adj ms	*small*
קְטַנָּה		adj fs	קָטֹן
קַל		adj ms	קָלַל
קֹלָהּ		noun ms + suff 3fs	קוֹל
קָלַל		verb	*to be light, to be fast*
	קַל	adj ms	*light*
קָם		Qal Perf 3ms or Ptc	קוּם

Entry	Related words	Form	Meaning/Look up Hebrew entry
קָמָה		Qal Perf 3fs	קום
קָמוּ		Qal Perf 3p	קום
קַמְנוּ		Qal Perf 1p	קום
קַמְתְּ		Qal Perf 2fs	קום
קַמְתָּ		Qal Perf 2ms	קום
קַמְתִּי		Qal Perf 1s	קום
קַמְתֶּם		Qal Perf 2mp	קום
קַמְתֶּן		Qal Perf 2fp	קום
קָרָא		verb	to call
קֶרֶן		noun fs	horn of animal
קֶשֶׁת		noun fs	קושׁ
רָאָה		verb	to see
רָאָה		Qal Perf 3fs	רָאָה
ראשׁ		noun ms	head
	רֵאשִׁית	noun fs	beginning, former time
רֵאשִׁית		noun fs	ראשׁ
רַב		adj ms	רָבַב
רָבַב		verb	to be many, become many
	רַב	adj ms	many
רָבָה		verb	to shoot
רֹבֶה		Qal Ptc	רָבָה
רֶגֶל		noun fs	foot
	רַגְלַיִם	noun f dual	feet
רום		verb	to be high; Hif to raise, exalt; Hof to be exalted
רוק		verb	Hif to empty
	רֵיק	adj ms	empty
רָחַק		verb	to be distant
	הַרְחֵק	Hif Inf abs	far away
	מֵרָחֹק	adv	in the distance

Entry	Related words	Form	Meaning/Look up Hebrew entry
רֵיק		adj ms	רוּק
רַע		adj ms	רָעַע
רָעֵב		verb	*to be hungry*
	רָעָב	noun ms	*famine*
רָעוֹת		adj fp	רָעַע
רָעִים		adj mp	רָעַע
רָעַע		verb	*to break in pieces, to be evil*
	רַע	adj ms	*evil, bad*
רָקַד		verb	*to leap, dance*
רָשַׁע		verb	*to be wicked*
	רְשַׁע	adj ms cstr	*wicked*
רִשְׁעֵי		adj mp cstr	רָשַׁע
רְשָׁעִים		adj mp	רָשַׁע
שְׂאִי		Qal Impv 2fs	נָשָׂא
שֵׁב		Qal Impv 2ms	יָשַׁב
שְׁבוּ		Qal Impv ms	יָשַׁב
שָׁבַע		verb	*to swear*; with בּ or with ל *to swear to (something)*
שָׁבַר		verb	Qal *to break*; Pi *to shatter*
שֶׁבֶת		Qal Inf cstr	יָשַׁב
שָׂדֶה		noun ms	*field*
שֶׂה		noun ms	*lamb, sheep, goat*
שׁוּב		verb	*to return*; Hif *to restore*; Hof *to be restored*
שׁוֹפֵט		Qal Ptc	שָׁפַט
שָׁחַד		verb	*to give presents, to bribe*
	שֹׁחַד	noun ms	*present, bribe*

Entry	Related words	Form	Meaning/Look up Hebrew entry
שָׁחָה		verb	*to bow down,* Hit *to worship*
שָׁחוֹט		Qal Inf abs	שָׁחַט
שָׁחַט		verb	*to kill, slaughter*
שְׁחַט		Qal Inf cstr or Impv ms	שָׁחַט
שׁוֹחֵט		Qal Ptc	שָׁחַט
שָׁחַק		verb	*to laugh*
שִׂיחַ		noun ms	*shrub*
שִׂיחִם		noun mp	שִׂיחַ
שִׂים		verb	*to put, place*
שִׁיר		verb	*to sing*
	שִׁירָה	noun fs	*song*
שָׁכוֹחַ		Qal Inf abs	שָׁכַח
שָׁכַח		verb	*to forget*
שְׁכֹחַ		Qal Inf cstr	שָׁכַח
שֹׁכֵחַ		Qal Ptc	שָׁכַח
שָׁכַם		verb	*to get up early*
	שֶׁכֶם	noun ms	*shoulder*
שִׁכְמָהּ		noun ms + suff 3fs	שָׁכַם
שָׁלוֹחַ		Qal Inf abs	שָׁלַח
שָׁלוֹשׁ		numeral	*three*
	שְׁלִישִׁי	adj	*third*
שָׁלַח		verb	*to stretch out, to send*
שְׁלַח		Qal Impv 2ms	שָׁלַח
שְׁלֹחַ		Qal Inf cstr	שָׁלַח
שֹׁלֵחַ		Qal Ptc	שָׁלַח
שְׁלִישִׁי		adj	שָׁלוֹשׁ
שָׁלַךְ		verb	*to throw*
שָׁלַם		verb	*to be whole, to be complete, to be at peace*
	שְׁלֹמֹה	pr noun ms	*Solomon*
שָׂם		Qal Perf 3ms or Ptc	שִׂים

Entry	Related words	Form	Meaning/Look up Hebrew entry
שָׁם		adv	*there*
שֵׁם		noun ms	*name*
	שְׁמוֹ	noun ms + suff 3ms	*his name*
שָׁמָּה		adv + ה of direction	שָׁם
שְׁמוֹ		noun ms + suff 3ms	שֵׁם
שָׂמוֹחַ		Qal Inf abs	שָׂמַח
שָׂמַח		verb	*to rejoice, be glad*
שְׂמֹחַ		Qal Inf cstr	שָׂמַח
שָׂמֵחַ		Qal Ptc	שָׂמַח
שָׁמַיִם		noun f dual	*heaven*
שְׁמָם		noun ms + suff 3mp	שֵׁם
שְׁמֹנֶה		numeral	*eight*
	שְׁמֹנַת	numeral cstr	*eight of*
שָׁמַע		verb	*to hear*
שָׁמֹעַ		Qal Inf abs	שָׁמַע
שְׁמֹעַ		Qal Inf cstr	שָׁמַע
שֹׁמֵעַ		Qal Ptc	שָׁמַע
שָׁמַעְתָּ		Qal Perf 2ms	שָׁמַע
שָׁמַר		verb	*to keep, to guard,* Hit *to observe*
	מִשְׁמָר	noun ms	*prison*
	מִשְׁמֶרֶת	noun fs	*injunction, charge*
	שִׁמֻּר	noun ms	*vigil*
	שֹׁמֶר	noun ms	*guard*
	שְׁמֻרָה	noun fs	*eyelid*
	שְׁמָרָה	noun fs	*watch, guard*
שְׁמֹר		Qal Impv 2ms	שָׁמַר
שִׁמֻּר		noun ms	שָׁמַר
שֹׁמֶר		noun ms	שָׁמַר
שְׁמֻרָה		noun fs	שָׁמַר
שָׁמְרָה		Qal Perf 3fs	שָׁמַר
שְׁמָרָה		noun fs	שָׁמַר
שָׁמְרוּ		Qal Perf 3p	שָׁמַר

Entry	Related words	Form	Meaning/Look up Hebrew entry
שִׁמְרוּ		Qal Impv 2mp	שָׁמַר
שִׁמְרִי		Qal Impv 2fs	שָׁמַר
שְׁמֹרְנָה		Qal Impv 2fp	שָׁמַר
שָׁמַרְנוּ		Qal Perf 1p	שָׁמַר
שָׁמַרְתְּ		Qal Perf 2fs	שָׁמַר
שָׁמַרְתָּ		Qal Perf 2ms	שָׁמַר
שָׁמַרְתִּי		Qal Perf 1s	שָׁמַר
שְׁמַרְתֶּם		Qal Perf 2mp	שָׁמַר
שְׁמַרְתֶּן		Qal Perf 2fp	שָׁמַר
שֶׁמֶשׁ		noun ms and fs	*sun*
שָׁנָה		verb	*to repeat*
	שָׁנָה	noun fs	*year*
	שְׁנֵי	numeral cstr	*two of, both of*
	שְׁנַיִם	numeral	*two, both*
	שֵׁנִית	adj	*second*
שָׁנָה		noun fs	שָׁנָה
שְׁנֵי		numeral cstr	שָׁנָה
שְׁנֵיהֶם		numeral + suff 3mp	שָׁנָה
שְׁנַיִם		numeral	שָׁנָה
שֵׁנִית		adj	שָׁנָה
שָׁעַר		verb	*to estimate value*
	שַׁעַר	noun ms	*gate*
שָׂפָה		noun fs	*lip*
	שְׂפָתַיִם	noun f dual	*lips*
שָׁפַט		verb	*to judge*
	שֹׁפֵט	noun ms	*judge*
	מִשְׁפָּט	noun ms	*judgement*
שְׁפֹט		Qal Inf cstr	שָׁפַט
שֹׁפֵט		noun ms	שָׁפַט
שְׂפַת		noun fs cstr	שָׂפָה
שְׂפָתַיִם		noun f dual	שָׂפָה
שָׁקָה		verb	Hif *to give someone a drink*

Entry	Related words	Form	Meaning/Look up Hebrew entry
שַׂר		noun ms	שָׂרַר
שָׂרָה		verb	Pi *to loose, set free*
	יִשְׂרָאֵל	pr noun ms	*Israel*
שָׂרָה		noun fs, pr noun fs	שָׂרַר
שָׂרוֹת		noun fp	שָׂרַר
שָׂרִים		noun mp	שָׂרַר
שָׂרַר		verb	*to rule, to be a prince*
	שַׂר	noun ms	*prince*
	שָׂרָה	pr noun fs	*Sarah*
שָׁתָה		verb	*to drink*
	מִשְׁתֶּה	noun ms	*feast, banquet*
תֹּאכְלוּ		Qal Impf 2mp	אָכַל
תֹּאמֶר		Qal Impf 2fs	אָמַר
תֹּאמַר		Qal Impf 3fs	אָמַר
תֵּבְךְּ		Qal Impf 3fs apoc	בָּכָה
תִּגְלוּ		Qal Impf 2mp	גָּלָה
תִּגְלִי		Qal Impf 2fs	גָּלָה
תִּגְּעוּ		Qal Impf 2mp	נָגַע
תֵּדַע		Qal Impf 2ms or 3fs	יָדַע
תֵּדְעוּ		Qal Impf 2mp	יָדַע
תֵּדְעִי		Qal Impf 2fs	יָדַע
תֵּדַעְנָה		Qal Impf 2fp or 3fp	יָדַע
תַּהַר		Qal Impf 3fs apoc	הָרָה
תּוֹרָה		noun fs	יָרָה
תּוֹרוֹת		noun fp cstr	יָרָה
תּוֹרַת		noun fs cstr	יָרָה
תַּחַת		prep	*beneath, under, instead of*
	תַּחְתָּיו	prep + suff 3ms	*under him* (or *it*)
תַּחְתַּי		prep + suff 1s	תַּחַת
תַּחְתֶּיהָ		prep + suff 3fs	תַּחַת
תַּחְתֵּיהֶם		prep + suff 3mp	תַּחַת

Entry	Related words	Form	Meaning/Look up Hebrew entry
תַּחְתֵּיהֶן		prep + suff 3fp	תָּחַת
תַּחְתָּיו		prep + suff 3ms	תָּחַת
תַּחְתֶּיךָ		prep + suff 2ms	תָּחַת
תַּחְתַּיִךְ		prep + suff 2fs	תָּחַת
תַּחְתֵּיכֶם		prep + suff 2mp	תָּחַת
תַּחְתֵּיכֶן		prep + suff 2fp	תָּחַת
תַּחְתֵּינוּ		prep + suff 1p	תָּחַת
תִּירְאִי		Qal Impf 2fs	יָרֵא
תֵּלֵךְ		Qal Impf 2ms or 3fs	הָלַךְ
תֵּלְכוּ		Qal Impf 2mp	הָלַךְ
תֵּלְכִי		Qal Impf 2fs	הָלַךְ
תֵּלַכְנָה		Qal Impf 2fp or 3fp	הָלַךְ
תַּמּוּ		Qal Perf 3p	תָּמַם
תְּמַלֵּא		Pi Impf 3fs	מָלֵא
תָּמַם		verb	*to be completed, be finished, be gone*
תִּמְשֹׁל		Qal Impf 2ms or 3fs	מָשַׁל
תִּמְשְׁלוּ		Qal Impf 2mp	מָשַׁל
תִּמְשְׁלִי		Qal Impf 2fs	מָשַׁל
תִּמְשֹׁלְנָה		Qal Impf 2fp or 3fp	מָשַׁל
תְּמֻתוּן		Qal Impf 2mp + parag נ	מות
תְּנַחֲמֵנִי		Pi Impf 2ms + suff 1s	נָחַם
תָּסֹב		Qal Impf 2ms or 3fs	סָבַב
תָּסֹבּוּ		Qal Impf 2mp	סָבַב
תָּסֹבִּי		Qal Impf 2fs	סָבַב
תְּסֻבֶּינָה		Qal Impf 2fp or 3fp	סָבַב
תָּעָה		verb	*to wander*
תַּעֲמֹד		Qal Impf 2ms or 3fs	עָמַד
תַּעַמְדוּ		Qal Impf 2mp	עָמַד
תַּעַמְדִי		Qal Impf 2fs	עָמַד
תַּעֲמֹדְנָה		Qal Impf 2fp or 3fp	עָמַד
תַּעַשׂ		Qal Impf 2ms apoc	עָשָׂה

Entry	Related words	Form	Meaning/Look up Hebrew entry
תִּפֹּל		Qal Impf 2ms or 3fs	נָפַל
תִּפְּלוּ		Qal Impf 2mp	נָפַל
תִּפְּלִי		Qal Impf 2fs	נָפַל
תִּפֹּלְנָה		Qal Impf 2fp or 3fp	נָפַל
תְּפַקֵּד		Pi Impf 2ms or 3fs	פָּקַד
תְּפַקְּדוּ		Pi Impf 2mp	פָּקַד
תְּפַקְּדִי		Pi Impf 2fs	פָּקַד
תְּפַקֵּדְנָה		Pi Impf 2fp or 3fp	פָּקַד
תַּפְקֵדְנָה		Hif Impf 2fp or 3fp	פָּקַד
תַּפְקִיד		Hif Impf 2ms or 3fs	פָּקַד
תַּפְקִידִי		Hif Impf 2fs	פָּקַד
תִּקַּח		Qal Impf 3fs	לָקַח
תִּקְטֹל		Qal Impf 2ms or 3fs	קָטַל
תִּקָּטֵל		Nif Impf 2ms or 3fs	קָטַל
תִּקְטְלוּ		Qal Impf 2mp	קָטַל
תִּקָּטְלוּ		Nif Impf 2mp	קָטַל
תִּקְטְלִי		Qal Impf 2fs	קָטַל
תִּקָּטְלִי		Nif Impf 2fs	קָטַל
תִּקְטֹלְנָה		Qal Impf 2fp or 3fp	קָטַל
תִּקָּטַלְנָה		Nif Impf 2fp or 3fp	קָטַל
תֵּרֶא		Qal Impf 3fs	רָאָה
תִּשָּׂא		Qal Impf 3fs	נָשָׂא
תֵּשֵׁב		Qal Impf 2ms or 3fs	יָשַׁב
תֵּשְׁבוּ		Qal Impf 2mp	יָשַׁב
תֵּשְׁבִי		Qal Impf 2fs	יָשַׁב
תֵּשַׁבְנָה		Qal Impf 2fp or 3fp	יָשַׁב
תִּשְׁלַח		Qal Impf 2ms	שָׁלַח
תַּשְׁלִךְ		Hif Impf 3fs	שָׁלַךְ
תִּשְׁמֹר		Qal Impf 2ms or 3fs	שָׁמַר
תִּשְׁמְרוּ		Qal Impf 2mp	שָׁמַר
תִּשְׁמְרִי		Qal Impf 2fs	שָׁמַר
תִּשְׁמֹרְנָה		Qal Impf 2fp or 3fp	שָׁמַר
תֵּשְׁק		Hif Impf 3fs apoc	שָׁקָה

Entry	Related words	Form	Meaning/Look up Hebrew entry
תֵּתַע		Qal Impf 3fs apoc	תָּעָה
תַּתְפְּקִידוּ		Hif Impf 2mp	פָּקַד
תִּתְקַדֵּשׁ		Hit Impf 2ms or 3fs	קָדַשׁ
תִּתְקַדְּשׁוּ		Hit Impf 2mp	קָדַשׁ
תִּתְקַדְּשִׁי		Hit Impf 2fs	קָדַשׁ
תִּתְקַדֵּשְׁנָה		Hit Impf 2fp or 3fp	קָדַשׁ

teach
yourself

modern hebrew
shula gilboa

- Do you want to cover the basics then progress fast?
- Do you want to communicate in a range of situations?
- Do you want to learn modern hebrew in depth?

Modern Hebrew starts with the basics but moves at an energetic pace to give you a good level of understanding, speaking and writing. You will have lots of opportunity to practise the kind of language you will need to be able to communicate with confidence and understand Israeli culture.

- Do you want to cover the basics then progress fast?
- Do you want to communicate in a range of situations?
- Do you want to reach a high standard?

Yiddish starts with the basics but moves at a lively pace to give you a good level of understanding and speaking, and reading and writing the Hebrew script. You will have lots of opportunity to practise the kind of language you will need to be able to communicate with confidence and understand the culture of speakers of Yiddish.

teach yourself®

From Advanced Sudoku to Zulu, you'll find everything you need in the **teach yourself** range, in books, on CD and on DVD.

Visit **www.teachyourself.co.uk** for more details.

Advanced Sudoku and Kakuro
Afrikaans
Alexander Technique
Algebra
Ancient Greek
Applied Psychology
Arabic
Aromatherapy
Art History
Astrology
Astronomy
AutoCAD 2004
AutoCAD 2007
Ayurveda
Baby Massage and Yoga
Baby Signing
Baby Sleep
Bach Flower Remedies
Backgammon
Ballroom Dancing
Basic Accounting
Basic Computer Skills
Basic Mathematics
Beauty
Beekeeping
Beginner's Arabic Script
Beginner's Chinese Script
Beginner's Dutch

Beginner's French
Beginner's German
Beginner's Greek
Beginner's Greek Script
Beginner's Hindi
Beginner's Italian
Beginner's Japanese
Beginner's Japanese Script
Beginner's Latin
Beginner's Mandarin Chinese
Beginner's Portuguese
Beginner's Russian
Beginner's Russian Script
Beginner's Spanish
Beginner's Turkish
Beginner's Urdu Script
Bengali
Better Bridge
Better Chess
Better Driving
Better Handwriting
Biblical Hebrew
Biology
Birdwatching
Blogging
Body Language
Book Keeping
Brazilian Portuguese

Bridge
British Empire, The
British Monarchy from Henry VIII, The
Buddhism
Bulgarian
Business Chinese
Business French
Business Japanese
Business Plans
Business Spanish
Business Studies
Buying a Home in France
Buying a Home in Italy
Buying a Home in Portugal
Buying a Home in Spain
C++
Calculus
Calligraphy
Cantonese
Car Buying and Maintenance
Card Games
Catalan
Chess
Chi Kung
Chinese Medicine
Christianity
Classical Music
Coaching
Cold War, The
Collecting
Computing for the Over 50s
Consulting
Copywriting
Correct English
Counselling
Creative Writing
Cricket
Croatian
Crystal Healing
CVs
Czech
Danish
Decluttering
Desktop Publishing
Detox

Digital Home Movie Making
Digital Photography
Dog Training
Drawing
Dream Interpretation
Dutch
Dutch Conversation
Dutch Dictionary
Dutch Grammar
Eastern Philosophy
Electronics
English as a Foreign Language
English for International Business
English Grammar
English Grammar as a Foreign Language
English Vocabulary
Entrepreneurship
Estonian
Ethics
Excel 2003
Feng Shui
Film Making
Film Studies
Finance for Non-Financial Managers
Finnish
First World War, The
Fitness
Flash 8
Flash MX
Flexible Working
Flirting
Flower Arranging
Franchising
French
French Conversation
French Dictionary
French Grammar
French Phrasebook
French Starter Kit
French Verbs
French Vocabulary
Freud
Gaelic
Gardening

Lithuanian
Magic
Mahjong
Malay
Managing Stress
Managing Your Own Career
Mandarin Chinese
Mandarin Chinese Conversation
Marketing
Marx
Massage
Mathematics
Meditation
Middle East Since 1945, The
Modern China
Modern Hebrew
Modern Persian
Mosaics
Music Theory
Mussolini's Italy
Nazi Germany
Negotiating
Nepali
New Testament Greek
NLP
Norwegian
Norwegian Conversation
Old English
One-Day French
One-Day French – the DVD
One-Day German
One-Day Greek
One-Day Italian
One-Day Portuguese
One-Day Spanish
One-Day Spanish – the DVD
Origami
Owning a Cat
Owning a Horse
Panjabi
PC Networking for Small
  Businesses
Personal Safety and Self
  Defence
Philosophy
Philosophy of Mind

Philosophy of Religion
Photography
Photoshop
PHP with MySQL
Physics
Piano
Pilates
Planning Your Wedding
Polish
Polish Conversation
Politics
Portuguese
Portuguese Conversation
Portuguese Grammar
Portuguese Phrasebook
Postmodernism
Pottery
PowerPoint 2003
PR
Project Management
Psychology
Quick Fix French Grammar
Quick Fix German Grammar
Quick Fix Italian Grammar
Quick Fix Spanish Grammar
Quick Fix: Access 2002
Quick Fix: Excel 2000
Quick Fix: Excel 2002
Quick Fix: HTML
Quick Fix: Windows XP
Quick Fix: Word
Quilting
Recruitment
Reflexology
Reiki
Relaxation
Retaining Staff
Romanian
Running Your Own Business
Russian
Russian Conversation
Russian Grammar
Sage Line 50
Sanskrit
Screenwriting
Second World War, The

Serbian
Setting Up a Small Business
Shorthand Pitman 2000
Sikhism
Singing
Slovene
Small Business Accounting
Small Business Health Check
Songwriting
Spanish
Spanish Conversation
Spanish Dictionary
Spanish Grammar
Spanish Phrasebook
Spanish Starter Kit
Spanish Verbs
Spanish Vocabulary
Speaking On Special Occasions
Speed Reading
Stalin's Russia
Stand Up Comedy
Statistics
Stop Smoking
Sudoku
Swahili
Swahili Dictionary
Swedish
Swedish Conversation
Tagalog
Tai Chi
Tantric Sex
Tap Dancing
Teaching English as a Foreign
  Language
Teams & Team Working
Thai
Theatre
Time Management
Tracing Your Family History
Training
Travel Writing
Trigonometry
Turkish
Turkish Conversation
Twentieth Century USA

Typing
Ukrainian
Understanding Tax for Small
  Businesses
Understanding Terrorism
Urdu
Vietnamese
Visual Basic
Volcanoes
Watercolour Painting
Weight Control through Diet &
  Exercise
Welsh
Welsh Dictionary
Welsh Grammar
Wills & Probate
Windows XP
Wine Tasting
Winning at Job Interviews
Word 2003
World Cultures: China
World Cultures: England
World Cultures: Germany
World Cultures: Italy
World Cultures: Japan
World Cultures: Portugal
World Cultures: Russia
World Cultures: Spain
World Cultures: Wales
World Faiths
Writing Crime Fiction
Writing for Children
Writing for Magazines
Writing a Novel
Writing Poetry
Xhosa
Yiddish
Yoga
Zen
Zulu